Labeling Women Deviant

Gender, Stigma, and Social Control

Labeling Women Deviant
Gender, Stigma, and Social Control

Edwin M. Schur
New York University

McGRAW-HILL PUBLISHING COMPANY
New York St. Louis San Francisco Auckland Bogotá
Caracas Hamburg Lisbon London Madrid Mexico
Milan Montreal New Delhi Oklahoma City Paris San Juan
São Paulo Singapore Sydney Tokyo Toronto

LABELING WOMEN DEVIANT
First Edition
98765
Copyright © 1984 by Edwin M. Schur

Library of Congress Cataloging in Publication Data

Schur, Edwin M.
   Labeling women deviant.

   Bibliography: p.
   Includes index.
      1. Women—Social conditions.   2. Deviant behavior—Labeling theory.
3. Sex discrimination against women.   4. Stigma (Social psychology).
5. Social norms.   I. Title.
HQ1206.S443   1984   305.4'2   83-10942
ISBN 0-07-554466-0

To My Daughters
Amy and Sarah

Preface

This book appears at a time when many of the topics it covers have moved to the forefront of public attention. The women's liberation movement has promoted an increased consciousness of sexism in general, and of its many specific manifestations. Both scholarly research and academic courses on women have reached an all-time high. As a combined result of activist efforts and social research, most of the patterned ways of labeling women deviant that are discussed in this text have now come under significant challenge. The time may not be too distant when it will be possible to discuss many of these patterns in the past tense. By and large, however, that time has not yet arrived.

The text is intended for use in courses on deviance, women, gender, sex roles, social problems, and contemporary American society. It is in part an outgrowth of seminars I have conducted recently—for undergraduates and graduate students—on the relation between gender and definitions of deviance. In trying to organize and teach these courses, I have found existing texts inadequate. Recently, several texts and readers concerned with women and crime have become available. But no book has systematically developed the broader deviance perspective as it relates to women, or covered the correspondingly wider range of substantive problems that I treat here.

Given the burgeoning nature of the field of women's studies, the literature on women's issues has become enormous. In this book I have opted to discuss a wide range of topics and to provide a general theoretical framework for analyzing them—either separately or in combination. Because of the scope of coverage attempted here, it has not been possible to explore all of the topics in the greatest depth or detail. I have, necessarily, been selective rather than encyclopedic—with respect to research data, interpretations, and even the choice of the topics themselves. I hope that readers will find the selections I have made and the theoretical framework I have developed to be useful and thought-provoking.

The analysis here grows out of my previous and rather extensive work on deviance, which for the most part has been informed by a "labeling" or social reactions perspective. It also reflects my long-standing experience in teaching courses on the family—with a special emphasis on gender conceptions and women's situation. Although I am not by temperament an activist, my early critiques of restrictive abortion laws (beginning in the 1950s) may have been a precursor of any underlying feminist advocacy revealed in the pages below.

During the several years in which these materials were being developed, I have received many helpful suggestions from colleagues and friends. I am especially grateful to Arlene Kaplan Daniels and Meredith Gould for their detailed and critical comments on an earlier, related paper. I appreciate too the suggestions and words of encouragement I received from David F. Greenberg, Daphne Joslin, Edward W. Lehman, Joan Brodsky Schur, and Patricia Cayo Sexton. The book no doubt also reflects ideas developed by various students in my seminars. Specific contributions by two of them, Philip Kasinitz and Nancy Larkin, are cited in the text. Detailed critiques of an earlier draft of this manuscript by Robert M. Emerson, Victoria Swigert and two other anonymous reviewers proved extremely helpful. I want finally to thank Jane Carey for her scrupulous typing of the manuscript, Ruth Flaxman for her copyediting, and Bert Lummus and Cindy Spiegel for their professional assistance and guidance in the production of this book.

Edwin M. Schur

Contents

PART I

Theoretical Framework

CHAPTER 1

Women and Deviance: A Sociological Perspective

One way or another, virtually every woman in our society is affected by the dominant definitions of deviance. If we were to look only at the officially recorded statistics on major criminal offenses, we might be led to conclude that being labeled deviant is overwhelmingly a male experience. However, such a conclusion would be quite unwarranted. Today sociologists recognize that deviance-designating goes well beyond such publicly proscribed and formally processed wrongdoing. It includes as well the numerous informal processes of routine social interaction through which individuals may be personally discredited or placed "in the wrong."

Once we adopt this broadened perspective, we are led to recognize that in our society being treated as deviant has been a standard feature of life as a female. With great regularity women have been labeled—and they still are being labeled—"aggressive," "bitchy," "hysterical," "fat," "homely," "masculine," and "promiscuous." Judgments such as these, and the social reactions that accompany them, represent a very potent kind of deviance-defining. They may not put the presumed "offender" in jail, but they do typically damage her reputation, induce shame, and lower her "life chances." These informal ways of defining and reacting to women should be of great interest to the sociologist. They help us to recognize perceptions and ideas that frequently dominate interaction between males and females. They also show how such daily interaction reflects, and in turn reinforces, the overall disparities in social and economic power between the sexes.

Throughout this book, we shall be seeing some of the ways in which this routine devaluation adversely affects females specifically and our patterns of social life more generally. As a consequence of the women's liberation movement, many women now are speaking out to document and condemn such treatment. These personal testimonies come from females who have been informally discredited, as well as from those who have been subjected to public and official deviance labeling.

Thus, a young woman notes of being scorned as overweight: "I always felt, when I went into some boutique, that all the salesgirls were staring at me and snickering, knowing that nothing in the store would fit me" (in Millman, 1980, p. 79). A (female) former mental patient asserts: "I was punished for questioning, for wondering, for trying to figure out who I was and what I should do and what it all meant" (Chamberlin, 1975, p. 45). Commenting on her male clients, a prostitute states: "What they've bought is being able to pay us, a piece of degradation, our degradation" (Jaget, ed., 1980, p. 103). And perhaps as an ultimate expression of their devaluation, even women who have been raped are often discredited and made to feel shame. One such victim reports that "I felt like I was a criminal when I was up there [testifying]" (in Holmstrom and Burgess, 1978, p. 224).

DEVIANCE AND STIGMA

These statements highlight some of the specific responses to women that we will be considering at length later in this text. As the statements begin to suggest, exploring the relation of women to definitions of deviance requires more than just research on female behavior. At one time, sociologists were heavily preoccupied with the study of individual "offenders." They believed that through such research they could unearth the causes of deviance. It is true that if we could obtain valid samples of persons who engage in a given behavior and of those who do not, comparative analysis might help us to answer certain kinds of causal questions. For example, we might learn which kinds of people were engaging in the behavior, and we could then determine in what respects, if any, they differed from those who were not.

However, from the standpoint of meaningfully and comprehensively understanding deviance, such an approach has serious limitations. This is so because "deviance" is a designation, a way of characterizing behavior. Often it is the very process of defining and reacting to the behavior or condition *as* deviant that is of greatest interest to the sociologist. Howard S. Becker emphasized this point in his oft-quoted statement:

> ... *social groups create deviance by making the rules whose infraction constitutes deviance,* and by applying these rules to particular people and labeling them as outsiders. From this point of view, deviance is *not* a quality of the act the person commits, but rather a consequence of the application by others of rules and sanctions to an "offender." The deviant is one to whom that label has successfully been applied; deviant behavior is behavior that people so label (Becker, 1963, p. 9; italics in the original).

These ideas, and the companion notion of stigma, or "spoiled identity" (Goffman, 1963), direct our attention to the devaluation phenomenon itself as the core ingredient common to all deviance situations. Women's deviance, like any deviance, is a social construct. It results, as Becker's statement indicates, from a particular kind of definition and response. The acts and individuals are not intrinsically deviant (Kitsuse, 1962; Erikson, 1962). Rather, they acquire their "deviantness" (Schur, 1979) through a characteristic process of meaning-attachment. In many respects, then, how people perceive and react to a given behavior or condition is what "counts most" socially. This is so because the very same behavior or condition may be defined and responded to differently by different persons.

A good example would be "promiscuity." Suppose that a particular unmarried woman maintains an active and varied sex life. While some people may condemn her as "promiscuous," others may view her and her behavior as "liberated." Note that these highly divergent designations do not stem from differences in the sexual behavior itself. On the contrary, the behavior has been the same; it is only the evaluation of it that has varied. Clearly, then, stigma does not automatically or unvaryingly attach to behavior. When tarnishing of a woman's reputation does occur, this outcome necessarily reflects the responses of specific other persons.

The outlook on deviance that we have briefly sketched out so far is usually referred to as the "labeling" perspective (for a variety of interpretations see Schur, 1971; Hawkins and Tiedeman, 1975; Suchar, 1978; Schur, 1979; Gove, ed., 1980; Rosenberg, Stebbins, and Turowetz, eds., 1982). Unfortunately, the concept of labeling is sometimes interpreted too narrowly. Thus critics of the approach (e.g., Gove, ed., 1980) often construe it as referring only to the direct stigmatization of particular individuals. At times in this book we will be exploring—as labeling-oriented analysts often have done—the nature and impact of the stigmatization process. But recent perspectives on deviance point to other aspects or dimensions of labeling as well. Becker begins, after all, by noting that "social groups create deviance by making the rules." Thus the "labels" themselves, the dominant concepts as to what constitutes deviance, become a major focal point for research and interpretation.

Once this "collective definition" aspect is brought under study, it is evident that the perspective urged by Becker is not a narrow social-psychological one. Indeed, as he points out in another, less frequently quoted passage, labeling is largely a matter of some persons or groups imposing their rules on others. Ultimately, then, who will be defined as deviant, and for what, is "a question of political and economic power" (Becker, 1963, p. 17). Contemporary deviance theory therefore stresses power and intergroup conflict as key determinants of deviance outcomes (Lofland, 1969; Schur, 1971; Hawkins and Tiedeman, 1975), and examines the development and conduct of collective struggles over public definitions of deviance (Horowitz and Liebowitz, 1968; Spector and Kitsuse, 1977; Edelman, 1977; Schur, 1980; Gusfield, 1981).

In this text, we are going to consider the situation of women in relation to several different aspects of deviance-defining. However, it is not possible in a brief work of this sort to give every aspect full or equal attention. As the reader should already suspect, the traditional focus on individual etiology—in this case, the "causes" of women's behaviors (some of which are deemed deviant)—is not a major one here. Our emphasis throughout this book will be on processes and patterns of deviance labeling.

The discussion will be organized around four main subtopics. To begin with, in Chapter Two we shall examine basic aspects of the stigmatization process itself. In daily interaction, women are often perceived and responded to primarily in terms of their category membership—as females, first and foremost. Such response may itself carry a certain degree of stigma, since relatively speaking femaleness appears to be a devalued status. Indeed, this dominant way of "seeing" and responding to women—whatever their behavior or situation—displays all the key features of stigma-laden typing which we find generally in reactions to "deviants."

Such categorical devaluation is reflected in and reinforced by numerous applications to women of substantively specific deviance labels. In this sense, we might even say that women have served as "all-purpose deviants" within our society. A large section of the book (Chapter Three) is devoted to a broad overview of these occasions for (or, a critic might say, pretexts for) labeling women deviant. What we will be looking at will be the proliferation of distinctively female "deviances." These presumed offenses emerge when women are perceived as having violated specific gender system norms—by behaving or even presenting themselves in ways deemed inappropriate for females.

Following this overview, we shall turn in Chapter Four to a counterpart phenomenon: the fact that major offenses *against* women, which we *profess* to consider deviant, in practice have been responded to with much ambivalence. That the female victims in such instances as sexual harassment, rape, and woman-battering have themselves often been treated as though *they* were the "deviants" again reflects the overall devaluation of women.

A fourth general topic—one of more traditional interest in sociology—also receives consideration. In Chapter Five, we will see how the classifying and processing of "cases" affects recorded deviance statistics, especially male-female rate differentials.

As sociologists recently have emphasized, recorded rates and trends in deviance are partly determined by the nature and extent of the deviance-classifying and processing activities and apparatus (Erikson, 1966; Kitsuse and Cicourel, 1963; see also Hawkins and Tiedeman, 1975). Such statistics necessarily reflect the policies and practices of agents and agencies of social control. Sociologists now define these terms broadly so as to include not only policers, punishers, and correctors, but also certain supposedly "helping" professionals and organizations. That most deviance-classifiers and processors have been men, and that the definitions and classificatory criteria they have applied have largely been developed by men, are obviously relevant to understanding the types and rates of recorded female deviance. We shall examine in particular two major examples: the role of psychiatrists in classifying women as mentally ill; and the influence of the criminal justice system in shaping women's officially recorded crime rates.

Two central themes will underlie our analysis of all these topics. One is the already suggested relation between stigma and social power. Women's vulnerability to stigmatization rests on their general social subordination, their relatively poor power position. At the same time, when women are effectively stigmatized, that reinforces their overall subordination and makes it more difficult for them to achieve desired goals. This is part of what labeling analysts mean when they note that stigmatization can become self-propelling or snowballing in its impact.

However, few if any of these analysts claim that stigma is fixed, invariant, absolute, or irreversible. On the contrary, most sociologists recognize that there are always variations in susceptibility and impact, based largely on the individuals' pre-existing power resources. And we know that individuals and especially organized groups may sometimes be quite successful in their efforts to counter stigmatization. Throughout this text, we shall be noting many points on which women's recent collective action has helped to produce change in specific patterns of deviance labeling. Unfortunately, a more general discussion of collective struggle and social change is beyond the scope of this work. A few preliminary comments on these matters are included in the book's brief concluding chapter.

A second and related underlying theme is signaled by inclusion of the term "social control" in this book's subtitle. As Becker's comments on power, cited earlier, imply, definitions of deviance operate to impose control. Some people control others by defining the latter's behavior as deviant. Many current definitions of deviance and ways in which they are used function to keep women under control, or in their "place", regardless of whether anyone has consciously intended that effect. Contemporary sociologists of deviance place a special emphasis on social control. Not only do they see control agents and agencies as being in a sense "contributors" to deviance problems, but they also recognize the extent to which deviance-definers may benefit through the labeling of others as deviant.

We must then take into account the various ways in which

men may gain, or think or feel that they do, as a result of the deviance labeling of women. Recent studies show that efforts at deviance-defining typically are grounded in the definers' perception that the "deviants" pose some kind of threat to their specific interests or overall social position (Becker, 1963; Gusfield, 1966; Cohen, 1974; Lauderdale, 1976; Spector and Kitsuse, 1977). There can be little doubt of the relevance of this notion to the situation of women. It is, indeed, axiomatic that male dominance depends upon female subordination. As we are going to see shortly, there are several more specific senses too in which men seem to find women, and especially the prospect of women's liberation, threatening.

THE GENDER SYSTEM

Labeling studies emphasize the uncertainty, variability, and relativity of deviance-defining. They make clear that the consensus on norms is far from absolute. Yet this is not to deny that—within a particular society, and at a given time—certain normative standards may be the *dominant* ones. Despite the significant changes that are occurring, the gender-related norms examined below maintain their dominance in the society at large. They continue to be reflected in public policy, and they also influence the "micropolitics" of routine interaction (see Emerson and Messinger, 1977). Their impact is repeatedly felt by women in numerous daily life situations.

Such norms, furthermore, still do comprise a "system," albeit one that is now in a considerable state of flux. To fully understand any one of the topics examined in this text, we need to examine its relation to that broader system. Exploring the deviance labeling of women highlights, in a way that past studies have not always done, the sociocultural connections between and among what often have been treated as separate "problems." From beauty norms to female crime-processing, from maternity norms to male crimes against women, from the diagnosis of female mental illness to sex discrimination at work—all these and many more women-and-deviance patterns are linked together. They all are shaped by, and constitute important parts of, an overall system of subordination and devaluation.

A composite exploration of such topics should help to enrich the substance and broaden the perspective of courses on deviance. At the same time, a systematic overview of women's situation presented in deviance and control terms should serve to complement existing works in the interdisciplinary field of women's studies. In approaching our topic from that standpoint, some preliminary comments about basic terminology and selective emphasis in the present text may be in order.

To begin with, we should note that the very terms "sex" and "gender" continue to give rise to uncertainty and confusion. Many laypersons use the two designations more or less interchangeably. Legal specialists and also literary analysts often use "gender" in referring to a person's biological sex. Social scientists tend to adopt the opposite approach, associating "gender" with nonbiological factors. Some, however, have developed such a preference for the term that they now use it indiscriminately in writing about any aspect of male-female difference. This tendency only adds further to the confusion, by obscuring the value of distinguishing between the biological and the nonbiological. In the present work, the term "gender" refers to the sociocultural and psychological shaping, patterning, and evaluating of female and male behavior. According to this usage, most "sex roles" are, strictly speaking, "gender roles." (Wet nurse and sperm donor are often cited, along with childbearer, as examples of true "sex roles"—that is, roles that can only be played by members of one biological sex.) But by the same token, it is "sex" and not "gender" to which we refer when we say that people are biologically female or biologically male (for general discussion of this distinction see Gould and Kern-Daniels, 1977; Richardson, 1981, pp. 4–7).

Even after we adopt a sociocultural focus, many important aspects of the gender system must remain outside the purview of this short volume. Primary attention is given here to those aspects that most directly help us to understand women's relation to definitions of deviance. For the most part, we are going to concentrate in this book on present-day American society. Hence we shall touch only slightly on the kinds of historical and cross-cultural research that have become very important in the field of women's studies. Similarly, this text includes little discussion of certain issues that have preoccupied specialists in that field—such as the rise of patriarchy (the system of male dominance), and the relative merits of different types of feminist theory.

Most of our references to the gender system will point to a particular aspect of that system which many general discussions of gender have slighted. We are going to focus primarily on gender as a normative system, a pervasive network of interrelated norms and sanctions through which female (and male) behavior is evaluated and controlled. This conception of gender as a scheme of interpersonal evaluations is, of course, implicit in most critiques of the concepts of "femininity" and "masculinity." That these rubrics are sociocultural constructs, and not simply objective "facts," is now widely accepted (for an overview of research and theory on this issue see Spence and Helmreich, 1978, Ch. 1). Since the notions of "femininity" and "masculinity" are central to the overall gender system, it is not surprising that many of the specific evaluations and practices considered below bear a close relation to them.

Diverse studies of the gender system have irrefutably shown how the subordination of women is sustained through their being socialized for, and restricted to, limited aspirations, options, roles, and rewards. The heavy significance of such factors, and of the basic learning processes and major societal institutions that produce and perpetuate them, is unquestionable. Equally important, although it has not been as systematically analyzed, is the role of interpersonal evaluation in ordinary life situations. In particular, social stigmatization must be recognized as a key mechanism that backs up and "enforces" many of the restrictions and limitations placed on women.

There are various ways, then, in which gender—as a sociocultural complex of meanings, behaviors, and assessments—is instilled and "reproduced." This book stresses what one recent text has termed "the reproduction of male dominance in everyday interactions" (Stockard and Johnson, 1980, pp. 10–19). As two other writers have succinctly stated: "Social interaction is the battlefield where the daily war between the sexes is fought. It is here that women are constantly reminded where their 'place' is and that they are put back in their place, should they venture out" (Henley and Freeman, 1979, p. 474). In emphasizing ongoing devaluation processes and the everyday uses of stigma-laden definitions to control female behavior, the present study is only able to touch in passing on certain key aspects of gender—including economic and occupational stratification by sex, and sex differences in the social-ization of children.

Our examination of the gender system is necessarily selective on another score as well. We are, among other things, going to be focusing on the myriad instances in which women are punished for violating or threatening to violate gender-related norms. But there is no denying that the gender system controls men too. Unquestionably, men are limited and restricted through narrow definitions of "masculinity" (see, for example, Fasteau, 1974; Pleck and Sawyer, eds., 1974; Farrell, 1975; David and Brannon, eds., 1976; Lewis, ed., 1981). They too face negative sanctions when they violate gender prescriptions. There is little value in debating which sex suffers or loses more through this kind of control; it is apparent that both do. However, as we are going to see below, women typically face a double-bind or no-win situation with respect to gender norms. Unlike the acknowledgment given to male "success," there is relatively little rewarding of women when they do "conform." Between pervasive stigmatizing, on the one hand, and low status acquisition on the other, women are liable to "lose either way." At any rate, since our main focus here is on women and deviance, the gender "problems" of men cannot re-ceive great attention. But the implications of male gender norms, as they affect women, will be an important concern throughout the book.

Some final comments are necessary regarding theoretical orien-tations to the gender system. Arlie Hochschild (1973) has identi-fied and compared four main perspectives adopted in studies of women. One, favored by psychologists, focuses on the nature of sex differences; a second emphasizes "sex roles and the norms which govern them;" a third treats "women as a minority group;" and the fourth, which she terms the "politics of caste" outlook, stresses power differentials and exploitation as a tool of control. As Hochschild notes, these alternative approaches reflect different intellectual traditions, tend to favor different "conceptual vocabu-laries," and may carry different implications with respect to social change and public policy.

In this text, the first orientation ("sex differences") receives little attention. Each of the other three approaches, however, provides some concepts and emphases that are useful for the analysis of women and deviance. Our central concept of "gender norms" has close ties to the study of "sex roles," even if the focus here on reinforcement in daily interaction departs somewhat from the more usual stress on socialization. In exploring the basic perceptions and responses through which women are devalued, the analogy to stigmatization of other "minority groups" will prove extremely useful. Finally, exploitation is going to be an underlying theme throughout this work; it becomes most explicit in Chapter Four on the victimization of women.

In developing an overview of women and deviance it is unnecessary, therefore, and might even prove counterproductive, to attempt to "choose" among these orientations. As I have suggested elsewhere (Schur, 1979) with respect to a similar issue in the deviance field, the sociological penchant for identifying supposedly competing "schools" should not lead us to neglect points on which otherwise different approaches may converge or complement each other. Because the topic of women and deviance is highly complex, to study it we may well need a varied arsenal of sociological concepts and outlooks.

SOCIOLOGISTS AND VALUES

During the last several decades, sociologists have become increasingly self-conscious appraisers of their own research and theorizing. They are somewhat less inclined than before to insist that sociology is a narrowly scientific, ethically neutral enterprise. Particularly in areas of great public interest and controversy, the centrality of value questions is readily apparent. One aspect of this centrality has long been recognized: the role of values in shaping the social action that sociologists are trying to study. In the field of deviance sociology, contemporary writers have reasserted the point Willard Waller stressed in discussing the nature of social problems: "The term *social problem* indicates not merely an observed phenomenon but the state of mind of the observer as well. Value judgments define certain conditions of life as social problems; there can be no social problem without a value judgment" (Waller, 1936, p. 922; and see Spector and Kitsuse, 1977; Schur,

1979). Essentially it is such value judgments and responses based on them that we must study if we are to understand how particular behaviors and people are treated as deviant.

Rather more controversial has been the issue of the sociologist's own values. There is wide recognition that a certain amount of selectivity inevitably occurs with respect to research topics and analytic priorities. But there is persisting disagreement as to whether such selectivity reflects, in the main, professional priorities or personal ones. Within the sociology of deviance, radical critics have charged that by only studying the status quo but not actively opposing it, deviance specialists implicitly reinforce dominant public definitions and indirectly help to sustain existing oppression (see especially Gouldner, 1968; Thio, 1973; Schwendinger and Schwendinger, 1975; Quinney, 1980; Balkan, Berger, and Schmidt, 1980; and Piven, 1981). According to these critics, a preoccupation with describing and analyzing the prevailing patterns of deviance-defining diverts sociologists from the critical task of asserting what the *real* problems are, and who the *real* "deviants" are.

The counterargument, of those the critics label "mainstream" sociologists, is that the first commitment of sociology is to the advancement of knowledge. Whatever conditions the sociologist personally might like to see prevail, those that actually do prevail must be documented and interpreted. Sometimes the counterargument asserts further that by exposing oppressive conditions in this systematic way, in the long run, sociologists may even promote desired changes more effectively than they would by actively engaging in public protest.

In recent years it has become increasingly common to assert that sociological studies of deviance—much as in other subfields of sociology—have displayed a systematic bias against women (see, for example, Klein, 1973; Millman, 1975; Smart, 1978; Adler and Simon, eds., 1979; Balkan, Berger, and Schmidt, 1980; Leonard, 1982; and see also the related analysis by Harris, 1977). Underlying this claim is an awareness that the discipline in general has long been dominated by men, and a conviction that consequently sociological analysis has one-sidedly reflected male interests, outlooks, and prejudices. As Jessie Bernard has put it, "Practically all sociology to date has been a sociology of the male world. The topics that have preoccupied sociologists have been the topics that preoccupy men: power, work, climbing the occupational ladder, conflict, and sex—but not women—or women only as adjuncts to men" (Bernard, 1973, pp. 20–21). In a similar vein, according to feminist critics, sociological theories, methods, and general "models" of the social order also have reflected male perspectives or been used in male-emphasizing ways (Bernard, 1973; also Millman and Kanter, 1975, Introduction).

With respect to the sociology of deviance, a number of specific charges exist. Among the most important are the following (see especially Klein, 1973; Millman, 1975; and Smart, 1978):

1. Deviance studies have paid insufficient attention to women. Researchers and theorists have focused heavily on explaining male offenses. These are the behaviors that they have deemed socially consequential and have "taken seriously."

2. When they have tried to explain female deviance, the typical "explanations" have reflected sex role stereotypes, have been grounded in myths about biological sex differences and women's "innate" psychological qualities, or have depicted woman's behavior as being totally governed by her sexuality and her relation to men.

3. Works on female deviance have tended, in particular, to depict women offenders as suffering from "pathology" or as being in some way "unadjusted." Rarely has female deviance been interpreted "appreciatively" as active rebellion or simple unwillingness to conform. Thus one critic suggests that many deviance specialists share the common public view that "it is only men who take a serious stand against society and its conventions" (Millman, 1975, p. 252).

4. Analyses not oriented to pathology have sometimes stressed the "functions" of female deviance. The critics have cited, in particular, an early analysis of prostitution (Davis, 1937) which will be discussed further in Chapter Four of this text. As they point out (see especially Klein, 1973; and Smart, 1978), a supposedly nonevaluative discussion of such a practice's "functioning" easily slides over into an assertion of its inevitability if not its "value," neglect of its exploitative character, and evasion of the fact that it is primarily "functional" for men —in ways that we might well not wish to tolerate.

5. By focusing on offenders, deviance studies have neglected their victims. Thus the suffering that women have experienced because of male deviance has not been a major area of investigation.

6. This failure to study suffering reflects the more general tendency for sociology to exhibit "systematic blindness to crucial elements of social reality," especially the role of emotions in social life (Millman and Kanter, 1975, Introduction).

7. Another way of making this point is to note that the very definition of "deviance" adopted by the specialists has been too narrow. As Millman (1975, p. 254) puts it, "certain topics have been underinvestigated in the study of deviance: particularly everyday deviance and control in interpersonal behavior and everyday accommodation and suffering with regard to deviance."

8. There has been a failure to investigate the impact of sexism on prevailing public definitions of deviance. This failure reflects a broader tendency to exaggerate the separateness of deviance, to neglect its relation to the sociocultural context within which it arises and is defined. As the present writer has suggested, sociologists must recognize that "a society gets the deviance it deserves" (Schur, 1979, Ch. 2).

These allegations offer, in varying degrees, constructive commentary on many of the deviance studies conducted prior to the 1960s. However, in order to assess the overall and continuing value of the critique, we need to keep several basic considerations in mind. While they no doubt deserve strong criticism, certain of the studies focused on by the critics (for example, Lombroso and Ferrero, 1895; Thomas, 1923; Glueck and Glueck, 1934; Davis, 1937; and even Pollak, 1950) are early ones that are not truly representative of contemporary outlooks. Not all of the criticized studies were undertaken by sociologists; thus, a number of the heavily faulted authors have been psychiatrists, psychologists, or lawyers. Furthermore, the critics' primary focus, mirroring the actual emphasis in early research on deviance, has been on studies of crime and delinquency. As such, their conclusions are not uniformly applicable to contemporary work in the substantively more inclusive field of deviance and control.

Within this more broadly defined field (which now covers "offenses" and "stigmas" of many kinds), current outlooks and emphases should serve to correct many of the errors committed by earlier investigators. Our discussion already has touched briefly on a few of these current themes. Especially relevant in evaluating the feminist critique are the following points:

1. Most contemporary sociologists of deviance reject notions of biological "causation" and of the "offender's" pathology (see particularly Taylor, Walton, and Young, 1974, Ch. 2; Suchar, 1978, Ch. 3; Schur, 1979, pp. 48–66; Higgins and Butler, 1982, Ch. 2). They refuse to make the "assumption of differentiation" (Matza, 1964; Matza, 1969) under which it is supposed that "deviants" and "nondeviants" are basically

different kinds of people, and that by comparing them we will learn the "causes" of deviance. With the widespread repudiation of such assumptions, it becomes increasingly unlikely that sociologists will view female deviance in biological or pathological terms.

2. The shift in primary focus, from studying "offenders" to studying deviance-defining and specific reactions to perceived deviance, similarly implies that the meaning of female deviance cannot be found merely in the attributes or assumed qualities of women themselves. We have noted already that recent work on deviance emphasizes processes of meaning-attachment. This suggests the importance of studying the *meanings* of women's deviance problems, rather than simply describing and counting behaviors. Recent studies emphasize too the "audience of reactors" (Erikson, 1962). It would seem to follow that to understand the relation of women and deviance, a major focal point for research must be male perceptions, outlooks, and behaviors.

3. A related shift in preferred research methodologies has made for greater flexibility in the ways in which deviance is studied (see Douglas, ed., 1972). The renewed interest in meanings has led sociologists to examine deviance situations from the standpoint of the subjective experience of the actors themselves. Thus, qualitative methods, such as observation, have become very important. If, as Bernard (1973, pp. 22–24) suggested, there has been "a *machismo* element" in the past preference for quantitative techniques (in which the researcher is always trying to "control" and manipulate the data), recent methodological trends indicate a moderation of this tendency.

4. This in turn suggests the recent deviance analyst's increased interest in the "everyday deviance and control in interpersonal relations" to which Millman referred in her critique. At least potentially, current perspectives point to the importance of deviance-defining in everyday life (see, for example, Goffman, 1963; Garfinkel, 1964; Douglas, ed., 1970; and Schur, 1979, pp. 66–69).

5. Actually, the substantive scope of the deviance field has been expanding in several ways. We have seen that recent work emphasizes stigmatization more than either "wrongdoing" or "maladjustment." Deviance sociology is no longer exclusively focused on blameworthy, disruptive, or "disturbed" acts. Deviance-defining is seen to occur with respect to stigmatized personal conditions (such as physical and mental disabilities), orientations and life-styles (homosexuality, bohemianism, etc.), and even belief systems (e.g., political "extremists" and religious "cults"). Individuals often are stigmatized not so much for specific acts as for being certain kinds of persons, for membership in a devalued category. As we shall see below, even the way individuals look—for example, women who are deemed "overweight" —can brand them as deviant.

6. From this focus on devaluation (see Sagarin, 1975; also Goffman, 1963) sociologists may increasingly recognize that to be female has itself amounted to occupancy of a "deviant" status. In any case, recent outlooks make it more likely than before that the topic of women and deviance will be examined in the light of our society's pervasive devaluation of the female sex.

7. Recent deviance studies, as we have noted, stress the significance of power resources and conflict processes (see Becker, 1963; Lofland, 1969; Schur, 1971; Hawkins and Tiedeman, 1975). We should expect, accordingly, that analyses of women and deviance will now have to take into account women's relatively low power in our society, and their continuing social, economic, political, and legal subordination.

8. Finally, the recent guiding conception of deviance as a "social construction" encourages attention to the relation between deviance and social change. If current deviance definitions have been "created" and imposed, then they can also be modified or removed. Today's deviance may be tomorrow's conformity. Women's relation to deviance has been defined primarily by men, who have monopolized the power to define. The future relation between women and deviance will depend on whether there are changes in the distribution of such power. Women's collective efforts to effect such changes therefore also become important factors which the sociologist working in this area must study.

It would be a mistake to assume glibly that these general developments already have eliminated the problem of sex bias in the sociology of deviance. What they point to is a potential for more even-handed research and analysis. The present text represents a preliminary effort to indicate systematically how the study of women and deviance might begin to fulfill that potential. Men continue to dominate the profession of sociology. It is unlikely, therefore, that sexist influences on sociological work will disappear overnight. Furthermore, even the newer outlooks on deviance remain subject to some of the criticisms noted above. It is true, for example, that most labeling analysts have had relatively little to say about systematic exploitation, direct victimization, and harsh suffering—a point stressed in Millman's critique (Millman, 1975; see also Piven, 1980).

On the other hand, a totally pessimistic forecast is not warranted either. There is reason to believe that the critics' claims of sex bias already have begun to move workers in the field toward correcting earlier imbalances. Nor are sociologists unaffected by ongoing social movements in the world at large. It is quite evident that the recent women's liberation movement has had a significant influence on deviance research, particularly as regards the selection of specific study topics. Even a cursory review of recent textbooks and journal articles on deviance quickly reveals that "women's issues" are being given much greater prominence than before. It also appears that characteristic approaches to and conclusions about such issues are undergoing considerable change.

SOCIOLOGY AND FEMINISM

The growth of programs and courses in sex roles, sex and gender, and the sociology of women also reflects the influence of feminist activity. A further consequence has been the heightening, among many sociologists in diverse specialties, of a dual commitment— to actively strive for women's liberation as well as to document and interpret the situation of women in our society (see Millman and Kanter, eds., 1975). Some conventional sociologists may see a danger here that there will be a confusion of professional and personal roles. Feminist-sociologists, on the other hand, insist that they are not introducing any personal bias but simply trying to counteract the distortions that have shaped the field in the past. Recent work in "feminist theory" (see, for example, Rosaldo and Lamphere, eds., 1974; Jaggar and Struhl, eds., 1978; Eisenstein, ed., 1979; Sargent, ed., 1981; MacKinnon, 1982; Janssen-Jurreit, 1982) suggests further that feminist and academic perspectives, far from necessarily being in conflict, can be brought together in an intellectually fruitful manner.

Although this text reflects many feminist ideas, our primary aim here is to develop a sociological rather than a feminist analysis. Nonetheless, the materials and ideas in this text may well have implications for the clarification and pursuit of feminist goals. It is usually said that the major aims of feminism are equality and liberation. The necessary and proper call for economic, political, and legal equality does not directly address a companion issue on which this book focuses. There is also a pressing need to eradicate the pervasive objectifying of women that is built into the very processes of seeing and responding to them. Perceptions of women must be humanized or "normalized," just as their options and place in the social system must be equalized and strengthened. This book also suggests the need to ask whether what is popularly deemed to constitute "sexual liberation" always enhances female liberation. As we are going to see below, there are considerable grounds for believing that the tendency to treat the two as identical is unsound.

How should feminists view the decision, on which this book is based, to depict women's situation in deviance and control terms? One feminist writer recently asserted: "Using deviance concepts conceals the moral and social ugliness of certain ways of doing things, by classifying those ways as normal. Using them also conceals evidence that there are other ways of doing things and evidence that many people are criticizing and resisting" (Addleson, 1981, p. 190; see also the call for "emancipatory feminist speech" in Elshtain, 1982a). This comment is most apt as applied to the processes through which, in much ordinary social interaction, women are treated as deviant. However, its applicability to the social scientist's analytic use of deviance concepts is debatable.

When sociologists explore the ways in which women have been treated as deviant, their analyses are more likely to document than to conceal the "moral and social ugliness" such treatment involves. Nor can they be held responsible for the incontrovertible fact that many people in our society continue to view certain patterns and restrictions that oppress women as being "normal." Finally, documenting these unpalatable but only too real aspects of women's present situation need not lead one to ignore the existence of active opposition or viable alternatives. Realism compels us, however, to recognize which patterns are (still) dominant and which are not. An understanding of that persisting dominance may indeed be a major prerequisite in attempting to effect social change.

SUGGESTED READINGS

Becker, Howard S., *Outsiders: Studies in the Sociology of Deviance*. New York: The Free Press, 1963. The modern sociological classic which focused attention on the interpersonal and collective "labeling" of deviance.

de Beauvoir, Simone, *The Second Sex.* tr. H. Parshley. New York: Knopf, 1953. A major statement on woman's condition, and a key influence on contemporary feminism.

Gornick, Vivian and Barbara K. Moran, eds., *Woman in Sexist Society: Studies in Power and Powerlessness.* New York: Signet Books, 1972. Essays on various aspects of women's devaluation and subordination.

Millman, Marcia and Rosabeth Moss Kanter, eds., *Another Voice: Feminist Perspectives on Social Life and Social Science.* Garden City, N.Y.: Doubleday Anchor Books, 1975. Feminist critique of research and theorizing in various subfields of sociology, including the sociology of deviance.

Oakley, Ann, *Subject Women.* New York: Pantheon Books, 1981. Comprehensive and current overview of different aspects of modern women's situation, by a British sociologist.

Rubington, Earl and Martin S. Weinberg, eds., *Deviance: The Interactionist Perspective.* 4th ed. New York: Macmillan, 1981. Representative studies illustrating recent research on deviance.

Schneir, Miriam, ed., *Feminism: The Essential Historical Writings.* New York: Vintage Books, 1982. Excerpts from writings of the nineteenth century feminists, intellectual and activist forerunners of the contemporary women's liberation movement.

Schur, Edwin M., *Interpreting Deviance: A Sociological Introduction.* New York: Harper and Row, 1979. A text which attempts to provide a synthesis of current deviance theory and research in sociology.

CHAPTER 2

The Devaluation Process

Deviance is a matter of definition. It lies, as many people now recognize, in the "eye of the beholder." This phrase nicely depicts the relativity of deviance and indicates the need to focus on the definer. It may be somewhat less effective in capturing the equally crucial idea of process. Beholding is itself a process, one that may seem "internal" but which in fact is much affected by the beholders' social experiences and ongoing interactions. Beholders, furthermore, do not just "sense" that certain behaviors or people are deviant. They also respond in various characteristic ways. It is through closely linked processes of beholding and responding that the "deviance" emerges.

Direct attention to these processes of meaning-attachment is what makes the recent approaches to deviance "interactionist" (Rubington and Weinberg, eds., 1981). There are, in this view, two central and necessary ingredients of any deviance situation: stigma-laden meanings, and the processes of perception and interaction through which they emerge and are applied. Another important theme in recent deviance analysis has been that of deviant statuses and identities (see Garfinkel, 1956; Becker, 1963; Goffman, 1963; Lofland, 1969; Matza, 1969, esp. Ch. 7; Schur, 1979, Chs. 4 and 5; Pfuhl, 1980, Ch. 5; Farrell and Swigert, 1982, Ch. 8). As mentioned in the last chapter, a specific act of offending behavior may not always be needed for "deviantizing" to occur. It is often what one is perceived to "be," more than what one is believed to have done, that gives rise to stigmatization.

These emerging outlooks have led sociologists to focus on the close similarities that exist among substantively varying types of devaluation. Studies of physical disability (see Davis, 1963; Scott,

22

1969; Higgins, 1980; also Campling, ed., 1981) and mental retardation (Edgerton, 1967; Mercer, 1973) have found that responses to persons with such continuing handicaps are in many respects very much like reactions to persons thought to have committed morally blameworthy acts. As Eliot Freidson noted in an important essay (Freidson, 1965, p. 79), "The simple moral dichotomy of responsibility does not allow for the halo of moral evaluation that in fact surrounds many types of behavior for which, theoretically, people are not held responsible, but which in some way damage their identities." While the extent to which homosexuals are held "responsible" for their orientation may vary, it seems evident that their case too (see Plummer, 1975; also Lewis, 1979; Wolf, 1980; Ettore, 1980) involves devaluation of an overall identity more than of specific acts.

The line between reactions to these types of perceived deviance and devaluing responses to racial and ethnic minorities, and to women, is in turn a hazy one. We are going to see, throughout this chapter, that classic analyses of racial and ethnic prejudice are extremely helpful in illuminating diverse examples of stigmatizing. In a recent study of the common stigma problems experienced by blacks, Jews, and homosexuals, Barry Adam (1978) describes the process all three groups have undergone as "inferiorization." It is significant that the same term had been used earlier by Juliet Mitchell, in her important analysis of woman's situation (Mitchell, 1973, p. 67).

As these parallels suggest, being treated as deviant often has less to do with specific offending acts than with the "kind of person" one is taken to be (see Katz, 1975, on "essences as moral identities"). Although it is not yet common in sociological discussions to find the mere condition of being a woman described in deviance terms, the recent focus on generic devaluation processes helps us to see their relevance. Similarly, while women's studies specialists seldom state explicitly that femaleness is a "deviant status," this basic idea has been implicit in most analyses of women's situation, at least since Simone de Beauvoir's discussion of woman's relegation to the role of inessential "other" (de Beauvoir, 1953; see also Gornick and Moran, eds., 1972, Introduction).

Sometimes the idea has become explicit. Thus feminist writer Mary Daly (1974, p. 65) has asserted, "To be female is to be deviant by definition in the prevailing culture." And social psychologist Judith Long Laws (1979, p. 4) similarly comments, "Males as a group constitute the dominant class and females are the deviant class. . . . In our society, male is normal (not merely different) and female is deviant, or Other." Being female, Laws goes on to note, "carries a stigma in and of itself, independent of other attributes with which it may be hyphenated" (ibid.). In this chapter, we are going to explore basic features of the devaluation process which are present in the stigmatizing of women. Thus our focus here will be on *how* women are stigmatized. Chapters Three through Five will deal more directly with substantive examples of stigmatizing—that is, with *what* it is (besides simply *being* women) that women are stigmatized *for.*

CATEGORICAL PERCEPTION
Master Status

Deviant statuses, Becker (1963) has emphasized, tend to exhibit a "master status" quality. They "override all other statuses and have a special priority." The imputation of an identity that is deviant "proves to be more important than most others. One will be identified as a deviator first, before other identifications are made" (Becker, 1963, p. 33; see also Hughes, 1945). Numerous studies have demonstrated that when individuals are "seen" in terms of a deviant status and identity (past or present)—be it "criminal," "homosexual," "madman," "prostitute," "drug addict," "cripple," or "retardate"—other people's responses to them are heavily influenced by that identification. The tendency is for that to be all the other persons "see." Such imputed deviant identity becomes, in the eyes of others, the individual's essential character; Goffman terms it a "virtual" social identity as distinguished from the actual one (Goffman, 1963, p. 2; see also Garfinkel, 1956).

Reactions to perceived deviance thus emerge through a process of categorical "typing" (Rubington and Weinberg, 1981, pp. 5–7). The individual is responded to, first and foremost, in terms of his or her presumed membership in the devalued category. Furthermore, once this categorical label is applied, people tend to impute to the individual various "auxiliary traits" they believe (however erroneously) to be "characteristic of anyone bearing the label" (Becker, 1963, p. 33; also Hughes, 1945). It can easily be seen that this process is central to the general phenomenon of "prejudice," and that it is therefore manifest in the categorical devaluation of persons on the basis of race, ethnicity, or religion (see Allport, 1958).

Much the same thing is true of responses to women. Since it is indeed a basic mode of human differentiation, we would expect biological sex to carry some "master status" implications. Yet in fact this does not hold true equally for the two sexes. On the contrary, being a female, more than being a male (and in even more distorting ways), "conditions all social interactions; whether or not the individual is conscious of her femaleness, others are" (Laws, 1979, p. 2). Individual women are perceived and reacted to at least initially, and often primarily, in terms of their femaleness. Only secondarily, if at all, do their other identities and qualities determine responses to them. They are perpetually thought to be acting "just like a woman." They regularly have ascribed to them numerous "auxiliary traits" which reflect much refuted but none-theless persisting "sex role stereotypes" (see Chafetz, 1974, p. 61; also Friedan, 1963; Epstein, 1971; Stoll, 1974; Rothman, 1978; Stockard and Johnson, 1980; Richardson, 1981).

One of the most widespread cultural indicators of the master status tendency is the "hyphenization" phenomenon. Although the practice has been widely criticized, it remains common to describe someone as a "woman-doctor," a "woman-executive," a "woman-novelist," a "woman-athlete," or as the apocryphal "woman-driver." Despite what one might infer from the fact that there are also a few instances in which comparable designations may be applied to men (e.g., "male-nurse," "male-secretary"), such usage clearly represents more than just a convenient means of noting numerically infrequent patterns. In either case, there is an imputation of "occupational deviance" (see Chapter Three). But in addition, since high status occupations and prized compe-tencies tend to be stereotypically "male," the hyphenated designa-tions of women imply a further "put-down." Because she is female, a woman is assumed not to have the same overall compe-tence for the prized role that a man would have. Hence she should be described and assessed only relative to the occupation's other female occupants, rather than in terms of universalistic (i.e., sex-neutral) criteria. (Or, as we shall see shortly, she must be labeled an "exceptional" female.)

Two well-known empirical studies also illustrate the master status aspect of femaleness. A study by Philip Goldberg (1968) relates closely to the assumptions underlying hyphenization, and also shows how women themselves may devalue other women. Goldberg had female college students read excerpts of six journal articles drawn from the professional literature of six different fields—two of the fields being stereotypically "male," two stereotypically "female," and two deemed stereotypically neutral. In preparing the study materials, Goldberg had systematically varied the sex of the indicated authors. For example, one set of respondents reading a given article believed it to have been written by John T. McKay, while for another set of respondents the identical writing was attributed to Joan T. McKay. Asked to evaluate the articles and their authors, Goldberg's respondents consistently rated the articles attributed to men more highly than the identical articles attributed to women. Although the apparent bias against women was strongest in the evaluations of articles from traditionally male fields, the ratings favored presumed male authors in all the fields. Of fifty-four points at which comparisons were possible (each of the six articles was followed by nine questions), three were tied, seven favored the "female" authors, and forty-four favored the "male" authors.

In her study of "token" female sales personnel in a large industrial corporation, Rosabeth Kanter (1977a; 1977b) explicitly used the master status concept in describing and analyzing the responses to these women displayed by male members of the sales force. Kanter found much evidence that these women were perceived and reacted to more as females than as fellow workers. Because they were only "tokens" (i.e., constituted a small numerical minority) their femaleness "stood out." Their "technical abilities were likely to be eclipsed by their physical appearance," and both "male peers and customers would tend to forget information women provided about their experiences and credentials, while noting and remembering such secondary attributes as style of dress" (Kanter, 1977a, p. 973). They were viewed as objects of sexual attention, they were not fully trusted, and male workers made jokes at their expense. Often, in dealing with customers and managers, they "felt themselves to be treated in more wifelike and datelike ways than a man would be treated by another man, even though the situation was clearly professional" (ibid., p. 981).

Treated as "outsiders," these women could not easily enter into the existing (male) camaraderie of the work force. They felt pressured to play out male stereotypes of female roles (such as "the mother," "the seductress," and "the pet"), and if they did not succumb to these "role traps" they were seen as "tough" types who should be kept at a distance. Kanter's analysis emphasizes the matter of numerical frequency. She sees the skewed sex ratio as significantly influencing these modes of interaction. A good deal of experimental research on groups supports this claim—by showing, for example, that the size of a numerical minority within the group affects its members' ability to withstand majority-imposed pressures to conform. Yet it should be realized that Kanter's study can be given a broader reading as well. Almost all the male responses revealed in her research that reflect the "master status" aspect of femaleness are found in most female-male interaction in our society, regardless of numerical frequencies in the particular situations. There is, then, a sense in which women in general continue to occupy a "token" position within our system as a whole. To recognize this is not to deny that there are variations in types and degrees of stigmatization—depending on the particular perceived "offenses" of women and on other features of the specific situation (including the numerical frequency factor).

The beliefs and attitudes revealed in these studies are no doubt undergoing considerable change at the present time. This is perhaps especially true with respect to women's own beliefs regarding female competence. It is not even clear whether Goldberg's findings were fully representative of attitudes held at the time of his research (for discussion of related studies see Stoll, 1974; Fransella and Frost, 1977, Ch. 3; and Spence and Helmreich, 1978). Since then, the women's liberation movement has promoted an increased public awareness of the full range of female competencies. (For more recent data see Levenson, et al., 1975; also England, 1979.) On the other hand, even among women, the tendency to evaluate males more highly may not yet have disappeared. For example, if one were to conduct today a nationwide survey exploring women's preferences in the choice of a personal physician, it is not at all clear that a systematic bias toward males would not be revealed.

If women's beliefs and attitudes are still ambivalent, men's perceptions and behaviors are probably even more resistant to change. Responses in direct interaction situations (of the kinds found in Kanter's research) frequently become habitual in character, almost reflexlike, *regardless* of the beliefs and attitudes—about the abilities of women, and so on—that males might express if questioned. Throughout the rest of this book, we are going to encounter repeated examples of the ways in which male reactions to women are heavily affected by the fact of their femaleness—even in situations where that condition ought to be quite irrelevant.

Maintaining Consistency

The individuals who are perceived as falling into a devalued category are typically thought of as comprising a unitary or homogeneous "type." According to Adam (1978, p. 43) for any given category of the "inferiorized" there is a "composite portrait." It is "founded on three axioms: the inferiorized are (1) a 'problem,' (2) all alike, and (3) recognizable as such without exception." One sees reflected in categorical devaluation an apparent urge to differentiate as much as possible between "them" and "us." Characteristically, the persons who offend or disturb are viewed as being basically different, not at all like the individuals who are responding to them (see Schur, 1979, pp. 48–66)—hence the special appeal of biological and psychogenic "explanations" of the behaviors of devalued persons.

As Gordon Allport stated of ethnic prejudice, it is "an antipathy based upon a faulty and inflexible generalization" (Allport, 1958, p. 10). This is another way of describing the process of categorical perception, and in particular the imputation of "auxiliary traits" which the responders associate with the master status. Yet a third way of describing the process is in terms of "stereotypes" (false preconceptions). In the classic statement on stereotyping, Walter Lippman (1922, pp. 81, 90) noted: "We do not first see, then define, we define first and then see. . . . We are told about the world before we experience it. We imagine most things before we experience them. And those preconceptions, unless education has made us acutely aware, govern deeply the whole process of perception."

Allport emphasized the role of "linguistic labels" in the classification of the devalued. He pointed out that "each label we use, especially those of primary potency [i.e., master statuses], distracts our attention from concrete reality. The living, breathing, complex individual—the ultimate unit of human nature—is lost to sight." The label, Allport observed further, "magnifies one attribute out of all proportion to its true significance, and masks other important attributes of the individual" (Allport, 1958, pp. 175–176). Two major types of complexity especially are masked through this categorical typing process: the range of individual variation within each category, and the considerable overlap between the supposedly contrasting categories. Apart from having in common the attribute on which they are being classified, the categorized persons are not "all alike." By the same token, many of them have some attributes (other than the basis for classifying) in common with those in the "opposing" category.

It follows from such variation that the "typers" are going to encounter, and not infrequently, cases that contradict their preconceptions. Studies in the sociology of deviance demonstrate a tendency toward selective perception and a recourse to selective depiction in dealing with such contradictions. We should recall that deviant statuses are thought to indicate essential character or "virtual" social identity. Research suggests that deviance-definers experience a need to maintain intact the preconceptions they have about the presumed deviants. Thus efforts at maintaining cognitive consistency are a central feature of the devaluation process (see especially Lofland, 1969, pp. 124–128, 146–153).

In recent deviance studies, this has been seen primarily in terms of the process of "retrospective interpretation" (see Garfinkel, 1956; Goffman, 1961a; Kitsuse, 1962; Lofland, 1969; Schur, 1971; Rosenhan, 1973; Snyder and Uranowitz, 1978). Once an individual has been identified as a deviant (of whatever sort), observers tend to reassess the person's overall character and specific behaviors—past and present—in the light of that new, devaluing identity. The person's "social biography" is reconstructed in such a way as to be consistent with the presently imputed deviance. In the process, qualities and actions that contradict preconceived images regarding the particular deviant "type" are largely ignored. The devaluation of women and racial minorities does not usually require such "*re*-reading," because the devalued master status has been evident and governing other peoples' responses all along. The continuous "reading" of such individuals, however, is similarly selective.

Because individual women in fact display so many highly varying qualities and achievements—many of which conflict with persisting sex role stereotypes—categorical typing often demands adoption of some consistency-maintaining procedure. A major one is selective inattention, simply not "noticing" whatever it is that contradicts the stereotype. Once noticed, however, a discrepant item must somehow be reconciled with the "type." Allport described the means by which this is usually accomplished as the "re-fencing" device. "When a fact cannot fit into a mental field, the exception is acknowledged, but the field is hastily fenced in again and not allowed to remain dangerously open" (Allport, 1958, p. 23).

The familiar example of this which is seen widely in connection with women's devaluation is the use of "exceptionalism" labels. When a woman achieves to an extent or in ways that stereotypical notions describe as beyond female capacities, it is assumed and said that she must be "exceptional." Again, this is not really a statement about statistical probabilities. It is not just an assertion that most women do not do these things, but rather an implicit claim that "typical," "normal," and even "natural" women do not and cannot do them. Such reasoning allows the categorical type to stand, as does the description of a woman who behaves contrary to type as "acting like a man," or as being "masculine." The numerous stigmatizings of women for violating gender norms considered throughout this book can be seen as mechanisms for maintaining preconceived cognitive categories, just as they are also mechanisms for keeping women, individually and collectively, "in line."

Objectification

Categorical devaluation implies treating people as objects. Others respond to the devalued persons in terms of their membership in the stigma-laden category. Individual qualities and actions become a secondary consideration. The stigmatized person is reacted to primarily as "an instance" of the category. At an extreme, he or she is viewed as having no other noteworthy status or identity. When that point is reached a person becomes—in the eyes of others, for all practical purposes—*nothing but* "a delinquent," "a cripple," "a homosexual," "a black," "a woman." The indefinite article "a" underlines the depersonalized nature of such response. Members of the devalued category are treated as being virtually indistinguishable from, and in many respects substitutable for, one another.

Stigmatized persons, then, are little valued *as persons.* Classificatory status tends to displace alternative criteria of personal worth. Under these circumstances, others may claim license—implicitly if not explicitly—to treat the stigmatized individuals in exploitative and degrading ways. The logical endpoint of this process would involve treating them exclusively as "nonpersons" or mere objects. Black slavery and the mass extermination of Jews suggest the directions in which extreme and systematized depersonalization can lead. The relegation of racial or ethnic minorities to servant status—and the associated pattern of masters and mistresses behaving in the presence of servants as though they simply were not there—also illustrates the tendency toward treating the devalued as nonpersons.

Recent studies in the sociology of deviance have highlighted the importance of similar objectification processes. The most dramatic examples involve the ritual "mortification" or "identity-stripping" undergone by new inmates in such "total institutions" (Goffman, 1961a; also Foucault, 1977) as prisons, mental hospitals, and military barracks. Dispossessed of personal effects and attire and perhaps even normal physical appearance (as when inmates' heads are shaved, etc.), one now becomes—for all intents and purposes—"a prisoner," "a mental patient," "a recruit." The assignment of identifying numbers to both prisoners and military recruits is a final and very clear indicator of this depersonalization. If becoming a soldier carries some positive status that offsets the negation, such compensatory features are not available to prisoners or mental patients.

For the inmate, depersonalized treatment is an everyday occurrence. David Rosenhan's (1973) "pseudopatient" study—in which his research confederates were admitted to mental hospitals on the basis of fabricated "symptoms"—documented this ongoing tendency. As we might predict, staff members constantly "re-read" the behaviors and biographies of the pseudopatients in light of the presumed mental illness. Beyond that, however, routine staff responses to the pseudopatients' normal and courteous requests for information revealed that the latter were being seen largely as nonpersons. Rosenhan reports (1973, p. 25), "The encounter frequently took the following bizarre form: (pseudopatient) 'Pardon me, Dr. X. Could you tell me when I am eligible for grounds privileges?' (physician) 'Good morning, Dave. How are you today?' (Moves off without waiting for a response)."

Other deviance studies have disclosed different facets of objectification. Research on social control agencies has found that "typification"—the rapid classification of cases in a scheme of preconceived "types"—is central to their work (see for example Sudnow, 1965; Scheff, 1966; Cicourel, 1968; Emerson, 1969; Wiseman, 1970; also Hawkins and Tiedeman, 1975). When the processed individual becomes a typical case, he or she is likely to be responded to by officials in the manner they adopt for "any such case." Under this "bureaucratization of deviance" (Rubington and Weinberg, 1981, pp. 130–131; also Hawkins and Tiedeman, 1975), the personal qualities, problems, needs, and even specific "offenses" of the processed individual will not always determine official response. Often, in fact, strictly organizational factors (such as work load, pressure of public opinion, and so on) may significantly affect processing outcomes.

Any formal classification of an individual as falling into a devalued category implies some degree of objectification. The person is being converted into a "case," and is likely to be treated at least partly in those terms rather than individual ones. This is equally true whether the classification be deemed "correctional," "preventive," or "therapeutic." Virtually all of the recent studies of the "labeling" of deviance illustrate this conversion-objectification process. Response is to the label, not the individual; and the label is difficult to shed because the individual's other attributes or current accomplishments are overshadowed by it.

Table 1 shows how some of these general features of objectification are central to the devaluation of women. As part of their overall subordination, women find that their individual uniqueness and full humanity are regularly slighted. Frequently they (still) experience not being taken seriously in matters that are thought to "count." And to the extent a woman is responded to largely in categorical terms, she may well come to feel she is being treated as a standardized "thing," rather than as a real person.

Objectification in this general sense appears in combination with, and is exacerbated by, the more specifically sexual objectify-

Table 1 *The Objectification of Women*

---

1. General Aspects of Objectification

---

a. each woman responded to primarily as "a female," an instance of the category; personal qualities and accomplishments of secondary importance

b. women seen as "all alike," therefore largely substitutable for one another

c. woman's imposed secondariness, as inessential Other, and her assumed innate passivity, implying objectlike status—as compared with actively engaged subject (male)

d. woman's subordination meaning that things can easily be "done to her"—e.g., discrimination, harassment, violence; also that she can be endlessly studied, advised, converted into "a case"

e. similarly, woman as easily ignored, dismissed, or trivialized; treated as childlike or even as a nonperson

f. her social standing deemed to attach vicariously, through men; likewise, many of her actions attributed to her relations with men

2. Specifically Sexual Aspects of Objectification*

---

a. woman responded to (by heterosexual males) first and foremost, and in almost any context, as objects of sexual attention; men socialized not to respond to females as full human beings; perpetual male gaping; routine sexual harassment

b. the cultural preoccupation with women's "looks"
    (1) male perception of woman as depersonalized body parts—"a piece of ass," etc.
    (2) cultural and economic uses of depersonalized female sexuality—media, advertising, fashion, and cosmetic industries; pornography
    (3) women as "decorative" and status-conferring objects, to be sought (sometimes collected) and displayed by men
    (4) women evaluated according to prevailing, narrow, "beauty" standards
    (5) induced female preoccupation with physical appearance; concern about ascribed deficiencies and continuous efforts to conform to "appearance norms"; corresponding tendency for women to see themselves (through male eyes) as objects, and to respond to other women as (competing) objects

c. women as "sexual property," to be bought, sold, and "owned" (by men); owner can treat largely as he wishes; lack of an exclusive "owner" tarnishes woman's "respectability"

d. woman as object in sexual behavior itself; assumed passivity; function is to please man, her satisfaction not important; not supposed to initiate sexual activity

---

*The listed aspects of sexual objectification pertain primarily to heterosexual responses and interactions; note, however, that lesbians are not entirely exempt from being treated in some of these ways, and also that male homosexuals are not necessarily free of these objectifying tendencies. This is all the more true with respect to the general aspects of objectification.

ing noted in the second part of Table 1. For most women in our society, being literally "seen" as a sexual object (if not being virtually "undressed" in the process) is an omnipresent feature of everyday life. One feminist writer recently asserted, "Sexual objectification is the primary process of the subjection of women" (MacKinnon, 1982, p. 541). While many observers might not go that far, few would deny that such objectification is extremely significant.

Objectification implies denial of personal autonomy. Presumably this is the basis for MacKinnon's reference to it as the "primary process" in woman's subjection. In the chapters that follow, we are going to see that objectification—in both its general and its sexual aspects—has a great bearing on many specific women-and-deviance patterns. Treating women as objects is central to perceptions of female deviance associated with "appearance norms" and "sexuality norms." As we shall note too, it is a key factor in sexual harassment. Rape and woman-battering, and also prostitution, reflect the treatment of woman as a "thing," as does pornography —in which explicitly visual objectification plays a particularly crucial role. In a somewhat different sense, female crime and mental illness will be seen to entail objectification, as individual women are submitted to standardized (and stereotype-laden) categorization and routinized "processing."

STIGMA AND ITS CONSEQUENCES

Is Womanhood Really Devalued?

To what extent, overall, are we justified in viewing femaleness as a devalued or "deviant" status, one that—as Laws put it—"carries a stigma in and of itself"? The strength of heterosexual attraction, professed male reverence for certain (limited) women's roles (e.g., motherhood), and the persisting dominance of conventional heterosexual marriage, together suggest how difficult it is to answer that question. As Sheila Rowbotham (1973, p. 34) notes, "The relationship of man to woman is like no other relationship of oppressor to oppressed. It is far more delicate, far more complex. After all, very often the two love one another. It is a rather gentle tyranny. We are subdued at the very moment of intimacy."

It seems clear that the devaluation of women is not total. On the other hand, there is massive evidence showing that it is indeed very substantial, and that its manifestations are extremely widespread. This book is not a general treatise on woman's situation. For a review of the depth and extent of sex inequality in our society, the reader must consult other sources (see, for example, Laws, 1979; Stockard and Johnson, 1980; Oakley, 1981). We can, however, at least briefly note here four major grounds for accepting the notion that womanhood is, on balance, a devalued status. The first has just been referred to: namely, the well-documented existence of pronounced sex inequality within our social and economic system. An evaluative component is inextricably linked with placement in such a scheme of stratification. Highly valued persons are not systematically relegated (in the way women have been) to the lower echelons of the socioeconomic and occupational prestige ladders. Occupancy of such positions, in turn, tends to be a basis for evaluating people unfavorably.

A second reason to accept the claim that femaleness is devalued has to do with the widespread categorical perception and objectification tendencies cited above. It should be apparent that some measure of devaluation is always present in these modes of perceiving and responding to women. At times this element is only implicit, but at other times it becomes quite explicit, even blatant. Women are routinely—and to an extent that we cannot simply attribute to the general impersonality of modern life—treated in ways that suggest they are being little valued for their own selves.

A third and closely related point is the pervasive devaluation of women in "cultural symbolism" (Stockard and Johnson, 1980, Ch. 1; see also, Firestone, 1971; Gornick and Moran, eds., 1972; and Goffman, 1979). Common language usage often trivializes, slights, derogates, or unnecessarily sexualizes woman (see Lakoff, 1975; Adams and Ware, 1979; Richardson, 1981, Ch. 2; also Thorne and Henley, eds., 1975). The same can be said about images of women in the mass media and advertising—some specific aspects of which we will consider below. Widespread public exposure to softcore pornography, let alone the hardcore varieties, currently adds much sexually objectifying imagery of the most blatant sort to this constellation of cultural symbols. (See Chapter Four for discussion of pornography.)

The fourth, and perhaps overriding, reason to view femaleness as devalued is reflected in the central concern of this text—namely, woman's relation to definitions of deviance. Both the multitude of specific "deviances" imputed to women under our gender system, and the failure to strongly condemn male offenses against women, illustrate the low value placed on femaleness. When the extensiveness of these phenomena is explored, the devaluation thesis is once again confirmed.

In the light of these four important types of evidence, the male claim that far from being devalued woman has been kept on "a pedestal" appears highly disingenuous. The treatment of women as "special" that this implies is itself a denial of their ordinary and full humanity. And the little "courtesies" (door opening, cigarette lighting, etc.) that often are cited in connection with the "pedestal" notion trivialize relations with women as well as seeming to deny their capacities for everyday living. Kate Millett's comment (1971, p. 37) on male chivalry is most cogent. She describes it as "a sporting kind of reparation to allow the subordinate female certain means of saving face. While a palliative to the injustice of woman's social position, chivalry is also a technique for disguising it."

A 1960 news account (*The New York Times,* August 10, 1960) nicely suggests the phenomenon of subordination *via* the "pedestal." The article reports a magistrate's criticism of a woman for wearing slacks to traffic court (thus illustrating in retrospect the changeability over time of one type of gender-related "deviance"). In lecturing the woman, the judge explained that he took the matter seriously because he held women on a high plane, and didn't want to see them brought down from "this pedestal." In subsequent reported comments to the woman's husband, the judge inadvertently revealed the true nature of the pedestal. Saying that he would not go out with his own wife if she were dressed that way, he told the husband to "clamp down a little," or else it would be "too late."

Perhaps the most positive thing that can be said about overall male responses to women is that they are ambivalent (see Goffman, 1977, on reflections of such ambivalence in routine interaction). Social psychologist Irwin Katz (1981) has suggested that ambivalence may be a fairly common feature of responses to stigmatized persons. Focusing on reactions to blacks and persons with physical handicaps, Katz reviews findings from his own and other experimental studies to support an "ambivalence" model. Because they hold a mixture of positive and negative attitudes toward and feelings about the stigmatized, other people experience special tension in contacts with them—tension that in turn must be reduced. Thus, research subjects in various experiments attempted to justify or compensate for harm they did to blacks or handicapped persons (e.g., by administering a shock), more than when the harm was done to white or nonhandicapped persons. In other experiments, research subjects were found more likely, under certain conditions, to "help out" a black or physically handicapped person than they were to help a white or nonhandicapped person.

At first glance, the ambivalence thesis seems applicable to the "gentle tyranny" of men over women. However, the consequences of dominant male responses to women may be such as to prevent the "positive" side of the ambivalent feelings from having much real social force. Such consequences (at least in the past) have included the partial "segregation" of women in a separate women's "sphere," the discouragement of aspirations and restriction of opportunities, the consistent subjection to objectifying treatment in ordinary interaction, and so on. As we shall note shortly, systematic "inferiorization" of this sort easily becomes self-fulfilling and self-perpetuating. It can create conditions that minimize the need for males to confront evidence contradicting their stereotypes, or to experience discomfort when they negate women. The same conditions may reduce the efforts of females to demonstrate their full potential. Under all of these circumstances, the "tokens" of affection and respect men may bestow on women hardly seem sufficient to refute the claim of (and women's experiences of) a pervasive devaluation.

Experiencing Stigma

Women face stigmatization on a number of fronts. As we have seen, a certain degree of devaluation attaches merely by virtue of being a female. On top of this, women may be more directly stigmatized and punished for a multitude of specific "deviances" discussed in the next chapter. These definitions of female deviance are, in fact, so extensive that virtually every woman becomes a perceived offender of some kind. When these facts are considered, together with the devaluation implicit in woman's general social and economic subordination, it becomes clear that the combined weight of the stigma women may encounter is considerable.

The more concrete stigma experiences of particular women, and the impacts these experiences have on them, are bound to vary a good deal. Labeling analysts (see Lofland, 1969; Schur, 1971; Schur, 1979) have emphasized that the individual's relevant resources (socioeconomic, psychological, group support, etc.) will affect his or her ability to resist stigmatization or to avoid some of its negative impact. To the extent femaleness carries a stigma, avoidance of the "labeling" itself—as may be possible when the stigmatized condition is not immediately evident to others (see Goffman, 1963)—is not an option for women. As Helen Hacker noted (1951) in her important early discussion of similarities in the situations of women and blacks, both suffer from "high social visibility."

Other things being equal, stigmatization usually implies a number of negative social and psychological consequences for the "marked" individual (E. E. Jones, et al., forthcoming; also Goffman, 1963). Typically, social reactions aim to "isolate, treat, correct, or punish" such individuals (Schur, 1971, p. 24), and overall, in one or another way, to "contain" them (Schur, 1980). Many of the specific definitions of female deviance considered below, as well as the sanctions used to uphold them, appear to serve functions of this sort. Practical consequences of an individual's being stigmatized and treated in these ways can include the reduction of his or her social acceptability, a blocking of important social and economic opportunities, a diminishing of overall life chances.

Studies of deviance and also of racial and ethnic minorities have paid special attention to the psychological consequences of stigmatization. The central concept in such analysis has been the self-fulfilling prophecy, the possibility that a false definition—if acted upon sufficiently—can, in effect, become true. Thus the individual who has consistently been treated as inferior—and who also has been denied the opportunities to develop and demonstrate the capacities that would disprove this—may even come to see himself or herself as inferior. This possibility obviously is closely tied to the "master status" and "nothing but" aspects of categorical perception. The individual may not be able to avoid "engulfment" (Schur, 1971; Schur, 1979) or "entrapment" (Kanter, 1977a) in the devalued role. Edwin Lemert (1951, p. 77) depicted as the extreme endpoint of a stigmatization process the devalued person's "ultimate acceptance of deviant social status and efforts at adjustment on the basis of the associated role."

Again, the likelihood of such an outcome will be affected by the specific individual's personal resources. Also important will be the nature and extent of the specific stigmatizing. As John Lofland points out, "Other things being equal, the greater the *consistency, duration* and *intensity* with which a definition is promoted by Others about an Actor, the greater the likelihood that an Actor will embrace that definition as truly applicable to himself" (Lofland, 1969, p. 122). Studies invariably conclude that as a general proposition, and notwithstanding some individual variability, systematic devaluation implies a strong likelihood of impaired self-esteem. It is extremely difficult to maintain favorable self-conceptions in the absence of validation (that is, reinforcement) by others. Furthermore, as Goffman has noted, stigmatized persons have themselves been socialized to accept the beliefs and values on which the stigma is grounded. Accordingly, "The standards he [or she!] has incorporated from the wider society equip him to be intimately alive to what others see as his failing, inevitably causing him, if only for moments, to agree that he does indeed fall short of what he really ought to be" (Goffman, 1963, p. 7).

Hence stigmatized persons often display what Allport called "traits due to victimization" (Allport, 1958, Ch. 9; see also, Hacker, 1951; Fanon, 1952, 1968; and Adam, 1978). These can include various patterns of withdrawal and defensiveness, passivity, ingroup hostility and identification with the oppressors, as well as seriously impaired self-esteem. The last-named consequence has been emphasized in studies of the psychological problems of black persons, which at times have found the impairment to verge on self-hatred and to kindle severe psychological despair and rage (see Kardiner and Ovesey, 1951; Fanon, 1952, 1968; Grier and Cobbs, 1968; also Ladner, 1972).

Self-esteem has been a major focus also in studies of women's situation. Thus Hacker (1951, p. 61) stated that "women reveal their introjection of prevailing attitudes toward them," and Daly (1974, p. 48) has noted further that "As contradictory, divided beings, the oppressed do not fully grasp the paralyzing fact that the oppressor, having invaded the victims' psyches, now exists within themselves. They are caught in a web of self-defeating behavior." Gornick and Moran (eds., 1972, xx) similarly charge sexism with having produced in women "an image of the self that paralyzes the will and short-circuits the brain, that makes them deny the evidence of their senses and internalize self-doubt to a fearful degree."

Three specific empirical studies have regularly been cited as providing evidence of impaired female self-esteem or low achievement motivation among women. In Mirra Komarovsky's early research (1946) on "cultural contradictions and sex roles," 40 percent of her female college student respondents—torn between "modern" and traditional "feminine" roles—admitted that they had occasionally "played dumb" on dates. They pretended ignorance of certain subjects, expressed surprise over getting high grades, allowed men to explain at length things they already understood perfectly, and so on. Other similar studies have not always confirmed these findings (see discussion in Tresemer, 1975), and no doubt there has been substantial change over the years (see Komarovsky's own more recent assessment, in Komarovsky, 1976). Informal observation suggests, however, that at least some significant vestiges of this general pattern of intellectually deferring to men do still persist today.

Also frequently cited as providing evidence of low female self-esteem is the Goldberg (1968) "John T. McKay/Joan T. McKay" study, discussed earlier as an illustration of the "master status" implications of femaleness. The title of Goldberg's research report, "Are Women Prejudiced Against Women?", underlines sharply the conclusion he drew from his subjects' devaluing journal articles when they were attributed to female authors. As we noted earlier, there is reason to think that the general tendency which this finding illustrated has not yet disappeared. Some questions have been raised regarding certain details of his findings (see Fransella and Frost, 1977, pp. 50–54), and again we can assume that women's likely responses have changed considerably since the time of his research (see Levenson, et al., 1975). Nonetheless, Goldberg's study remains an instructive one—for its implications regarding self-esteem, as well as for its illustration of categorical perception and response.

The third regularly cited study has more directly to do with what social psychologists call "achievement motivation." Matina

Horner (1968) had college students write stories based on the initial cue, "After first term finals, Anne finds herself at the top of her medical school class." The stories female students produced included many unpleasant themes; they felt that Anne's success would have negative consequences—including social rejection, imputations of nonfemininity, and consequent self-doubts and unhappiness. Horner's and subsequent studies found that cues about men did not elicit this type of story, either from female or male respondents—though some research has found males and females responding similarly to the female cue (for discussion see Stoll, 1974, Ch. 6; Tresemer, 1975; Spence and Helmreich, 1978, pp. 73–84; Laws, 1979, pp. 60–74; Stockard and Johnson, 1980, pp. 162–165). Horner concluded that women tend to display a "motive to avoid success."

Many commentators have argued that Horner's findings do not tell us about real or basic female "motivation." Rather, it is claimed, they reflect realistic female concern about the likely consequences of high occupational achievement. Women, in this interpretation, are not negatively oriented to success as a general goal, but they reasonably fear being maligned or punished for such success. In similar fashion, Kanter (1977a, p. 986) suggests that what has been taken to be "fear of success," may really amount to fear of being in the "token" position. Of course, if women are cowed into lowering their aspirations or limiting their efforts, it may not matter much whether this happens because of an abjuring of success goals or a realistic fear of punishment. Either way, and however indirectly, the overall devaluation of females would again be taking its toll.

Responding to Stigma

The topic of women's overall response to devaluation and subordination is not one that can be explored fully in this short text. A few points will be noted briefly here, and some additional comments will be included in the book's final chapter. There is little doubt that women's individual and collective responses to being stigmatized are undergoing rapid change at the present time. Recent gains achieved by the women's liberation movement are especially likely to affect occupational expectations and aspirations (see Garrison, 1979) and hence "achievement motivation." It is evident too that the dominant overall valuation of women within the society is becoming *somewhat* more positive.

Yet many of the specific definitions of female "deviance" to be discussed below appear highly resistant to change. In addition, the direct visual objectifying of women (i.e., perpetual male gaping at their bodies) continues to be commonplace. Most of the evidence we have concerning women's feelings about such objectification is unsystematic. No doubt some women would say they enjoy being stared at, that it makes them "feel good about themselves." But perhaps more representative are the personal accounts in which women describe the practice as highly demeaning (e.g., "being looked over like a piece of meat in the market") and as reflecting underlying male hostility and contempt. For at least the two general reasons just cited, it would be very misleading to say that the stigmatization of femaleness is a thing of the past. By the same token, it is probable that few women are totally unaffected by the impact of persisting devaluation on their self-conceptions.

Deviance research and studies of racial and ethnic minorities have emphasized various patterns of social accommodation that tend to characterize relations between the stigmatized and the stigmatizers. Even when they reject the imposed definition of their "essential character," stigmatized persons frequently find it necessary to compromise with their oppressors. They "make various less than satisfactory accommodations, usually relinquishing a certain amount of their freedom of choice and action in order to make life tolerable" (Schur, 1979, p. 319). Hacker (1951) noted that similar "accommodation attitudes" were adopted by blacks and women, and Adam (1978) more recently has described strategies for "coping with domination" found in common among blacks, Jews, and homosexuals. One prevalent pattern involves accepting a certain amount of social segregation. In the case of women, immersion by default in a stereotypical "women's world"—child-rearing, housekeeping, personal grooming, women's clubs, and so on—illustrates this tendency. So too does an induced willingness not to pursue various possibly desired but stereotypically "male" options and activities.

Another significant type of accommodation, suggested by some of the specific studies cited earlier, involves exhibiting stereotypical "feminine" characteristics in the course of ordinary interactions with men. Contrived helplessness, seductiveness, flattery, eagerness to please, and excessive deference exemplify this general pattern. As should be apparent, both major types of accommodation involve partial acceptance of the aforementioned "role engulfment." Or, to put this another way, they involve a playing out of male stereotypes, a partial willingness to adopt some standard version of the "deviant role" (see Schur, 1979, pp. 319–320; also Scott, 1969; Adam, 1978).

The recent "rebirth of feminism" (Hole and Levine, 1971) has been reducing both the necessity for women to strike such accommodations and the social approval they are likely to receive for doing so. Women's liberation activity has entailed a general affirmation of femaleness from which all women should derive some benefit. Direct involvement in "consciousness raising" (Dreifus, 1973) or in collective political action is likely to enhance self-esteem and to provide group support for self-affirming decisions and behaviors (see Adam, 1978, pp. 122–124). It is important to recognize, however, that large segments of the female population have not been directly involved in the women's liberation movement. Fewer and fewer American women may be willing to model themselves after the so-called "total woman" (Morgan, 1975). Yet a good many women either purport to "accept" traditional definitions, or else submit to them—albeit with reluctance and distrust.

We shall return briefly to the topic of the women's liberation movement at the end of this book. The central point to be made here is that, while recent developments have encouraged a less compromising confrontation with stigma, liberation advocates should not exaggerate the ease with which the thoroughgoing devaluation of females can be overturned. In her recent discussion of the "powers of the weak," Elizabeth Janeway (1980) sensibly urges women to capitalize on their strengths instead of adopting a defeatist stance. It is true that power is a "relationship," that those in power invariably seek legitimacy (see also Wrong, 1980, Ch. 5, on "the interaction of coercion and legitimation"), and that men and women share overriding common interests that should govern their relations. But whether these facts are sufficient to ensure an "ordered" (proper, equitable, agreed-upon) use of power in male-female relations, such as Janeway envisions, is not at all clear.

As we already have noted, sociologists emphasize the role of relative power in determining definitions of deviance. The stigmatized almost always have something "to bargain with" in "stigma contests" (Schur, 1980). At the same time, however, the very recognition of their "stigmatized" status implies, after all, that they currently do not have the upper hand in the power equation. The next three chapters, exploring the substance of the still-dominant deviance definitions which are applied to women, should show that these points are highly relevant to a depiction of woman's situation today. The social analyst, in summary, should note the strength of changes currently underway and the undoubted prospects for further change. Alongside those projections, however, we need to acknowledge the presence of considerable resistance to change, and the consequent persistence of significant devaluation tendencies.

UNDERLYING PERCEPTIONS OF THREAT

This comment about resistance to change suggests an additional theme in recent deviance analysis that is applicable to the devaluation of women. As noted in Chapter One, efforts at deviance-designation usually rest on a powerful group's perception of some threat posed by the "deviants." The perceived threat may be quite specific, or it may be diffuse and "symbolic"—for example, the fear of a powerful segment of the population that its overall standing, or position of dominance, is about to be undermined (Gusfield, 1966; Gusfield, 1967; Cohen, 1974; Spector and Kitsuse, 1977; Schur, 1980).

It is the perception of a threat, regardless of whether that perception is well founded, that triggers the efforts at systematic devaluation. In an ingenious laboratory experiment, Pat Lauderdale (1976) established experimental groups in which subjects were asked to discuss and evaluate social work dossiers. Each group included one of Lauderdale's research confederates, who was instructed to adopt "deviant" positions in the group discussions. In some instances, but not in others, Lauderdale also introduced a "threat" condition—members overheard a statement that their group might have to be discontinued. Later, the subjects were asked to rank the members of their groups in terms of preference for working with them again. Although the "deviant" was consistently ranked lower than other group members, this difference was greatly heightened under the "threat" condition (despite the fact that the nature of the "deviance" itself was essentially the same).

As Lauderdale concluded (1976, p. 660), the "moral boundaries" —that is, the deviance-definitions—"move independently of the actual behavior of the individuals defined as 'deviant.' "

Male perceptions of threat appear to be a major factor underlying the devaluation of women. Such perceptions likewise constitute a central basis for resistance to change in this area. Most readily apparent is the fact that many men find the prospect of women's "liberation" threatening. In general terms, the nature of this threat perception is obvious: men fear that their overall position of dominance is under severe challenge. Beyond this we can note a number of more specific aspects of perceived threat. Some of these (especially those pertaining to the economics of male domination) are manifest and readily understandable. Others (sexual or psychological in nature) are more subtle and deep-seated, and considerably less "rational."

Male fears of having to face hiring, promotion, and salary competition from women represent the most straightforward type of economic threat perception. Not as often or as openly acknowledged, but clearly at stake, is male control of the entire system of economic institutions—the sphere that "counts" most in a capitalist society. In addition, the prospect of women becoming economically independent threatens to remove one of the key foundations of their individual and collective subordination. Finally, woman's liberation threatens the "political economy of sex" (Rubin, 1975; see also Lévi-Strauss, 1949, 1969; Collins, 1971)—in which women are valued as commodities, to be "exchanged" by men. (We shall return to this theme in Chapter Four, when we consider prostitution and pornography.)

When one turns from economic aspects of perceived threat to sexual and psychological ones a further complexity is apparent. Here the threat of women's liberation seems to be intertwined with a male tendency to experience the very condition of femaleness as threatening. A term Charles Suchar (1978, p. 1) has used to cover the variety of substantive perceptions that may underlie deviance-defining applies well in this case. Men find women highly "unsettling." If femaleness itself poses some kind of threat, then it becomes all the more important to keep it under control. Male fears of this sort, furthermore, heighten the tendency to think of women in categorical terms, and to emphasize their supposedly fearful biological characteristics.

Psychodynamic interpretations, particularly, imply that men find women sexually threatening. One aspect of this is men's fear that they will not be able to satisfy women sexually. Thus Dorothy Dinnerstein (1977, p. 62) refers to the "archetypal nightmare vision of the insatiable female." Andrea Dworkin (1974, p. 48) similarly refers to the implicit "cannibal" persona that co-exists with a more benign beauty imagery of women: "She is devouring and magical. She is devouring and the male must not be devoured." In his psychohistorical study of nineteenth-century American writings on women's sexuality, G. J. Barker-Benfield notes that the demands of female sexuality were widely seen as undermining male work energy and economic acquisition. Thus he reports one leading writer's belief in "a direct relation between man's primary economic activity and copulation; the latter was demanded of men by women and demanded always potentially excessively." If a man gave in to such demands, he would be "drained of his life's blood and enslaved by woman's appetite, and he would fail in business" (Barker-Benfield, 1977, p. 196).

More recently, male fears of female sexuality may have been exacerbated by the Masters and Johnson (1966) research demonstrating that most women are capable of experiencing multiple orgasms. Mary Jane Sherfey, in her systematic study of the biology of female sexuality, suggests that women's powerful sexual drives may lie behind their social subordination. She thus comments that "The strength of the drive determines the force required to suppress it" (Sherfey, 1973, p. 139). Also potentially contributing to male perceptions of female sexual threat has been the attention recently paid to the clitoral, as opposed to the vaginal, orgasm (see Masters and Johnson, 1966; Lydon, 1970; Shulman, 1972; Sherfey, 1973; Laws and Schwartz, 1977, pp. 56–61). Men fear not merely that they will fail to satisfy women, but that they could become largely dispensable as sexual partners. From that standpoint, as we shall consider further in the next chapter, lesbianism might well be perceived by heterosexual men as constituting an ultimate threat to male sexuality.

Dinnerstein (1977) has discussed additional aspects of femaleness which she asserts men find psychologically threatening. She refers to a "carnal ambivalence" toward woman, who is taken to represent unpredictable nature, the body—and hence, mortality. Man has "magic feelings of awe and fear, sometimes disgust . . .

toward all things that are mysterious, powerful, and not himself ... woman's fertile body is the quintessential incarnation of this realm of things" (Dinnerstein, 1977, p. 125). Such ambivalence is fueled further by the fact that woman (first experienced in her all-enveloping motherhood role) also symbolizes absolute power and recalls the situation of complete dependency. As a result, women evoke "the terror of sinking back wholly into the helplessness of infancy" (Dinnerstein, 1977, p. 161). All this heavily rests, according to Dinnerstein (and see also Chodorow, 1978), on the arrangements and norms through which the mother in our society has exclusive responsibility for childrearing. Both Dinnerstein and Chodorow argue that until there is a significant sharing by men of that responsibility it will not be possible to substantially modify our overall system of male-female relations.

Finally, it has been suggested that women—and especially the prospect of equality for women—may somehow be perceived as a threat to male identity itself. According to Barker-Benfield, "Men's continued insistence on inexorable difference and separation seems to have indicated an anxiety that the sexual distinction would not be sustained" (Barker-Benfield, 1977, p. 209). In this point we can see a link between the psychodynamics and the social dynamics of gender. Gender norms and arrangements are concerned with maintaining "boundaries" (see Douglas, 1966)—moral, social, and also psychological.

Imputed male superiority and male social dominance require female "deviance" and subordination. Thus Dworkin asserts: "The truth of it is that he is powerful and good when contrasted with her. The badder she is, the better he is" (Dworkin, 1974, p. 44). As noted earlier, the sustaining of "masculinity" (as presently construed) requires the existence of a counterpart "femininity." Change on one side of the equation invariably affects—and in some sense "threatens"—the other side as well.

SUGGESTED READINGS

Adam, Barry D., *The Survival of Domination: Inferiorization and Everyday Life.* New York: Elsevier, 1978. Sociological analysis of similarities in the problems and responses to stigmatization of blacks, Jews, and homosexuals.

Allport, Gordon W., *The Nature of Prejudice.* Garden City, N.Y.: Double-day Anchor Books (1954), 1958. The classic discussion of social psychological aspects of prejudice. A major treatment of categorical perception processes.

Dinnerstein, Dorothy, *The Mermaid and the Minotaur: Sexual Arrangements and Human Malaise.* New York: Harper Colophon Books, 1977. Psychoanalytically oriented analysis of ambivalence toward women and its relation to the gender system as a whole.

Goffman, Erving, *Stigma: Notes on the Management of Spoiled Identity.* Englewood Cliffs, N.J.: Prentice-Hall, 1963. Insightful analysis of how stigmatized persons deal with social devaluation in their everyday interactions.

Lofland, John, *Deviance and Identity.* Englewood Cliffs, N.J.: Prentice-Hall, 1969. A sociologist's exploration of factors which affect the individual's susceptibility to deviance labeling.

Schur, Edwin M., *Labeling Deviant Behavior: Its Sociological Implications.* New York: Harper and Row, 1971. Critical overview of the "labeling" perspective on deviance.

PART II

Substantive Applications

CHAPTER 3

Women's Deviance Through Gender Norms

Perceptions of female deviance, as we noted at the outset, transcend the categories around which conventional deviance courses have been organized. Our focus in this chapter is going to be on deviance definitions routinely applied to women in their everyday lives. Under the gender system as presently constituted women are subject to an enormous array of increasingly questioned, but still dominant norms. These norms, which cover virtually all aspects of women's behavior and regular life situations, imply corresponding "deviances" for which women are likely to be stigmatized. Although there are in many of these areas counterpart gender norms governing male behavior, we are going to concentrate here on those which directly affect women. Therefore, the substantive examples we will be considering in this chapter are, as it were, "distinctively female offenses."

While these norms sometimes may be buttressed by formal definitions and procedures (as in psychiatric diagnosis and legal rulings) they operate for the most part on a level of informal interaction. Yet their pervasiveness and their continuous application to women, in various combinations, more than make up for whatever they may lack in formality. Compounding this widespread vulnerability to deviance-defining is the fact that women are often subjected to norms that contradict one another. As a consequence their efforts to conform to one standard may be treated as deviance when viewed from the standpoint of the opposing one.

To an extent this reflects a general condition of complex modern societies. Extensive role-overlap and role conflict imply that often behavior may be both "conformist" and "deviant" at the same time—depending on which set of expectations governs the evaluation (see Schur, 1979, pp. 100–102). However, the labeling of women as "deviant either way" seems to go beyond what one would expect from this overall social complexity. It reflects the uniquely high degree of "structural ambivalence" (Oakley, 1976, pp. 80–90; also Komarovsky, 1946) that has dominated thinking about women's roles. It reflects as well the generic stigma—ascribed merely on the basis of *being* a woman—which was discussed in the last chapter.

MAJOR TYPES OF GENDER NORMS

With the possible exception of books on etiquette (see Goffman, 1956), most gender norms are unwritten, and as just noted they tend to be imposed in the course of ordinary interaction. We can infer their existence from some of the standardized ways in which women (and men) behave, from various constraints they report experiencing, and especially by observing how and when sanctions are imposed to keep them "in line." Since virtually every aspect of female (and male) behavior is evaluated in gender terms, there is no single definitive or exhaustive way of specifying and classifying gender norms. Table 2 suggests one way of organizing some of the most important substantive examples. It is not possible here to discuss all of these with any thoroughness. Instead, this chapter will begin with but a brief overview of the various categories. Then, three of the categories—appearance norms (the female beauty cult and related "deviances"), maternity norms (with a special focus on the abortion issue), and sexuality norms (with particular attention to lesbianism)—will be singled out for special consideration.

If we think of the system of gender norms as a mechanism for the social control of women, then these three categories would seem to be especially pivotal. Beauty norms govern the visual objectification of women, a key aspect of their overall objectified status. Maternity norms govern what often has been viewed as the primary traditional female role, and could be taken more generally

Table 2 Gender Norms and Female Deviance

Major Category of Norms	Typical "Offenses" and Deviance "Labels"
1. Presentation of Self	
a. emotions	too little emotion ("cold," "calculating," "masculine"); *or* too much emotion ("hysterical"); *or* various "wrong" emotions (different types of "mental illness")
b. nonverbal communication	"masculine" gestures, postures, use of space, touching, etc.
c. appearance	"plain," "unattractive," "masculine," "overweight," "fat," "old," "drab," "poorly made up"; *or* "overly made up," "flashy," "cheap"
d. speech and interaction	"unladylike," "bossy," "competitive," "aggressive"; *or* "timid," "mousy," "nonentity"
2. Marriage/Maternity	
a. marital	"spinster," "old maid"; *or* "unmarried," "divorcée," "widow"; *or* "unwed mother"; *or* "sleeps around"
b. maternity	voluntary childlessness ("selfish"); *or* abortion ("killer"); *or* "unwed" motherhood; *or* "unmaternal," "unfit mother," etc.
3. Sexuality	
a. behavior	"oversexed," "nymphomaniac," "promiscuous," "loose," "cheap," "whore"; *or* "cock-teaser," "cold," "frigid"
b. orientation	"butch," "dyke," "queer," etc.
4. Occupational Choice	in a "man's" job, "tough," "aggressive," "castrating," "ball-buster," etc.
5. "Deviance Norms"	norm-violation "inappropriate" for females (e.g., armed robber, political revolutionary)

as emblematic of controls over personal autonomy. That sexuality norms are central to women's subordination is also readily apparent. Control over female appearance, autonomy, and sexuality—this might indeed serve as a capsule statement of what male domination entails.

The various norms depicted in Table 2 have all contributed to keeping woman in her "place." They have defined and limited the roles and behaviors deemed appropriate for females. In a sense, then, they have all been elements in what largely remains the dominant definition of "femininity." This point is underscored by the frequency with which perceived female norm violators are given the deviance label "masculine." As acknowledged above, many of these norms now face serious challenge. However, the cumulative force of this normative system continues to be substantial, even if some of the specific norms are less regularly or less strongly invoked than before. Let us next consider very briefly those categories in Table 2 which are *not* going to receive further attention in this chapter.

Presentation of Self

Once we recognize that there are norms governing how we "present" ourselves to others (Goffman, 1959), we can see the enormous potential for gender-based deviance-defining to occur in routine interaction. There are, to begin with, patterned expectations regarding the emotions that women and men are supposed to display, and even to feel. It is widely recognized that our gender system incorporates assumptions as to the emotional qualities that are "natural" to the two sexes. What is less often noted is the related element of interpersonal evaluation, the phenomenon of implicit emotion norms. Arlie Hochschild (1979; and see Goffman, 1961b) has suggested that "feeling rules" specify the emotions it is deemed appropriate to experience, as well as to display, in various kinds of situations. We engage in "emotion management" —evoking, shaping, or suppressing feelings of different kinds—in order to avoid committing "affective deviance."

Perhaps the best-known emotion rule in our present gender system is that men are supposed to suppress their feelings, to display little emotion of any sort (see especially Pleck and Sawyer, eds., 1974; Farrell, 1975; Lewis, ed., 1981). There is little doubt that men are unfairly denied by being consigned to this unfeeling state. However, woman's situation with respect to emotion norms may be even less enviable. As Table 2 suggests, females are subject to multiple and alternative imputations of affective deviance. They are believed to be "innately" emotional, and are expected to act accordingly—up to a point. Yet women's actions are regularly dismissed as being the results of their "emotionalism," and the deviance label "hysterical woman" is frequently applied. Even when this extreme is not reached, women often are perceived as displaying the "wrong" emotions.

If a woman does not openly demonstrate stereotypically "feminine" qualities—warmth, nurturance, supportiveness, and so on—she is likely to be defined as "cold," "calculating," "manipulative," and "masculine." Correspondingly, her direct display of emotions that are prized or accepted in men—such as coolness, assertiveness, aggressiveness, and anger—will usually be disapproved. Thus women are susceptible to negative sanctioning for several types of emotion norm violations. And when women themselves internalize the norms, they may even condemn themselves for such violations. On top of all this, women are expected —in line with prevailing gender assumptions (male impassivity, etc.)—to carry a heavy burden of "emotion management." As we shall see in Chapter Five, both the "deviant-either-way" nature of female emotion norms, and the heavy strains such norms impose, are significant elements in the diagnosing (and also the experiencing) of mental illness among women.

Of all the norms relating to presentation of self, those having to do with physical appearance are probably the most significant; they are discussed in a separate section below. But other nonverbal aspects of self-presentation also bear a close relation to the control of women through gender-based definitions of deviance. As Nancy Henley and Jo Freeman (1979, p. 475) have suggested, "If women are to understand how the subtle forces of social control work in their lives, they must learn as much as possible about how nonverbal cues affect people, and particularly about how they perpetuate the power and superior status enjoyed by men."

Henley (1977) has provided an excellent review of research on the gender implications of different aspects of nonverbal communication. Citing Goffman's early (1956) observation that relations between persons of unequal status are "asymmetrical," she discusses numerous studies illustrating that norms governing posture, gesture, movement, use of space and time, touching, facial expression, and so on, reflect and support the low power position of women. Table 3, reproduced from Henley's work, summarizes the major findings from such research. As the table indicates, the male-female differences shown there follow the same pattern gen-

Table 3 **Gestures of Power and Privilege: Examples of Some Nonverbal Behaviors with Usage Differing for Status Equals and Nonequals, and for Women and Men**

	Between Status Equals		Between Status Nonequals		Between Men and Women	
	Intimate	*Nonintimate*	*Used by Superior*	*Used by Subordinate*	*Used by Men*	*Used by Women*
Address	Familiar	Polite	Familiar	Polite	Familiar?*	Polite?*
Demeanor	Informal	Circumspect	Informal	Circumspect	Informal	Circumspect
Posture	Relaxed	Tense (less relaxed)	Relaxed	Tense	Relaxed	Tense
Personal space	Closeness	Distance	Closeness (option)	Distance	Closeness	Distance
Time	Long	Short	Long (option)	Short	Long?*	Short?*
Touching	Touch	Don't touch	Touch (option)	Don't touch	Touch	Don't touch
Eye contact	Establish	Avoid	Stare, Ignore	Avert eyes, Watch	Stare, Ignore	Avert eyes, Watch
Facial expression	Smile?*	Don't smile?*	Don't smile	Smile	Don't smile	Smile
Emotional expression	Show	Hide	Hide	Show	Hide	Show
Self-disclosure	Disclose	Don't disclose	Don't disclose	Disclose	Don't disclose	Disclose

*Behavior not known

Source: From *Body Politics* by Nancy M. Henley. © 1977 by Prentice-Hall, Inc. Published by Prentice-Hall, Inc., Englewood Cliffs, NJ 07632.

erally found in interaction between any persons of unequal status. This underscores the fact that they are "not sex differences, they are power differences" (Henley, 1977, p. 192). The findings presented in Table 3 can be read in two ways. They indicate the dominant behavior patterns researchers have observed in male-female interaction—patterns that reflect and reinforce female subordination. But they also imply patterns of approval and disapproval. Women (or men) will be punished if they depart from the pattern, if they violate the norm. To appreciate how significant such everyday perceptions of deviance are, we need only ask ourselves just what people mean when they say a woman is insufficiently "feminine." In many if not most instances, superficial nonverbal mannerisms, along with physical appearance, become major determinants of such judgments.

Erving Goffman (1979) has shown how the depiction of women in magazine and newspaper advertisements similarly reflects and reinforces the system of male dominance. Goffman reproduces, classifies, and interprets five hundred or so ads—not primarily with an eye to their substantive content, but rather with a focus on subtleties of body placement, depicted posture and gesture, and implied attitude. His study makes clear that at this level of pictorial presentation too women invariably are cast into subordinate roles. Female figures in the ads are smaller than the male ones, are placed lower, and their postures and gestures (knee-bends, "canting postures," prostration, etc.) signal subordination. Styles of holding are asymmetrical (males holding females more), and male attire is, according to Goffman, more formal and serious. Depictions of attitude and implied emotion also reflect common stereotypes. Thus Goffman concludes that women in the ads smile more and "more expansively" than do men. In addition, they are allowed what Goffman terms "licensed withdrawal." They are shown gazing off from the scene of the action, being psychologically "away," acting dreamily, averting their gazes, and appearing to communicate primarily with themselves or with inanimate objects. This research by Goffman was, of course, one step removed from actual human behavior, and it did not deal explicitly with definitions of deviance. Nonetheless, "gender display" of the sort he documents both reflects and reinforces (much as do the Henley findings) prevailing evaluations as well as prevailing behavior patterns.

Two examples of a different kind of "gender display" further illustrate the extent to which nonverbal cues are built into prevailing conceptions of "femininity." When biologically male transvestites (cross-dressers) succeed in "passing" as women (see Feinbloom, 1976), their success is almost entirely due to their mastery of what we conceive of as a "feminine" presentation of self. Likewise, when biologically male transsexuals (who sincerely believe that they are "really" women, "trapped" in the wrong kind of body) seek sex-change operations, it has been common for (primarily male) physicians to require that they first demonstrate that they can "pass" socially as women (Raymond, 1979). Indeed, it is only because they accept common stereotypes of "femininity" (including those concerning "feelings" and other nonverbal cues) that biologically male transsexuals can believe in the "wrong body" phenomenon at all. The "deviance" of transsexuals and transvestites seems twofold—they are condemned in part for trying to "steal" the other (biological) sex's appearance and "body language," and more generally for unacceptably blurring boundaries of sexual identity that people wish to believe are clear-cut.

Speech and interaction norms have received somewhat more attention than norms of nonverbal communication. While much has been written about sexist language usage, more relevant for our purposes here is the normative regulation of speech *by* (rather than about) women. Speech norms for women are trivializing in their substance, and at the same time their existence provides the basis for numerous imputations of "verbal deviance." As Robin Lakoff (1975) notes, the socialization of young girls to adopt a special, supposedly genteel "women's language" places them in an untenable situation. If a girl does not learn to talk "like a lady" she will be dismissed as unfeminine. However, if she does conform, her views will be dismissed because they will not have been presented in the manner called for in significant and serious discourse. According to Lakoff, higher education merely makes a woman "in effect a bilingual." Caught between two "languages," she may "never feel really comfortable using either, and never be certain that she is using the right one in the right place to the right person" (Lakoff, 1975, pp. 6, 7).

The prescription for "woman's language" includes specific norms governing speech content, intonation, and amounts and occasions of speaking. Women's speech is supposed to be more "polite" (e.g., no swearing) and less decisive than men's (Lakoff cites the frequent use of the "tag-question"—such as "John is here, isn't he?"), and to incorporate trivial descriptions (e.g., preoccupation with color gradations—such as lavender, mauve, beige, etc.) and slightly precious adjectives ("adorable," "sweet," "lovely," and "divine"). The wrong speech intonation, as implied by our earlier discussion, can easily earn a woman either the "hysterical woman" or the "cold bitch" label. As to speech frequency, it may be a common assumption that women talk more than men (and do less?), but it is primarily about inessential matters and about themselves that women are encouraged to talk.

Though women may be expected to carry the burden of sustaining everyday nonwork-oriented conversation (Fishman, 1978), males may nonetheless maintain dominance through greater license to interrupt (see West and Zimmerman, 1977). Women are expected, in cross-sex interaction, to converse in responsive and supportive if not deferential ways (see discussion of various findings in Adams and Ware, 1979), and in matters that really count to remain relatively quiet. Passivity and deference are, of course, norms that govern not merely speech but women's more general participation in interaction situations. A classic finding emerged from the Chicago Jury Project's intensive studies of mock jury deliberations. This early research (in the 1950s) suggested that when an important group task is to be undertaken, women are not expected to take a leadership role and will not be inclined to do so (Strodtbeck, James, and Hawkins, 1957).

There seems little doubt that speech and interaction norms are now undergoing significant change. Given women's growing access to higher status and more "responsible" occupational roles, this is understandable. At least when the "token" situation Kanter (1977a, 1977b) described has been transcended, female passivity and deference in speech and interaction will have to be more widely seen as dysfunctional, as well as unfair. Nevertheless, a caution similar to that voiced above in connection with the "playing dumb on dates" and "John T. McKay/Joan T. McKay" findings may be appropriate here. This pattern too, and the deviance perceptions associated with it, have not yet disappeared. In many situations, men continue to dominate routine interaction, and women continue to face disapproval if they refuse to acquiesce.

Marital and Occupational Norms

These norms may be considered together as major examples of "status norms" affecting women. That is, rather than being concerned with how women should behave in general, such norms specify which established social positions (statuses) women should occupy. The importance of both marital and occupational norms has been extensively discussed and documented in many popular as well as professional works. Our brief discussion here will focus on the ways in which such norms establish a basis for deviance imputations.

Marital Norms.   There are many specific aspects of the prescribed marital role which, despite their undoubted connection with the overall devaluation of females, cannot be treated in this short account. These include, for example, the nature and social appraisal of housework (see Oakley, 1976), the economic implications of unpaid work in the home, women's heavy childrearing responsibilities, sexual relations within marriage, and other similarly important topics. Our main concern here is with something different—the very fact of *marriage as a prescribed role.*

Given the changes that have been occurring in living arrangements, sexual behavior, and attitudes toward the family, some observers assert that today marriage is merely one of many options that people may choose. Available evidence, however, does not support such an extreme claim. Although the view of marriage as a required ingredient of "normal" adult womanhood has eased somewhat, this norm—if no longer absolute—still has great strength. Judith Laws and Pepper Schwartz (1977, p. 137), in a work highly sympathetic to the notion of diverse options, acknowledge that (heterosexual) monogamous marriage remains "the expected relationship." While our conceptions as to what marriage should be like may be in flux, "The *idea* of marriage and its potential is still powerful. It is a sacred script, one we have trouble rejecting because it is so central a part of our socialization and adult expectations" (ibid., p. 139).

Studies have regularly shown that in our society, marriage as a major life goal and psychological preoccupation has traditionally been a more crucial element in the socialization and experience of females than of males (see the discussion of various findings in Stockard and Johnson, 1980, pp. 258–259). Women's marriageability has been seen as a key test of their "attractiveness" and, ulti-

mately, their "femininity." Such evaluations will necessarily
persist (in some degree) as long as the pattern in which women are
expected to "market" themselves for marriage continues in force.
It remains true today that a woman who is unmarried—particularly if others deem that condition to be involuntary—faces stigma
on that account. And if the woman herself has doubts as to
whether she really "chose" singlehood, some degree of self-depre-
cation is likely to follow as well.

There is no evidence of substantial change in these responses,
notwithstanding such publicized phenomena as unmarried cohabitation, high divorce rates, and "alternative lifestyles"—including
voluntary singlehood. The U.S. Census Bureau reported in 1979
(see *The New York Times,* June 27, 1979, pp. A1, B5) that the
number of households containing two unrelated adults of opposite
sexes had doubled since 1970, reaching a total of 1.1 million.
Various studies (see Macklin, 1978; also the general review by
Cole, 1977) have found that unmarried cohabitation is especially
widespread among college students. For the most part, however,
such cohabitation has not been adopted as a permanent alternative
to marriage, nor does it appear to have significantly affected the
overall negative evaluation of singlehood.

Although high divorce rates have long been cited by those
predicting the demise of the conventional family, the co-existence
—at least until very recently—of high remarriage rates, following
both divorce and widowhood, appeared to belie the claim of general disillusionment with marriage (see Skolnick, 1978, pp. 234–
237). Current projections of the future state of affairs must be
highly uncertain. Since change in this area appears to be occurring
quite rapidly, the inevitable time lag in reporting research findings
becomes a special problem. It is undeniable that certain significant
changes are occurring—including a higher age at first marriage,
and a conscious decision by some persons never to marry . In the
aforementioned Census Bureau report, it was also found that the
proportion of women aged 25–29 who had never married had risen
from 10.5 percent in 1960 to 18 percent in 1978, up 70 percent. To
what extent these findings imply permanent singlehood (as opposed to deferred marriage), let alone voluntary permanent singlehood, is of course not clear.

The effect of recent changes on the overall tendency to stigmatize unmarried women appears, however, to have been minimal.
From his interview study of single adults, Peter Stein (1981) con-

cluded that such individuals now experience and report positive advantages to being single, as well as persisting disadvantages and problems. Yet despite his apparent efforts to counterbalance the exclusively negative depiction of singlehood in previous accounts, Stein was forced to acknowledge the persisting denial of legitimacy to such a choice. "In the absence of marriage these single adults noted the importance of substitute networks of human relationships that met their needs for intimacy, sharing and continuity. While pressures from external sources to leave singlehood continued, their membership in various support networks and in validating reference groups enabled them to discount negative evaluations" (Stein, 1981, p. 16). There is good reason to believe these negative evaluations continue to be applied more strongly to unmarried females than to unmarried males.

An often-cited indicator of this is the difference in terms used to describe female and male single persons. There really are no male equivalents of "spinster" and "old maid" (both of which have an explicitly sexual, as well as marital reference), and there is no female counterpart of the somewhat more positively tinged term "bachelor." The use of all of these terms may now be on the decline. Yet the terms that continue to be widely used—"unmarried woman" and "single man"—themselves imply differential evaluation of female and male singlehood. Woman in this situation is not merely on her own, she is deficient.

Only when other statuses besides marriage are viewed as being equally important for women will this common deviance perception recede. Until then, for females particularly, it will be true that "as a social category, singles are devalued and degraded" (Richardson, 1981, p. 271). It is only possible to note in passing two special versions of singlehood—the situations of the divorced woman and the widow. Stigmatizing the "divorcée" appears to have declined considerably in recent times, though devaluing imputations of "loose" sexuality do persist. The widow experiences, along with other single persons, many specific problems (and some unique to her situation), but it is unlikely that deviance imputations are among the most important of these. The stigma attached to living as a lesbian is discussed separately in a later section of this chapter.

At several points below, we shall return to marriage norms— for they are closely interwoven with the norms governing both maternity and sexuality. This will be evident, in particular, when we consider "unmarried" or "unwed" motherhood. The very fact that the situation usually is described in those ways, rather than as "single motherhood" is significant. It underscores the devaluation of single mothers, and shows that their perceived offense lies partly in a violation of marital norms. They also, of course, violate maternity norms, in the same process.

Occupational Norms. Occupational norms are grounded in the well-known phenomenon of occupational segregation by sex (see Epstein, 1971; Coser and Rokoff, 1971; Mitchell, 1973; Oakley, 1976; Hartmann, 1979; Laws, 1979, Ch. 1; Stockard and Johnson, 1980, Ch. 4). Presumably, under the most restrictive "traditional" definition of approved women's roles, just about any work outside the home has been perceived as deviant. Although this perception no longer seems to be the dominant one, there continue to be social circles in which terms like "working wife" and "career woman" carry disparaging connotations. One writer has suggested, furthermore, that the hidden agenda of certain "New Right" political movements involves efforts to stabilize the family "by removing women from the wage labor force" (Eisenstein, 1982, p. 577).

For the most part today, however, a woman's perceived "occupational deviance" lies not in simply having a job, but rather in having the "wrong" kind. The tendency toward sex typing, or sex labeling (Laws, 1979, pp. 30–37) of jobs—while now under continuous challenge—has not significantly altered. Although today more women are working than before, "they are not working in more jobs. Women are concentrated in relatively few jobs, while men are spread over a much broader range" (ibid., p. 22). Over the past several decades, actually, sex concentration in major occupational groupings (e.g., female concentration in clerical jobs and service occupations; male concentration in professional, managerial, crafts, farming, nonfarm laboring, etc.) has increased overall, leading to a greater "polarization" of female and male labor forces (ibid., pp. 25–27).

As Laws observes, the sex labeling of specific jobs is to an extent arbitrary and seems to follow only one rule: "men and women should be doing different things, whatever those things might be" (ibid., p. 31). By and large, she goes on to note, "female" jobs tend to exhibit the following characteristics: they offer low pay; they usually require skills women are thought to possess anyway—thereby reducing the need for on-the-job training; they do not require career continuity; and they involve relatively little specialization (ibid., pp. 34–37). As Chafetz (1974, pp. 56–66) has shown, furthermore, common sex stereotypes strongly support the concentration of females in the less-prestigious occupational categories. If one arrays the stereotypically assumed traits of women and men according to whether they are "helpful" or "harmful" in acquiring and performing well in high-prestige occupations, the preponderance of "harmful" traits for females (e.g., frivolous, emotional, passive, insecure) and "helpful" ones for males (logical, practical, ambitious, etc.) is striking. (However, for recent survey data on the prestige of women's occupations, see England, 1979.)

There are numerous other aspects of occupational segregation that cannot be taken up here—including "male" and "female" specializations within occupations (e.g., within the medical profession, surgery for males and pediatrics for females) and the even more pervasive phenomenon of "matched" male and female occupations (doctor/nurse, chemist/lab assistant, pilot/stewardess, orchestra conductor/orchestra musician, etc.). Stereotyped beliefs and traditional socialization practices have long sustained occupational sex typing. The stigmatizing of those who violate such norms of occupational choice (males as well as females) supports and reinforces these widely inculcated definitions. Negative reactions to the occupational "deviant" constitute a powerful sanction, because being in a job that is "sex role incongruent" (Laws, 1979, p. 32; also Safilios-Rothschild, 1972, pp. 309–315) may cause others to question one's basic "femininity" (or "masculinity").

Specific responses to women's occupational deviance will, of course, vary from situation to situation. In certain contexts, the aforementioned "token" patterns identified by Kanter (1977a; 1977b) will emerge. In other instances—perhaps particularly when women enter what have traditionally been viewed as ultra-masculine occupations (e.g., coal mining, professional athletics, the military, firefighting)—more overt derogation may occur. When male workers' conceptions of their "masculinity" are closely linked to the nature and conditions of their work, they are especially likely to feel threatened by female job entrants.

Several common elements of response are likely to be found in most situations of female occupational deviance. Consciousness of the deviant's femaleness will be heightened (actually, as we have noted, such consciousness is always high—even in situations where women hold stereotypically female jobs—but as Kanter points out it may well become even more central in "tokenism" situations). Consciousness of the female's "deviance" also will be high, and she will be devalued, restricted, and otherwise punished for it. Finally (and we shall return to this point in Chapter Four, on victimization of women) male workers may convince themselves that a woman who commits such occupational deviance deserves "whatever she gets." As an extension of the notion that she has disdained male "protection," such a woman may be treated as "fair game" for whatever assaults—verbal or physical, sexual or otherwise—male workers decide to "dish out." In such a situation, then, a specific imputation of deviance to the woman is used to "justify" diverse forms of male deviance directed toward her.

Deviance Norms

A final category of gender norms has to do with what may be called "appropriate and inappropriate deviance" (Schur, 1979, pp. 102–104). Among the various "standard" norm violations—that is, violations of widely agreed-upon norms which in theory apply to both men and women—some more than others are treated as being "appropriate offenses" for females. These perceptions tend to reflect stereotypical assumptions regarding woman's "nature." Hence, those "deviances" in which the offender acts in an aggressive or highly committed way (e.g., armed robber, political revolutionary) may be seen as "male." Offenses that tend to be passive or submissive (e.g., mental illness—especially "depression," being the "accomplice" to a crime, etc.) or that are closely linked to traditional women's roles (e.g., shoplifting) are thought of as being appropriately "female."

We shall consider this theme more thoroughly in Chapter Five, where we are going to examine the possible impact of such gender-based evaluations on the classification and processing of offenders and consequently on the recorded deviance statistics. As we will see, such statistics inevitably reflect classification and processing decisions, criteria, and activity levels. To an extent, we have the types and rates of deviance we seek out and process, and these efforts in turn may reflect our preconceptions as well as our fears.

APPEARANCE NORMS AND FEMALE DEVIANCE

Norms governing women's physical appearance, and perceived violations of them, deserve special attention in this book. As discussion above already has implied, such norms constitute a central element in the objectification and devaluation of females. They crucially influence the life goals and routine practices to which girls and young women are socialized. Concern about meeting these norms continues to pervade women's lives. Under prevailing criteria of personal worth, negative evaluations of physical appearance are likely to have a powerful impact on women's self-conceptions. Male socialization and ongoing male perceptions and behaviors are also heavily affected by the dominant prescriptions for female beauty. The preoccupation—of both men and women —with female appearance is, furthermore, a key ingredient in the "commoditization" of women's sexuality, which we will be considering in several later sections of this text.

Visual Objectification

Woman as object is not just a figure of speech. Females are not merely thought of as objects, they are *literally seen* as objects. The art critic John Berger (1977, p. 47) has commented that "*men act* and *women appear.* Men look at women. Women watch themselves being looked at. This determines not only most relations between men and women but also the relation of women to themselves. The surveyor of woman in herself is male: the surveyed, female. Thus she turns herself into an object—and most particularly an object of vision: a sight." Actually, one might better stress that she has "been turned" into an object, for women have not had much real choice in this matter. Even today few women feel free to ignore the dominant beauty prescriptions. On the contrary almost all must to some extent recognize that "becoming an attractive object is a role obligation" (Laws, 1979, p. 181).

Additional elements in women's visual objectification—imposed passivity, being placed on display, and being viewed as "sexual property"—were suggested in Thorstein Veblen's classic discussion of the functions of women's clothing (Veblen, 1899, 1934, pp. 167–187). Elegant dress, according to Veblen, "should not only be expensive, but it should make plain to all observers that the wearer is not engaged in any kind of productive labour" (ibid., p. 170). Veblen observed further that women's dress, in particular, serves to indicate such leisure. He cited such restrictive garments as the corset, which he claimed was "in economic theory, substantially a mutilation, undergone for the purpose of lowering the subject's vitality and rendering her permanently and obviously unfit for work" (ibid., p. 172). On this last point there has been, actually, some dispute. Critics of "tight-lacing" have regularly emphasized its constraining and debilitating effects (see, for example, Roberts, 1971; also Dworkin, 1974, Ch. 6; Lauer and Lauer, 1981, pp. 209–223). However, at least one historian (Kunzle, 1977) has claimed to the contrary that the practice was for the most part adopted voluntarily, and that it was used by women as a means of sexual and self-expression—"confining the waist in order to throw out the bust" (ibid., p. 579).

At any rate, the more general process in which woman is made into "a sight" and treated as an object for display remains a major target of feminist opposition. It was this process against which activists demonstrated at the 1968 Miss America pageant in Atlantic City, New Jersey (Morgan, 1978, pp. 62–67; also Hole and Levine, 1971, pp. 123–125). Through that protest, feminists were trying to show "to the public at large that beauty contests were as much an expression of social/political oppression as the more obvious manifestations of discrimination such as job and wage inequities" (Hole and Levine, 1971, p. 124). Although that demonstration obtained considerable publicity for the new women's movement, its overall results were mixed. The protesters themselves were widely assigned deviance labels ("bra-burners," etc.), and fifteen years later there is not much evidence that the beauty pageant phenomenon or mentality has been significantly reduced.

The persistence of beauty contests is, perhaps, the least important type of evidence that the visual objectifying of women is endemic to contemporary American culture. Among the many other more significant indicators are the following: female beauty imagery as the central device in much contemporary advertising; the amount of women's time, energy, and thinking that is devoted to self-beautification efforts (and the associated fact that weight, hair styles, clothing, and cosmetics continue to be staples of "women's talk"); the fact that female beautification supports several major industries—fashion, cosmetics, advertising (in large measure), and a substantial "diet industry"; and, most notably, the everyday behavior of men in our society—the aforementioned perpetual staring at women's bodies, the acceptability in the male subculture of supposedly "appreciative" references to a passing woman's body parts, such as "what an ass," "what a pair of tits," etc. The normative implication of all this for women is succinctly captured in the term "vital statistics"—a basis for evaluating female physical appearance of which there is no male counterpart.

We have already noted (see Table 1, in Chapter Two) various aspects of the visual objectification of women. Sociological and feminist critiques of the "cult of female beauty" have especially emphasized the following points: physical appearance is much more central to evaluations of women than it is to evaluations of men; this emphasis implicitly devalues women's other qualities and accomplishments; women's "looks" thereby become a commodity and a key determinant of their "success" or "failure"; the beauty norms used in evaluating women are excessively narrow and quite unrealistic; cultural reinforcement of such norms conveys to the ordinary woman a sense of her perpetual "deficiency."

The last two points are particularly significant in affecting perceptions of female deviance. As Una Stannard has stated, "the modern cult of women's beauty has nothing to do with what women naturally look like" (Stannard, 1972, p. 194; see also Densmore, 1972). Nonetheless, from girlhood on females are continuously exposed, especially through advertising and the mass media, to highly unrealistic "role models." The "ideal beauties" in the media, Stannard goes on to observe, "are always there to keep women permanently insecure about their looks, and that includes the great beauties as well. Indeed, the more beautiful a woman, the more she dreads time and younger beauties; for generally the beautiful woman's opinion of herself has depended almost solely on her looks" (Stannard, 1972, p. 196).

The ever-present danger of being deemed physically unattractive has, in fact, been a quite explicit theme—perhaps even the single most dominant one—in much advertising aimed at women. Commenting on the use of cosmetics, Germaine Greer has noted that "when they are used for adornment in a conscious and creative way, they are not emblems of inauthenticity: it is when they are presented as the real thing, covering unsightly blemishes, disguising a repulsive thing so that it is acceptable to the world that their function is deeply suspect" (Greer, 1972, p. 346). Sociological researchers often conclude that the media and advertising do not "create" behavior patterns or value priorities, they only "reinforce" them—in effect, merely giving people "what they want." But usually these conclusions have been based on limited studies aimed at testing only short-term and direct media effects.

In the case of female beauty norms, and women's related perceptions of themselves as likely norm-violators, the "mere reinforcement" claim is not entirely convincing. Sheila Rowbotham's (1973, p. 109) statement indicates why:

> The cosmetics industry has mushroomed and created needs as well as products. The female who is the cosmetic ideal is more or less unattainable, no sooner captured she appears in another form. Playing on insecurity and anxiety the advertisers market goods which actually create new fears. Vaginal deodorants make people anxious about sexual odour. Acting on the assumption that women regard themselves through men's eyes as objects of pleasure, advertising and the media project a haunting and unreal image of womanhood. The persistent sense of dislocation between the unrealized female self and the projected female stereotypes has contributed to a sense of failure.

We shall return shortly to the question of whether recent changes in advertising have significantly altered its contribution to the visual objectification of women.

A related aspect of the cult of female beauty deserves mention here—its effects on men. Critics have frequently deplored the unrealistic and limited role models provided for women. They less often have noted that "ideal beauty" imagery at the same time provides what might be called "object models" for men. Widespread imagery of this sort encourages and in a sense "trains" men to visually objectify women. It also provides physical criteria of assessment, according to which men are likely to find real women deficient. The social as well as psychological ramifications of this —most of which lie beyond the scope of this text—must be considerable. Objectified evaluations of female physical appearance must influence the course of most heterosexual relationships to an extent and in ways that go beyond what the basic mechanisms of sexual attraction or the normal human tendency to fantasize sexually (see May, 1980) would necessarily imply. Likewise, the visual objectification of women becomes a major element in the world of work, as we shall see when we examine the topic of sexual harassment of female workers. Indeed, as already noted, conditioning of men to literally "see" women as objects rather than as persons affects both the commission of and the sociolegal response to all of the serious offenses against women discussed in Chapter Four.

Negative Body-Consciousness

Under these circumstances, that part of a woman's self-conceptions which has to do with her physical appearance—her general attractiveness and, perhaps especially, her body shape—is routinely under siege. An array of associated behavior patterns emerges, and several related "disturbances" are formally diagnosed. Both the acknowledged disturbances and the more general behavior patterns strongly reflect "negative body-consciousness" —women not "feeling good about" their physical attributes.

Overweight and Stigma. Various studies have made clear that persons perceived to be significantly overweight are responded to negatively (see, for example, Allon, 1982). In early experiments young children were shown drawings of children with various physical disabilities, and asked to rank them ("tell me which boy —or girl—you like best," "next best," etc.). The drawing of an obese child received a lower (more negative) ranking overall than those of children having a facial disfigurement, sitting in a wheelchair, having a hand missing, or having crutches and a leg brace (Richardson, Goodman, Hastorf, and Dornbusch, 1961). In a related study, five samples of adult respondents were given the same type of test. They, too, "with few exceptions, ranked the overweight child as least likable" (Maddox, Back, and Liederman, 1968). The researchers concluded that their data (from these and other tests) "overwhelmingly support the [existence of an] essentially negative evaluation of overweight hypothesized to be characteristic in our society" (ibid., p. 10; see also discussion in Clinard and Meier, 1979, pp. 536–538).

Sociological analyses of group weight control programs have similarly recognized the stigma associated with being perceived as overweight. Natalie Allon discusses as latent functions of such groups the provision of opportunities for tension release, group support, and an atmosphere in which members can discuss various topics of concern which could not be so "easily discussed with the non-stigmatized" (Allon, 1975, p. 60). Although Barbara Laslett and Carol Warren (1975) conclude that diet groups can use the stigma on overweight to advantage—in effect, branding the members as being "essentially fat" in order to reinforce their efforts to keep thin—this technique itself rests on the strength of the stigma members confront in the outside world.

Marcia Millman (1980), who has done extensive interview and observational research in organizations for the overweight, discusses fatness explicitly in deviance terms. Dismissing the claim that we are concerned about overweight because it is unhealthy, she notes, "Many other things we do to ourselves are unhealthy, yet they do not incite the same kind of shame, hostility, and disapproval. Furthermore, many people have strong reactions to weight even when a person is not fat enough for health to be affected" (Millman, 1980, x). Fatness, Millman emphasizes, carries powerful symbolic meaning in our culture. As a result, being perceived as overweight deeply affects a person's overall identity. Fat persons are reacted to in (devaluing) categorical terms, and their self-conceptions may be shaped accordingly. There is a tendency, furthermore, to hold fat persons responsible for their condition— at least implicitly. Fatness is not viewed simply as a physical state, but also as evidence of some basic character defect. The overweight person, "especially if she is a woman, probably suffers more from the social and psychological stigma attached to obesity than she does from the actual physical condition. In a wide variety of ways she is negatively defined by her weight and excluded from full participation in the ranks of the normal" (ibid., xi).

Case studies Millman presents illustrate the strong devaluation fat women regularly experience. For example, a young woman who was about twenty-five to fifty pounds overweight during college and in her twenties wrote in an autobiographical account:

> I always felt that the first thing anyone would notice is that I was fat. And not only that I was fat, but that they would know *why* I was fat. They would know I was neurotic, that I was unsatisfied, that I was a pig, that I had problems. They could tell immediately that I was out of control. I always looked around to see if there was anyone as fat as me. I always wondered when I saw a fat woman, "Do I look like *that?*" (Millman, 1980, p. 80)

The stigma-imposing "master status" aspect of fatness is underscored when we consider the contrasting assessments of thin people. Except in extreme cases (such as anorexia nervosa, discussed below) we infrequently identify and categorize people as "thin." This fact indicates too that these responses do not follow directly from biological condition alone. They vary because of differences in sociocultural meaning and emphasis. There is much reason to believe, furthermore, that the stigma-laden meanings attached to overweight have greater impact overall in our society on women than on men. It is true that many of the findings cited thus far imply stigma regardless of sex. And there is little doubt that males who are extremely fat will incur devaluation. Nonetheless our gender system's greater emphasis on female appearance does make a difference.

Women more than men present weight-related "disturbances," exhibit significant concern about their weight, and involve themselves in frequent weight control efforts. It is revealing that several evaluatively neutral terms used to describe fat men—"stocky," "heavy-set," "portly"—are not matched by counterpart terms for fat women. As Goffman notes in his study of advertising's "gender display," the fact that male figures in the ads are bigger than female figures reflects our society's tendency to define male physical weight positively—as a symbol of the "social weight" (power, authority, prestige, etc.) accorded to men (Goffman, 1979, p. 28).

Compulsive Eating and Anorexia Nervosa. As the very term "overweight" implies, the classifying of persons as being excessively fat necessarily involves use of some (to an extent, arbitrary) standard of "normal" weight. A leading psychoanalytic specialist on eating disorders has stated: "Having followed patients over many years I have come to doubt the validity of approaching the whole obesity problem with the assumption that a definite height-weight relationship and a definite fat-lean tissue proportion are 'normal' for all people just because they are found in the majority" (Bruch, 1973, p. 113). Likewise, three researchers on the stigmatizing of overweight comment that "professionals particularly, but also laymen, can and do determine when body weight is socially deviant. Insofar as this is the case, these definitions . . . can be rate-producing or rate-reducing; that is, the incidence of socially deviant overweight is a function of shared definitions of *best* weight and tolerable deviations from that standard" (Maddox, Back, and Liederman, 1968, p. 15).

The fact that definitions of overweight are socially constructed does not, however, make them any less real in their consequences. Despite the possibility that therapists may sometimes overdiagnose weight-related disturbances in female patients, the phenomenon of pervasive negative body-consciousness among women is all too real. This phenomenon reflects, furthermore, the stigma-either-way tendency that females confront in connection with various gender norms. Fat women are the ones who are most blatantly devalued. At the same time, however, the woman who meets the norm of fashionable thinness easily becomes convinced that she is not thin enough or that she cannot "let down her guard" lest she become a norm-violator. In addition, psychodynamic interpretations suggest that gender norms may be an important factor in the "causation" of formally diagnosed weight-related disorders. Thus for some women fatness itself may represent an effort (conscious or unconscious) to avoid certain kinds of gender-based devaluation. Among other women, the "relentless pursuit of excessive thinness"—Bruch's (1978, ix) succinct characterization of anorexia nervosa—may also be tied closely to gender norms, representing an ultimately unsatisfactory "over-conformity."

According to one therapist, compulsive eating is a way of dealing with the pressures and limitations imposed by the gender system.

> Fat is a response to the many oppressive manifestations of a sexist culture. Fat is a way of saying "no" to powerlessness and self-denial, to a limiting sexual expression which demands that females look and act a certain way, and to an image of womanhood that defines a specific social role. Fat offends Western ideals of female beauty and, as such, every "overweight" woman creates a crack in the popular culture's ability to make us mere products (Orbach, 1979, p. 21).

Since compulsive eating is overwhelmingly a woman's problem, we should expect that it somehow reflects the "experience of being female in our society." Notwithstanding the stigma of overweight, compulsive eating—at an unconscious if not conscious level—"is linked to a desire to get fat," and "getting fat is a very definite and purposeful act connected to women's social position" (ibid., pp. 5, 28, 31).

Orbach goes on to identify a number of more specific psychodynamic functions sometimes served by fatness. It may help a woman to avoid being treated as a sexual object; express her unwillingness to compete with other women; symbolize "substance and strength" otherwise denied her; or represent a nonverbal "statement" when her verbal assertiveness has been squelched. Many women, Orbach claims, are afraid of being thin because they believe that the socially prescribed state of thinness denies them the power of self-definition. Getting fat is a way for women to "reappropriate" that power, while at the same time expressing their deep-seated anger over imposed limitations.

Anorexia nervosa (see Boskind-Lodahl, 1976; Bruch, 1978; Crisp, 1980; Palmer, 1980; Sours, 1980) represents the other side of the fatness coin—a "relentless" and ultimately excessive striving to achieve conformity by staying thin.

> Usually of average weight, the dieting anorectic decides to lose ten to fifteen pounds initially but often goes on to drop to 50 percent of her body weight and sometimes dies. The common, self-starving pattern of the anorectic is a persistent need to diet; she manages to live on no more than 400 calories a day which eventually results in generalized body wasting, sunken, glazed eyes, a cage of chest bones, a hollow abdomen, and emaciated limbs reminiscent of the most gruesome photojournalistic reports of concentration camp victims during World War II (Sours, 1980, p. 3).

The reference here to "she" is appropriate, since virtually all observers agree that its incidence among males is only around one-tenth that found among females.

Although anorexia has a long psychiatric history (ibid., Ch. 3), it has been an object of greatly increased attention and discussion in recent years. One specialist therefore comments cautiously, "It is difficult to be certain whether all this attention to the disorder has led to an increased rate of recognition or whether the condition has become more common" (Palmer, 1980, p. 4). Other observers less equivocally state that "anorexia nervosa has become more common" (Bruch, 1978, ix), one writer even asserting that its recent increase is "incontestable" (Sours, 1980, p. 281). According to Sours (ibid., p. 3), anorexia "now affects tens of thousands of young women of high school and college age and appears to be increasing rapidly in most countries where there is an affluent, well-educated segment of society" (ibid., p. 3).

To the extent the term "anorexia nervosa" (nervous loss of appetite) implies a lack of interest in food it is quite misleading, for in fact anorectics are greatly preoccupied with food and eating (Crisp, 1980, pp. 3–6). "Whatever their inner feelings, or however inaccurately they interpret or report them, anorexics [some writers use this term, some use "anorectics"] do not suffer from lack of appetite, but from the panicky fear of gaining weight" (Bruch, 1978, p. 4). Another specialist makes the same point perhaps even more strongly in asserting that "the anorexic has a phobia of her normal body weight" (Palmer, 1980, pp. 2–3). Therapists frequently recognize that the food-and-weight preoccupation of the anorectic is in one sense but an extreme point on a continuum of preoccupations shared by most adolescent girls. But they also note the obvious qualitative differences in symptomatology (e.g., severe emaciation, and eventually various other symptoms associated with malnutrition—including cessation of menstruation) and claim that there are important behavioral and psychodynamic differences as well (see discussion in Sours, 1980, pp. 4–8, 221–226; and Bruch, 1978, especially Ch. 5).

Explanations of the disorder's specific causation vary, though psychiatrists tend to stress maturational problems connected with puberty and adolescence (see Crisp, 1980, Chs. 6 and 7) and various patterns of abnormal family interaction (see Sours, 1980, Ch. 6; also Bruch, 1978). One therapist emphasizes a striving for perfection, of the kind often found among runners and professional dancers (Sours, 1980). Many accounts suggest that the parents of anorectics—who typically are described as having had privileged, seemingly "perfect" childhoods—tend to be extremely demanding, and that at some point the girl becomes convinced she is failing to meet their expectations. Regardless of the psychodynamics in particular instances—or even classes of cases—all professional commentators on anorexia recognize the central relevance of our culture's prescriptions (i.e., gender norms) regarding the physical appearance of females. And by the same token, virtually all specialists note as highly significant the female-male difference in incidence of the disorder.

The anorexia scenario represents a playing-out of variations on the overall cultural theme. Thus, in discussing family dynamics, Bruch observes, "Quite often these mothers are unusually weight-conscious and preoccupied with some flaw in the perfection of their bodies" (Bruch, 1978, p. 27). Another writer (Boskind-

Lodahl, 1976) offers an explicitly feminist interpretation of anorexia and bulimia. In her experience, these women grew up with unusually strong needs for achievement, recognition, and reward. Male approval, in particular, was seen as a sign of their success in perfecting "the female role." When they subsequently experienced male rejection—directly, or even implicitly through a failure of men to pursue them—the onset of the disturbance was triggered. A common theme in all these accounts of anorexia, then, is of special relevance for our purposes. The disturbance involves females fearing that they are or will become "fat," that they are or will become insufficiently "attractive"—in other words, a fear of being seen as visually deviant. This fear leads, in turn, to a set of behaviors that culminates in the labeled "deviance" of anorexia.

A special version of anorexia, or a related disorder (accounts differ on this technical point), is termed bulimia. These cases involve periodic eating "binges" followed by induced vomiting. According to one specialist, "The gorging-vomiting group of anorexia nervosa patients makes up at least 25 percent of all cases of the disorder" (Sours, 1980, p. 245). A recent journalistic discussion of bulimia stated, "Psychotherapists at eating disorder clinics around the country say the secretive phenomenon, which nearly always starts with a stringent diet to lose weight, is now epidemic on college campuses" (Brody, 1981, p. C1).

Bruch (1978, p. 84) describes binge eating as follows:

> Anorexic patients who indulge in binge eating . . . have in common the conviction that the food they feel compelled to gulp down cannot be integrated or would be damaging and therefore has to be removed from the body by vomiting. Once this symptom complex develops, it has a tendency to become more severe and resistant to treatment. In order to bring the food up again, larger and larger quantities have to be consumed. The sums spent on this routine are prodigious. Each one becomes a specialist in the type of food she uses, ranging from meals, one on top of the other, in gourmet restaurants to emptying the freezer at home in night orgies of broiled steaks, to junk food bought by the carload in the nearest supermarket. Whatever it is, it is washed down by quarts of milk and other fluids to make it easier to regurgitate.

In addition, according to another authority (Sours, 1980, pp. 246–247, 247), "Fear of insufficient food for a binge and privacy for vomiting can induce in the bulimic a profound tension state," and

"The combination of bulimia and vomiting becomes 'habit forming,' taking on an autonomy which eventually seems independent
from the original conflicts over food." This combined dieting-
gorging-purging phenomenon clearly reflects the contradictory
feelings about "fat" and about the female role to which Orbach
(cited above) gives much attention.

Fear of Visual Deviance. It must be emphasized that these formally
diagnosed disturbances represent only the most extreme cases of
"negative body-consciousness." Such cases do show us where the
conflicts and pressures generated by restrictive appearance norms
potentially can lead. More significant, however, is the extent to
which virtually *all* women in our society feel compelled to make
continuous efforts not to "violate" these norms. Commercial exploitation of the theme of never-ending female "deficiencies" virtually guarantees that those efforts will never be fully successful.
The very size of the "market" for appearance aids suggests the
pervasiveness of female concern and conformity-seeking effort.
According to a recent discussion of the cosmetics industry (*The
New York Times,* Nov. 16, 1980, p. 22E), estimated consumer ex-
penditures on cosmetics and personal hygiene products (in 1979)
included the following: cosmetics—$2,656,800,000; women's hair
products—$1,913,400,000; women's fragrances—$1,828,300,000;
skin preparations—$1,552,400,000; feminine hygiene—$770,100,-
000; diet aids—$388,800,000.

As well as being the chief consumers of cosmetics and other
self-presentation aids, women probably are the main purchasers
of mass-marketed "beauty tip" books and the primary obtainers
of purely "cosmetic" plastic surgery. These patterns too reflect the
impact on women of the constantly reiterated female deficiency
theme, and their consequent susceptibility to diverse offers of
(usually male) expert advice and assistance (Ehrenreich and English, 1979). We do not have systematic data regarding recourse to
cosmetic plastic surgery, but the extent to which such services now
are advertised in daily newspapers implies a substantial population of potential "patients." According to one writer, there has
been a recent "explosion in the field of cosmetic surgery." And he
goes on to note, "Today, good plastic surgery can rejuvenate flac-
cid breasts, sagging buttocks, jelly stomachs, bags beneath the
eyes, droopy lids, wrinkled foreheads, feathered lips, crow's-feet,

and much else that was once thought to be an inevitable part of the aging process" (Hoge, 1980, p. 52; see also Al-Issa, 1980, pp. 291–295).

This last statement suggests a further point of importance concerning appearance norms. The extreme cultural emphasis on female physical appearance is a key element in the heightened devaluation of females as they get older. Youthfulness in either sex is likely to be prized in our "narcissistic" society (Lasch, 1979, Ch. IX). But because of the cult of female beauty it has been without question a more crucial asset for females than for males. If a woman's looks are treated as her major resource, she simply cannot "afford" to lose them. The natural aging process, therefore, necessarily has evoked among women a great deal of appearance-related anxiety. Advertising at the very least strongly reinforces such anxiety. As one critic recently noted:

> Commercials assure us that you're never too young to feel anxious about growing old. In one TV spot, a Unesco assortment of women offers testimonials to the miracle properties of "X" cream. "I'm 36!" says a Scandinavian, anticipating our cries of disbelief. "I'm 41!" says another. "I'm 50!" "I'm 26," and so on.
>
> The assumed pride in looking younger than one's age is but a momentary balm against the implied, underlying sting: the horror of actually *being* that age (Haskell, 1982, p. C2).

We do not really know just how much or in what precise ways such messages affect the women exposed to them. In one small local survey of married women with adolescent children, Alice Rossi asked respondents (among many other things) what age they would "most like to be." She writes (Rossi, 1980, p. 23), "None of the women reported wanting to be older than they were, while half wanted to be under thirty years of age. Women in their late thirties and early forties wanted on an average to be six years younger than they were (mean actual age = 39.5, desired age = 33.6), but the older women, now in their late forties and early fifties, wanted to be fifteen years younger than they were (mean actual age = 47.5, desired age = 32.9)." At the same time, she found that "actual age has no independent effect on wanting to be young" when one examines it along with the respondents' scores on an "aging-symptoms index" (based on their ratings of nine factors—body shape, energy level, sex life, hair condition, etc.—

as being "better five years ago," "no change," or "better now"). Rossi concludes, "When life is going well, the women seem to be saying, they have no desire to be younger than they are. But, for many middle-aged women, life does not go well" (ibid., pp. 24–25).

Trends and Prospects

In this brief section on appearance norms, it has not been possible to provide in-depth discussion of such topics as fashion, the use of cosmetics, or the role of advertising. Opinions differ strongly regarding the extent to which such phenomena help to "cause" the objectification of women and the oppressiveness of appearance norms. Presentation of self, including appearance, will always be a significant factor in interpersonal relations (Stone, 1962; also Goffman, 1959). There is little doubt too that physical appearance will invariably be an element in sexual attraction. The sociological and feminist critiques do not necessarily deny this. They assert only that the emphasis in our society on (a narrowly defined version of) female beauty represents a gross and harmful distortion of what is natural, and that mass marketing helps to perpetuate that emphasis.

It may be asked whether there have been recent changes (in beauty norms and images, and in the marketing of them) which imply a more natural depiction of females. Today's advertising without question reflects an awareness of the women's liberation movement. In particular, women in the ads no longer are depicted exclusively as housewives and mothers. Yet if current ads show women in diverse work situations and more generally describe them as actively pursuing their own chosen goals, there is no corresponding evidence to suggest that the "woman as sex object" element in advertising has been significantly displaced. On the contrary, a standard technique is simply to place the old imagery in a new context, thereby exploiting two types of sales appeal. Thus, one sociologist who has studied advertising aimed at the "new woman" (Kasinitz, 1981, p. 27) notes that "the 'Cosmo girl' is not the romantic housewife or sexy secretary; she is the sexy executive vice president." And, he goes on to comment more generally, "The 'new woman' is presented as a dichotomy: totally 'feminine' (in the traditional sense), sexy and submissive, when *she* wants to be, yet tough, assertive, successful and fulfilled, when *she* wants to be" (ibid., p. 28; see also Cagan, 1978; Ehrenreich and English, 1979, pp. 285–297; and Gordon, 1983).

We know that, in actual fact, women are not by and large free to choose whether they do or do not wish to be "feminine" and "sexy"—unless they are prepared to face the negative responses they will elicit if they violate the norm. Most women today, no matter how successful, still "are not free to stop playing the beauty game" (Stannard, 1972, p. 192). It is possible that some beauty norms are becoming a bit less restrictive. For example, clothing manufacturers recently have shown increased interest in producing fashionable clothes for "large-size" women (*The New York Times,* March 22, 1980, p. 18). This development, however, appears to reflect recognition of the existence of a large consumer "market" more than it does any inclination to relax appearance norms. The segregative implications of marketing such clothes as a special "line" and of displaying and selling them in a separate "department" within a clothing store suggest that the stigma on largeness even here continues to maintain considerable force.

Other recent trends that might have provided a basis for reducing the coercive power of appearance norms also have proven ineffective in this regard, again partly because the marketers were quick to anticipate and exploit them commercially. Thus our culture's recent preoccupation with self-awareness and body-awareness (see Schur, 1976; Lasch, 1979), health and physical fitness, might have fostered a more wholesome and nonjudgmental approach to physical appearance. Yet there is little evidence this has occurred. If anything, the overall effect seems to have been to make the achievement of "perfection" (e.g., in body shape) even more obligatory than before. And as regards the adoption of a more relaxed and "natural" appearance, commercial interests have promptly responded by creating and promoting a "natural look" in cosmetics and attire.

Finally, the somewhat increased attention recently to men's physical appearance, clothing, and "beautification" does not seem to imply any relaxing of the pressure on women to conform visually. Viewed in combination with the recent emphasis on female sexual assertiveness (see Schur, 1976; Ehrenreich and English, 1979, pp. 297–311), this trend seems at most to suggest the possibility that in the future there might be "equal objectification" of heterosexual males. If women increasingly were to "see" and respond to men as men have traditionally seen and responded to them, the change—while it might represent a kind of equalization —would not be a very satisfactory one. Males would then have to share the burden of coercion imposed by appearance norms. But it is by no means clear that the similar burden on women would thereby have been removed or even reduced.

MATERNITY CONTROLS

As Nancy Chodorow (1978, p. 9) notes, "Women's mothering is a central and defining feature of the social organization of gender and is implicated in the construction and reproduction of male dominance itself." It is not surprising, then, that this is an area in which women's behavior is subject to considerable normative regulation. Such regulation is necessary for a number of reasons: motherhood imposes social and psychological costs as well as providing benefits (see Bernard, 1975; Oakley, 1976; Skolnick, 1978, pp. 294–298; Laws, 1979, pp. 122–151); increasingly, exclusive responsibility for childrearing conflicts with women's other aspirations and opportunities; there is no verifiable and invariant "maternal instinct" that will ensure high female commitment to the maternal role.

In a significant early analysis of the notion of "maternal instinct," Leta Hollingworth suggested that given the lack of confirming evidence we should "guard against accepting as a fact of human nature a doctrine which we might well expect to find in use as a means of social control" (Hollingworth, 1916, p. 20). Such control is effected through a number of "social devices for impelling women to bear and rear children" (the title of Hollingworth's study), including especially, inculcation of the "personal ideal" of maternity as the sign of a "normal woman." More recently, Oakley (1976, p. 186) has referred to a "myth of motherhood" comprising three related assertions: "all women need to be mothers, all mothers need their children, all children need their mothers. Popular fiction, pseudopsychology, and the pronouncements of so-called 'experts' faithfully reproduce them as facts rather than as unevidenced assumptions."

Norms relating to motherhood further uphold and strengthen the maternity ideal. They back up early socialization and its general cultural supports. Perceived violations of these norms include at least the following major "offenses": intentional nonmotherhood, "unwed" motherhood, and "unfit" motherhood. Thus we find in this area, again, a tendency for women to be "in the wrong" whatever they do. They can be punished if they decide they don't want children, or if they have children under the wrong circumstances; and if they do have children under the right circumstances (i.e., conventional marriage), they still face deviance labeling in connection with their efforts at child*rearing*. Because these maternity norms are closely tied to restrictions on sexuality, living arrangements, and life options generally (including work options), they illustrate (as we noted earlier) the broader pattern of controlling female autonomy.

Violations of Maternity Norms

Voluntary Childlessness.   In our "pronatalist culture" (Laws, 1979, p. 122), a married woman's decision not to have any children constitutes a significant norm-violation. One interview study of "voluntary childless wives" found that women who made such a choice reported being routinely subjected to direct and indirect pressure to have children, and they also experienced various types of deviance imputations. "All of the wives interviewed feel that they are to some extent stigmatized . . . and that there exists an ubiquitous negative stereotype concerning the characteristics of a voluntarily childless woman, including such unfavorable traits as being abnormal, selfish, immoral, irresponsible, immature, unhappy, unfulfilled, and non-feminine" (Veevers, 1974, p. 505). At the time of that research it appeared, furthermore, that "existing social movements concerned with population or with feminism" provided such women with "relatively little intellectual or emotional support" (ibid., p. 508).

Bernard (1975, p. 42) notes that a major goal of organizations such as NON (National Organization for Non-Parents, founded in 1972) is the removal of the social stigma that now attaches to nonmotherhood. She goes on to observe that such stigmatization is abetted by psychiatric efforts to "explain" nonmotherhood—in terms of underlying "narcissism" and the like. Although the specifics of such explanations tend to vary, their importance lies—

according to Bernard—in the "implications of deviance" they all present. "Not one 'explains' the women who prefer nonmotherhood as strong, autonomous women able to resist coercive pressures. No one emphasizes their strengths. It is always something bordering on the pathological" (ibid., p. 46).

Recent research by Kathleen Gerson (1981) suggests that today women of optimal childbearing age often find themselves torn between the personal and social costs of not having children, on the one hand, and the costs of having them, on the other. Yet despite increased recognition (at least in certain social circles) of the potential costs of motherhood, it is no doubt still true—for the population as a whole—that females who choose not to bear children at all are viewed as falling into "a deviant category" (Veevers, 1977, p. 367). Thus, those of Gerson's respondents who had opted for childlessness did not do so "easily or without conflict. The social and psychological importance placed upon children and motherhood remains enormous. Opting for a choice with so little historical precedent or cultural legitimacy thus meant weathering disapproval and personal self-doubt" (Gerson, 1981, p. 263). Gerson goes on to discuss various "coping strategies" such women adopt. The need to utilize these strategies indicates the persistence of stigma. The success of such coping efforts is bound to vary, depending on the individual's personal strengths and social circumstances.

"Unwed" Motherhood. Conformity not only requires having children but also having them within the approved context of conventional marriage. As we already have seen, the very terms used for childbearing outside of marriage—"unwed" or "unmarried" motherhood, and also "illegitimacy" itself—indicate both the character of the norm-violation and the strong social disapproval attaching to it. The first two terms underscore, furthermore, that this is deemed to be a *female* offense. Invariably it is discussed as a motherhood situation or problem, although obviously fatherhood is equally involved. As a leading researcher on the topic has pointed out, "Although biologically he is half the cause of illegitimacy, the ratio of studies of the unmarried father to studies of the unwed mother is approximately one to twenty-five" (Vincent, 1961, p. 3). Dominant norms and values, Vincent goes on to note, define the unwed father "as a less crucial social problem, and thus a less important research subject, than the unwed mother" (ibid.).

Social stigmatization displays the same pattern of inequality. There really is no widespread deviance labeling of "unwed fathers." To a degree, stigmatizing of the female may sometimes be offset by a retrospective labeling of the male as a "sexual exploiter." Thus Vincent comments (ibid., p. 81):

> ... the male passes the "masculinity test" when he pursues and obtains sexual favors from the female, but fails it when he refuses to shield her and to provide for her when she becomes pregnant. The female fails one aspect of the "femininity test" when she acquiesces to an illicit sexual union, but passes another aspect of it when she accepts motherhood and completes her pregnancy in the traditionally heroic manner—alone and condemned. By following this course, she partially diverts the censure from herself to the father, who traditionally should protect her and provide for the baby.

By and large, however, it is the female who must bear the brunt of the disapproval and who is assigned the primary responsibility for dealing with the situation (for an in-depth study of the problems of unmarried mothers, see Rains, 1971). The differential evaluation is evident from the fact that whereas there is, to speak of, no popular imagery of the "unwed father," stereotypes of the "unwed mother" are common. Usually the term evokes "an image of a female who is the polar opposite of the 'good woman' (or 'nice girl'). She is 'promiscuous,' slatternly, insatiable and/or ungovernable—unable to act in her own best interests" (Laws, 1979, p. 205). In actuality, as Laws goes on to point out, " 'Illicit' pregnancies do not ... result from a situation of unshackled female sexuality; quite the contrary. The majority of illicit births documented in the research literature germinate in ordinary dating and courtship relationships" (ibid.).

The important large-scale study done by Vincent in the mid-1950s (see Vincent, 1961, Chs. 4–6) pointed up this ordinariness in the relationships that produce out-of-wedlock pregnancies, and also the diversity of social backgrounds found among "unwed mothers" (once data on cases seen in private practice are added to those from public health and welfare agencies). Likewise, he found that the familial background and personality characteristics of unwed mothers did not differ significantly from what would be found generally among females of similar race and age. According to Vincent, contrary stereotypes of illegitimacy (depicting it, in particular, as being almost entirely a lower-class phenomenon) were used by middle-class parents to buttress their own social control efforts. Thus, " 'Only poor, ignorant, and mentally ill girls do become pregnant out of wedlock' is the obverse of 'nice girls don't' " (ibid., p. 16).

Psychological "explanations" of illegitimacy, as a British researcher notes, enable one to give the unmarried mother "some personal sympathy and understanding . . . without condoning a deviation from sexual norms" (Gill, 1977, p. 239). Most present-day students of illegitimacy emphasize, however, the need to examine this pregnancy outcome in broader societal focus. Statistics on illegitimate births must especially be interpreted in relation to those on such "alternatives" (Hartley, 1975, pp. 251–258) as effective use of contraception, abortion, and marriage as a result of pregnancy. Low rates for the latter necessarily imply high rates of illegitimacy. Considerations of that sort seem clearly relevant in interpreting the higher illegitimacy rate among blacks than among whites: in 1977, the estimated number of illegitimate births per 1,000 unmarried women aged fifteen to forty-four in the United States was 13.7 for whites and 79.4 for blacks (see Reiss, 1980, pp. 207–213).

Joyce Ladner, who is highly critical of attempts to interpret the behavior of black women from a white middle-class perspective, claims, on the basis of her research among lower-class blacks: "There are no 'illegitimate' children in the low-income Black community as such because there is an inherent value that children cannot be 'illegally born.' There are, however, 'unauthorized' births because these children are not born within the limitations and socio-legal context defined by legislators and other people in the majority group who *create* and *assign* labels to the minority group" (Ladner, 1972, pp. 213–214). William Ryan, who sees the stigmatizing of unwed mothers as a major example of "blaming the victim" (Ryan, 1972), notes that the apparent black acceptance of illegitimacy reflects inequality in access to the alternatives.

> The poor and the Negroes are, to put it simply, denied equality of choice at each of these points. Being forced to rely on public medical care, they are far less likely to receive accurate and effective contraceptive information; lacking a job, the man is less able to offer the refuge of marriage; and finally, their babies are viewed, in terms of adoption, as "hard to place." Black babies and babies of mixed racial parentage, who are classified as black, are a less readily marketed product in the adoption exchange; they are lumped together with those having genuine defects (ibid., p. 102).

The overall rate of illegitimate births in the United States has increased substantially over the past four decades (although the sharpest increase occurred between 1940 and 1960). In 1977 the overall estimated number of illegitimate births per 1,000 unmarried women aged fifteen to forty-four was 26.0, whereas in 1940 it had been only 7.1 (see Reiss, 1980, pp. 207–213). This increase suggests that the "alternatives" mentioned above are not keeping up with premarital (or extramarital) pregnancies. It may also reflect increased levels of sexual activity among the unmarried (ibid., pp. 211–212). To the extent the latter is true, some writers argue, our society's contradictory reactions to sex are revealed in responses to the unwed mother. Cultural encouragement of sexual behavior is widespread, yet the consequence of such behavior leads to stigmatization (see Vincent, 1961, pp. 241–245).

In particular, cultural ambivalence regarding female sexuality may influence one of the most important "alternatives" to illegitimacy—effective use of contraception. Kristin Luker's interviews (Luker, 1978) with clients at a California abortion clinic (who were predominantly white, middle class, and had an average age of twenty-two) showed this influence at work. Among the reasons why Luker's respondents had engaged in "contraceptive risk-taking" was their belief that practicing contraception on a regular basis would amount to an acknowledgment that they regularly engaged in sexual activity. "A woman who plans is actively anticipating intercourse; in the terminology of the women interviewed, she is 'looking to have sex' " (ibid., p. 46). Such women, Luker's interviewees reported, lose status. Thus, one respondent noted that "women who are too active are contemptuously referred to by both men and women in her circle as 'rabbits.' One way to avoid this definition is to have each and every sexual encounter be unanticipated, and hence free from the stigma of being continuous" (ibid., p. 47). Although Luker studied women who obtained abortions, similar contraceptive risk-taking also leads to illegitimate births. In both cases, we see again the vicious circle of deviance labeling that women confront. Fear of being seen as deviant in their sexual conduct leads to behavior that produces a result for which they may well be stigmatized—abortion (see discussion below), or "illicit" motherhood.

The legal status of children born out of wedlock has been modified somewhat in recent years. "New laws have removed the fact of illegitimacy from the birth record in many states, though not yet in a majority . . . the child has acquired the right to inherit from his or her mother (and in many states to inherit from the father as well)" (Goode, 1982, p. 42). Yet Goode goes on to assert that while modern legislation attempts to protect both mother and child, "It is an illusion to suppose that by some combination of liberal social welfare laws, the child will somehow be given a position exactly equal to that of a legitimate child" (ibid.).

Social stigmatization of the mother may (again, in limited social circles) be lessening somewhat, but often it remains substantial. Gill has noted that unwed mothers today, unlike their counterparts in Victorian times, are not forced into the "secondary deviance" of a life of prostitution (Gill, 1977, pp. 249–251). Nonetheless, as he notes further, "The impact of the label at the primary level is clearly significant," and "Much of what unmarried mothers do once they become pregnant [e.g., trying to get married, leaving town to have the baby, seeking an abortion] may be interpreted as attempts to reduce the degree of stigmatisation to which they are subjected" (ibid., p. 251).

A development which has been given considerable publicity in recent years is that of intentional childbearing out of wedlock. Some women now wishing to exercise that "option" may be in relatively good positions—socioeconomically, or through subcultural support—to ward off the stigma such behavior could entail. (The issue of lesbian motherhood is especially complex; it is discussed in a later section of this chapter.) Yet many people still may view such a "willful" violation of maternity and marriage norms as constituting an even more serious "offense" than simply being "caught" in an unwanted pregnancy. When a group of irate parents recently sought to have an unwed pregnant forty-one-year-old Long Island schoolteacher dismissed, the persistence of stigma was dramatically exposed. One of the complaining parents commented on her condition by saying, "You don't have to go into an X-rated movie if you don't want to, but you can't get away from it with her up in front of a classroom" (quoted in *The New York Times,* December 20, 1982, p. D12; see also *The New York Times,* December 27, 1982, p. A18). Laws and Schwartz have concluded that in general single motherhood "is still a comfortable option for only the economically and psychologically independent woman. While other women can and do have children out of wedlock, the penalties are much higher for them since economic assistance from the state is received only in exchange for their right to decide what kinds of relationships will characterize their personal lives" (Laws and Schwartz, 1977, p. 164).

Goode, who stresses that even sexually permissive societies disapprove of childbirth outside of marriage, makes a cautious forecast for the future. He rejects the claim that "there will be a strong, *continuing* trend toward viewing illegitimacy as no more than an unimportant, private decision. Rather, living together may become still more common as a phase of courtship, but having a child will remain an event in which the state, the grandparents, and the kin network believe they too have a stake" (Goode, 1982, p. 49). As a contrast to this conservative assessment we might note the radical conjecture by feminist Shulamith Firestone (1971, pp. 205–242), that artificial reproduction might eventually become a major factor facilitating revision of the gender system. If that were to happen, females might achieve a kind of ultimate reproductive autonomy. Having children would be separated not only from marriage but also from heterosexual intercourse itself. It is difficult to see how, under such circumstances, "illegitimacy" could be deemed a major female "offense" or a significant social problem.

"Unfit" Motherhood.   Conceptions of the "unfit" mother also reflect the dominant cultural tendency always to place the female "in the wrong." The labeling of males as "unfit fathers" is no more common than the designation of them as "unwed fathers." This sex differential is grounded both in the notion that childrearing as well as childbearing is a key (if not "innate") aspect of female "normality," and in the sociocultural arrangements under which childrearing is almost exclusively a female responsibility (Chodorow, 1978; also Dinnerstein, 1977). Allegations of unfit motherhood, furthermore, reflect a more general norm of the gender system which Laws terms "vicariousness." In this instance, "It is understood that when a woman undertakes the responsibility of parenthood, she subordinates her own needs, desires, or priorities to the welfare of the child" (Laws, 1979, p. 126).

Because males are not assigned major "responsibility" for parenthood, by the same token they are not readily held to be "irresponsible" parents. Females are—on a wide variety of alleged grounds, and often without much apparent need to provide evidence substantiating the charge. Almost any aspect of a woman's personal conduct—including her friendships, general life-style, drinking behavior, apparent psychological condition, and perhaps even physical appearance and self-presentation—may be cited to support a claim that she is an unfit mother. Sexual activity (deemed to be "excessive" or "improper") is an especially common "basis" for such claims, and sometimes sexual orientation or preference is used in this way (see discussion of lesbian mothers, below).

These labeling processes are most blatantly evident when a woman's fitness as a mother becomes a matter of legal or official concern—as in child custody cases, applications to adopt children, and the administration of various public welfare programs. Equally significant, however, is the more general anxiety most mothers in our society experience over the possibility of being (informally, if not formally) labeled "negligent," "uncaring," or "bad" childrearers. Anxiety of this sort has been very strongly generated by the public controversy over "working mothers." Again, and here more specifically, we find a double standard in evaluation and even in research: "Nobody has yet studied the impact of the father's employment–work role on his relationship with his children. In the dual-job family, it is the working mother who constitutes a problem because childcare is a mother's duty" (Oakley, 1976, p. 210).

Diverse developmental, social adjustment, and psychological difficulties of children have, accordingly, been attributed to "maternal deprivation" (see Rutter, 1981; also Laws, 1979, pp. 126–151; Oakley, 1976, pp. 203–221; and Bernard, 1975, esp. Ch. 5). This concept arose out of psychiatric studies—conducted by John Bowlby, Rene Spitz, and others in the 1940s and early 1950s—of the psychological damage that could result when infants were raised in institutional settings. That aspect of the research appears to have been sound, and to have led to specific reforms in the field of residential childcare. Yet the notion of maternal deprivation often was given a much broader reading, even when there was little evidence that it could validly be applied to other childcare situations.

In his exhaustive and scrupulous critical reassessment of the concept, Michael Rutter noted that "the very existence of a single term, 'maternal deprivation', has had the most unfortunate consequence of implying one specific syndrome of unitary causation" (Rutter, 1981, p. 124). As Rutter goes on to show, the worst effects even of institutional childraising may not have to do with the mother or with a deprivation of maternal care but rather with a lack or distortion of care in general. In addition, extensive research has now shown that the child can develop necessary bonds of attachment (a more general focus in Bowlby's later work) with a person or persons other than the mother—and that such persons do not have to be female. Finally, various studies have noted individual differences in children's responses to so-called deprivation.

On the basis of these and related findings, Rutter concluded:

> The concept of "maternal deprivation" has undoubtedly been useful in focusing attention on the sometimes grave consequences of deficient or disturbed care in early life. However, it is now evident that the experiences included under the term "maternal deprivation" are too heterogeneous and the effects too varied for it to continue to have any usefulness. . . . That "bad" care of children in early life can have "bad" effects, both short-term and long-term, can be accepted as proven. What is now needed is a more precise delineation of the different aspects of "badness," together with an analysis of their separate effects and of the reasons why children differ in their responses (Rutter, 1981, p. 130).

The recent growth of day care programs to provide working mothers with expanded childcare assistance has led to further research which bears on the maternal deprivation question. As Rutter points out, however, the situation of group *day* care in which a parent remains a key figure for the child and actively participates in his or her overall care is not to be equated with institutional childrearing with parents not at all involved (Rutter, 1981, pp. 154–156). Nonetheless, comparisons between day care and home care may be useful. A report on what is perhaps the most systematic controlled comparison study to date concludes that "a child's attendance at a day care center staffed by conscientious and nurturant adults during the first two and one-half years of life does not seem to produce a psychological profile very much different from the one created by rearing totally in the home. This conclusion is based on our formal assessments as well as informal observations of the children over the 2½ year period" (Kagan, Kearsley, and Zelazo, 1978, pp. 260–261).

Kagan and his associates acknowledge that their general conclusion—that good day care "does not seem to have hidden psychological dangers"—"flies in the face of much popular belief" and should be accepted with caution (ibid., pp. 261–262). They recognize that the day care children in their study came from "intact and psychologically supportive families" and attribute their results partly to the special salience that the mother and the home situation continued to have for these children. Noting too the competent and nurturant character of the group care that was provided, they emphasize that "these findings do not imply that *any* day care context would produce the same pattern of results" (ibid., p. 265). Although Rutter similarly advises caution in thinking about the effects of day care, he too evidently concludes from the available evidence that ultimately it is the quality of care—in the group situation and in the home—that makes the most difference. He believes that "some of the more alarming stereotypes about day care can be rejected," while at the same time he urges further research as an aid to "decisions on what type of care is most suitable for which children in which circumstances" (Rutter, 1981, p. 177).

Notwithstanding such findings—and the evidence from studies of childrearing in the Israeli kibbutzim (Bettelheim, 1970) and American communes (Berger, Hackett, and Millar, 1974) that children are not necessarily harmed by arrangements providing less-than-continuous involvement with the mother—Oakley's conclusion no doubt still holds true: "Employed mothers often feel guilty. They feel inadequate, and they worry about whether they are doing the best for their children" (Oakley, 1976, p. 211). Actually, much the same thing might be said regarding most mothers in our society—those who are not employed outside the home as well as those who are. The fact that maternal insecurity and guilt appear to be extremely widespread suggests another important facet of the unfit motherhood designation. This seemingly insurmountable concern about maternal fitness reflects a general aspect of women's situation of which we shall consider additional examples as we proceed—namely, their vulnerability to and control through the assessments and advice of specialized "experts," most of whom are male.

Barbara Ehrenreich and Deirdre English, in their sociohistorical analysis of such advice-giving over the past century and a half (Ehrenreich and English, 1979), show how motherhood—along with other female behaviors and conditions—came to be seen as "pathology." Childrearing, it seems, was too important to be left to mothers alone! Medical and other specialized expertise would have to be marshalled, so that children could be cared for in accord with the most up-to-date scientific knowledge. Unfortunately, scientific findings and advice in this area tended to be inconsistent and to fluctuate greatly over the years. As Ehrenreich and English indicate, women were first told they should be consciously "permissive," then they were instructed to relax and go by "instinct," still later they were alerted to the aforementioned danger of "maternal deprivation," only to confront shortly thereafter a warning that they must avoid the opposing peril of "overprotecting" the child (ibid., Ch. 7). By calling attention to the numerous pitfalls of childraising (some of which were without question real) the advocates of scientific motherhood made women increasingly insecure about simply doing what seemed "natural" or "right." Their childrearing confidence thus undermined, they became ever more dependent on expert advice.

Thus an endless circle of uncertainty, confusion, and insecurity was set in place. Childrearing norms were confusing and often contradictory, and on top of that they tended to change rapidly from year to year. The likelihood of a woman's being viewed as (or viewing herself as) a violator of one or another of these norms therefore became extremely high. And here again, the pervasive and generalized *fear* of committing such "offenses" affected women even more than did the actual responses to specific instances of perceived norm violation. To an extent, as Ehrenreich and English go on to suggest (ibid., Ch. 8 and "Afterword"), very recent developments—the new female "assertiveness," preoccupation with "careers," concern with "relationships," etc.—may imply a somewhat diminished involvement with childrearing. It should be noted, however, that books of advice on raising children remain extremely popular, and that large numbers of women feel the need to rely on them regularly for guidance. As long as conformity to expert-propounded norms is a requirement of good motherhood, female concern about being labeled "unfit" will persist as well.

The Medicalizing of Childbirth

A closely related development has been the medicalizing (one might, in a sense, even say the "deviantizing") of childbirth itself. Pregnancy and birth have come to be seen primarily as "problems"

—as troublesome "medical" conditions or events which require at all times the intervention of physicians. To an extent, this perception reflects a more general sociocultural tendency that social critic Ivan Illich terms "the medicalization of life" (Illich, 1976). As sociologists have indicated (see Freidson, 1971), both the emphasis on health in our culture and the medical profession's need to bolster its status and expand its "jurisdiction" have encouraged an ever-widening conception of the conditions that require medical management and treatment. In this connection, sociologists now recognize that frequently medicine functions as "an institution of social control" (Conrad and Schneider, 1980, Ch. 9).

Medicalization of childbirth, however, also reflects a more specific and long-standing pattern in the relations between women and the predominantly male medical profession. Ehrenreich and English (1979, p. 39) note that the witch trials of the middle ages "prefigured—with dramatic intensity—the clash between male doctors and female healers in nineteenth-century America" (see also Ehrenreich and English, 1979; Arms, 1977, pp. 14–20). Barker-Benfield (1977) suggests that the expansion in America of medical practices relating to women was heavily colored by deep-seated male ambivalence regarding female sexuality. The growth of obstetrics and gynecology reflected "male apprehensiveness over woman's generative power, and the desire to control it" (ibid., p. 62). Gross insensitivity to female patients, glib and questionable diagnoses of diverse ailments, and unnecessary (essentially punitive) sexual surgery—such as removal of the clitoris or the ovaries—were among the worst consequences of this male ambivalence.

A conception of childbirth as a medical "problem" that could be dealt with only by the skilled medical practitioner also was promoted. Male obstetricians waged an extensive campaign to discredit and drive out of practice the female (and, it should be stressed, female-oriented) midwife. "Since birth was unnatural, it was liable to affect the 'patient's' health in any number of unpredictable ways, with which only a fully trained expert was qualified to cope" (ibid., p. 63; see also Ehrenreich and English, 1973; Wertz and Wertz, 1979; Rothman, 1979; Dye, 1980). In an effort to gain a monopoly of supervision over childbirth and to bolster their professional standing, obstetricians emphasized the problematic aspects of maternity. Thus, a leading study of the history of childbirth notes:

> Doctors were on the lookout for trouble in birth. That seemed to them to be their primary purpose. They found a lot of trouble—so much, in fact, that they came to think that every birth was a potential disaster and that it was best to prepare each woman for the worst eventualities. In line with that perception, doctors increased their control over the patients during labor and delivery, rendering them more powerless to experience or participate in birth. Women acceded to the doctors' increasing control because they also believed that their methods would make birth safer (Wertz and Wertz, 1979, p. 136).

It was out of such a background that what two recent observers have called the "medical frame of reference" (Graham and Oakley, 1981; see also Shaw, 1974; Rothman, 1979; Rothman, 1982) came to dominate childbirth. In this set of outlooks—which Graham and Oakley contrast to the perspectives of mothers themselves (Graham and Oakley, 1981)—reproduction is viewed as an isolated medical event requiring specialized expertise, having specific medical goals (i.e., mainly the negative ones of avoiding mortality and morbidity), and calling for preventive efforts even at the cost of what in most cases will prove to have been unnecessary caution. The overriding themes, then, in this evolving medical perspective are evident: *professionalization* in the management of childbirth; *prevention* of anticipated disorders and complications as the major focal point of this management; and *hospitalization* as the only site in which such efforts can be carried out properly. The entire process was to be organized around medical needs, medical procedures, and medical convenience.

In the United States today (and also in Canada and Great Britain) this approach is heavily emphasized, and significant deviations from it are strongly discouraged. Under this system, "the pregnant woman soon finds herself in the midst of an autonomous world of authoritarian rule to which *all* patients must conform if they are to regain their health and return to society" (Arms, 1977, p. 63). Feminists and sociologists studying the health care provided to females have criticized the system on many grounds. A major claim is that childbirth has been unnecessarily and unwisely technologized in ways that prevent women from experiencing it as a natural, biological occurrence. Thus, Suzanne Arms (1977, p. 26) refers to the history of childbirth as "a chronicle of interferences in the natural process." Among the specific interferences which she and other authors discuss critically—and which they often assert are completely unnecessary in over 90 percent of the cases—are the following: fetal monitoring to detect any complication that may arise in the early stages of labor; use of drugs to induce early labor; use of various types of anaesthesia during delivery; use of forceps and related techniques in delivery; performance of an episiotomy (surgical incision in perineal tissue at the opening of the vagina to ease the birth process)—which is now virtually routine; and frequent recourse (excessive, according to the critics) to surgical delivery through Caesarean section. Insensitivity (and, again, use of some questionable technological "advances") in prenatal care, the impersonalized and bureaucratic setting and procedures of the modern hospital (including excessive separation of mother and newborn baby), and the disapproval of midwife-assisted home births, provide additional grounds for criticism.

Some of this critique is based on the desire to return to a more "natural" birth process. There is also concern that some of the medicalized techniques pose serious risks to the fetus or create unnecessary pain or discomfort for the mother. But beyond all this is the fact that increasingly women are finding the dominant procedures oppressive. As Wertz and Wertz comment, "What had begun in the 1920s as a pursuit of safety, comfort and efficiency, a shared effort by doctors and patients to have the 'best' for birth, had become by the 1950s and 1960s an unpleasant and alienating experience for many women. Technical routines to control natural processes compounded with social routines to process the patient no longer seemed warranted by the danger of birth but seemed instead to stand in the way of a humane and meaningful delivery" (Wertz and Wertz, 1979, p. 173). Physicians and hospitals recently have made some concessions to these feelings, but usually not to the extent of dramatically altering the overall approach to maternity care.

For example, many hospitals today permit the mother (and the father) to utilize some form of "natural" or "prepared" childbirth (Romalis, 1981; Rothman, 1981)—with breathing exercises, training in the timing of contractions, the baby's father in the delivery room, and so on. However, there is no guarantee in such cases that medicalized techniques will not eventually be used during labor or delivery should they be deemed necessary. Sometimes "natural" and medicalized techniques are routinely used in combination.

Furthermore, many obstetricians tend to be less than enthusiastic about the "natural" approach, and to indicate that at the outset:

> The voice of professional authority is hard to counter. The woman is clearly being primed in the initial interview for acceptance of a medical definition of birthing. She hears from her doctor that it is unusual for women to have nonmedicated births, that she might be putting the baby at risk to achieve her goal, that guilt results from trying and failing, and that there is nothing unnatural about medication, or even a Caesarean (Romalis, 1981, p. 70).

Similarly, while the category of nurse-midwives is now often accorded a certain amount of standing, these midwives for the most part are relegated to a subordinate role in the hospital system—often having to use the standard medicalized techniques in order to function as "a member of the obstetrical team" (Rothman, 1981, p. 159). Finally, although many hospitals have tried to create a more sympathetic environment for labor and delivery, and arrangements that minimize mother-newborn separation, the strong resistance to midwife-assisted nonhospital births has not abated.

At the heart of the controversy over medicalized childbirth lies the general issue of female autonomy versus professional (and primarily male) control. Two English researchers who interviewed women in antenatal clinics noted, "The women interviewed both in York and London reported very few areas in which they were able to exercise choice about the kind of maternity care they had. From the moment they first saw a doctor about the pregnancy, decisions were made for them. . . . This lack of control experienced by mothers extended right through their antenatal careers" (Graham and Oakley, 1981, p. 61). This situation reflects not only female vulnerability and induced deference, but also the standard socialization of physicians—who are trained to depersonalize the patient, to view her situation (particularly in childbirth) from a narrow medicalized perspective, as well as to forcefully assert their professional authority (see Carver, 1981; Young, 1981).

Insensitivity to the female patient is an issue that extends across the whole gamut of medical practice. Some further maternity-related areas in which critiques of medicalization have been made include the prescribing of drugs during pregnancy and the emphasis on women (rather than men) practicing contraception (Merkin, 1976; Roberts, 1981; also Gordon, 1977), treatment of infertility (see Rothman, 1979, Ch. 5), and medical attitudes toward breast-feeding (ibid., Ch. 7; also Oakley, 1976, pp. 194–195). A sense of the way in which women may experience their contacts with the medical practitioner as a kind of imposed social control is starkly conveyed in the following description of the routine gynecological examination, written by a female physician:

> The doctor enters the room fully clothed and very proper, plus or minus white coat. Here we have two very symbolic themes: that of rape—the fully dressed male and the naked anonymous woman—and that of submission—the woman on her back, knees in the air, her most vulnerable parts exposed. Under the circumstances vaginismus [involuntary contraction of muscles around the vaginal opening] is hardly surprising. Then, of course, if because of the muscle tightening the examination *is* painful, it is the woman's fault because she "won't relax."
>
> Since a woman's first visit to her gynecologist usually includes a pelvic exam and Pap smear, this sets the tone for the doctor-patient relationship. Clearly this is not a partnership situation. There is no question who's boss, who has the authority. The stage is set for the doctor to tell the woman what's good about her and what's bad, what she should do about this or that, and what her relationship with him will be in the future (Carver, 1981, p. 123; on the pelvic examination generally, see Emerson, 1970).

Female encounters with the medical profession tend, then, to mirror in at least some respects the general power differential between females and males in the society at large. In this situation, too, the tendency to respond to a woman in categorical terms exacerbates the professional norm of objective impersonality to which the medical practitioner is expected to conform. Drawing an analogy between American gynecology and Nazi medicine—as radical feminist Mary Daly has done (Daly, 1978, Ch. 7)—will strike many as being grossly excessive. Nonetheless, it is clear that women in our society frequently perceive male doctors—regardless of their actual personal motivations—as agents of control more than as kindly helpers. Women feel that medicine again places them "in the wrong"—guilty if they voice their own wishes and viewpoints, guilty if childbirth does not go smoothly, ashamed of pregnancy, and finding it difficult to feel good about being biologically female.

Restricting Abortion

Restrictions on abortion epitomize the control of women through gender norms. Although the public controversy over abortion is sometimes said to promote "single issue politics," in fact the issue of abortion is very closely tied to other aspects of women's situation. The stigmatizing of women for terminating unwanted pregnancies has closely reflected both of the phenomena discussed immediately above: the effort to sustain norms governing motherhood, and the role played by the medical profession in evaluating and regulating female behavior. Norms relating to sexuality, discussed further below, are also very much involved in attitudes and policies toward abortion. Above all—and it is for this reason that it has become perhaps the preeminent "women's issue"—abortion forcefully poses for women the question of personal autonomy.

As one writer recently has put it, "The struggle for reproductive self-determination is one of the oldest projects of humanity, one of our earliest collective attempts to alter the biological limits of our existence. Women died in this struggle, and still do, though their deaths today are due more to prohibitions and illegalization than to necessary risks in birth control" (Gordon, 1977, p. 403). Until recently, abortion was not usually treated as a standard topic in the sociology of deviance (but see Schur, 1955; Schur, 1965; also Rossi, 1966). This omission—like the failure to pay attention to offenses committed directly against women—did provide some support for the claim, (Chapter One) that deviance studies reflected an anti-female or "phallocentric" bias. The heated public conflict over abortion policies has forced sociologists recently to take a greater interest in this topic.

Over the years women regularly have faced stigma for obtaining abortions. Yet the definition of an approved abortion, and the laws and regulations governing and limiting the performance of this simple surgical procedure, always have been formulated and administered by men—who have dominated legislatures, the judiciary, and the medical profession. Commenting on "the hypocrisy of the masculine moral code," Simone de Beauvoir wrote:

> Men universally forbid abortion, but individually they accept it as a convenient solution of a problem; they are able to contradict themselves with careless cynicism. But woman feels these contradictions in her wounded flesh; she is as a rule too timid for open revolt against

masculine bad faith; she regards herself as the victim of an injustice that makes her a criminal against her will, and at the same time she feels soiled and humiliated (de Beauvoir, 1953, pp. 491–492).

Historian James Mohr (1979) has shown that prior to 1800 there were no laws restricting abortion in the United States. Passage of such legislation during the nineteenth century was in large measure attributable to a vigorous campaign in favor of legal restriction waged by the overwhelmingly-male medical profession. These efforts constitute a good example of the general processes of "moral enterprise" and "creation" of a new deviance category, as well as of the "medicalization" tendencies noted in the last section. Mohr cites a number of reasons for this campaign, including the profession's wish to strengthen its overall standing and to curtail competition from unlicensed (usually female) practitioners. Especially noteworthy is Mohr's further contention, "Regular physicians were among the most defensive groups in the country on the subject of changing traditional sex roles" (Mohr, 1979, p. 168). He goes on to comment, "To many doctors the chief purpose of women was to produce children; anything that interfered with that purpose, or allowed women to 'indulge' themselves in less important activities, threatened marriage, the family, and the future of society itself" (ibid., p. 169).

From the late 1800s until the late 1950s statutes in most American states proscribed abortion unless it was "necessary to preserve the life of the mother." By the 1950s this legal criterion was no longer medically meaningful, since advances in medicine had greatly reduced the danger of life-threatening conditions during pregnancy. On the other hand, doctors were beginning to view as "indications" for abortion a few conditions not covered by the law's exception—notably, German measles early in pregnancy, and the taking of certain drugs by pregnant women. These conditions did not threaten the mother's life, but they did pose a serious danger of fetal abnormality. Since technically abortion in such a situation—and also in cases of pregnancy through rape or incest —was not permitted, hospitals had to be extremely cautious about allowing the procedure, but they did sometimes stretch the law in such instances (see Calderone, ed., 1958; Schur, 1965; Lader, 1966). Medical subterfuge was also engaged in to provide some abortions on psychiatric grounds, with the hospital certifying that if abortion was not granted the woman was likely to commit suicide (i.e., the operation, as per the legal exception, was necessary to preserve her life).

Because of the ever-present threat of legal prosecution, hospitals created "therapeutic abortion" committees to rule on abortion applications (Lader, 1966; Lader, 1973). It is generally recognized that this system discriminated against low-income ward patients. However, all women who experienced this bureaucratic "processing" found it demeaning:

> Even wealthy and influential women who had some chance of getting through TA committees, were forced to crawl and beg before godlike doctors (almost always male), who had been granted by the state supreme power over a woman's right of choice in childbearing. Women had to perjure and degrade themselves to comply with the system, paying exorbitant fees to psychiatrists for "letters of approval" that would convince the committee a patient was on the point of suicide. Even worse was the "punishment syndrome." After approving abortion, one committee reversed itself on discovering the woman was unmarried. Another committee reported, "Now that she has had her fun, she wants us to launder her dirty underwear" (Lader, 1973, p. 22).

Punitiveness was likewise evident in the requirement some physicians imposed, that the abortion-seeking woman must agree also to undergo sterilization, as a condition of terminating her present pregnancy (Schur, 1965, p. 22; also Luker, 1978, p. 8).

The overall result of the "abortion board" system was that very few abortions were performed in hospitals (Schur, 1968, pp. 138–139). This did not mean, however, that the legal and administrative restrictions were resulting in far fewer pregnancies being terminated. On the contrary, this shutting off of legal options for the most part simply diverted abortion seekers to illegal practitioners, and indeed provided economic incentives that supported a thriving black market (Calderone, ed., 1958; Schur, 1965; Lader, 1966; Schur, 1968). A statistical committee of abortion experts in 1955 estimated the annual number of induced abortions in the United States to be somewhere between 200,000 and 1,200,000 (Calderone, ed., 1958, p. 180). Of these, only about 8,000 were hospital-approved. Under these circumstances male physicians widely displayed professional timidity, if not hypocrisy, by making what was in effect an "implicit referral" to the illegal abortion-

ist—and sometimes such referral was explicit—when they refused
to perform abortions themselves.

Critiques of this "criminalizing" of abortion (Schur, 1965;
Lader, 1966; Packer, 1968; Schur, 1968) noted that these laws were
virtually impossible to enforce. Since the "offense" involved a
consensual transaction, in most instances there was no citizen-
complainant on whom investigators and prosecutors could rely for
evidence. The demand for abortion, furthermore, was so widespread and strong that illegal practitioners (particularly given the
financial incentive) could be counted on one way or another to
provide the services that were not available legally, despite the
risks they incurred in doing so. If restrictive laws did not significantly deter abortions, they did however ensure that a great many
women would obtain them under conditions of serious risk. Estimates of death from illegal abortion went as high as 10,000 annually; it should be noted that *hospital* abortion, in the early months,
is usually an extremely safe procedure. According to a 1966 account, "Deaths from abortion have doubled in New York City in
the last decade. The principal victims are the deprived minority
groups" (Lader, 1966, p. 66). Medical complications short of death
were extremely common. Some were produced by illegal practitioners who were untrained or who could not be sufficiently careful. Others resulted from attempts at self-induced termination,
which typically preceded recourse to the abortionist.

Under this system of illegality, the quality and safety of abortion services a woman obtained was almost entirely dependent on
her ability to pay. Thus poor women were placed in by far the
greatest danger. But all women who found they had to obtain
illegal abortions underwent, at the very least, an unpleasant experience. In addition they were made conscious of their "criminality," for under the statutes they were technically guilty of a
criminal offense. Nancy Howell Lee's study (Lee, 1969) of the
efforts of relatively affluent and knowledgeable women to locate
illegal abortionists showed that a considerable search—including
the pursuit of "false leads"—might be necessary. Furthermore,
"About a third of the women felt they had no choice about the
abortionist they went to, and less than a third said they chose their
abortionist on the basis of trust in the recommendation they received" (ibid., p. 77). Even women who were quite competent to
deal with such a situation in practical terms may have recognized

nonetheless the possibility of stigma. Thus one of Lee's respondents stated, "I've sometimes felt very ashamed of my cowardice when the subject came up and people started talking nonsense about it But there is so much prejudice against women in my field of work that I just couldn't afford to give people a reason to talk and sneer and feel superior" (ibid., p. 112).

Beginning around the mid-1950s a strong movement developed (Sarvis and Rodman, 1974, Ch. 1; Humphries, 1977) in favor of reforming these highly restrictive abortion laws. At first, the movement involved primarily efforts at public education, calls for research, scholarly conferences, and the like. The reference to "reforming" the laws is pertinent, because in the movement's early stages most of the advocates of change sought only—at least initially—to modify the existing statutes. It should be noted that although doctors had been instrumental in administering the restrictive system, the medical profession did come to play a significant role in this reform movement. Individual physicians, and then increasingly medical organizations, favored wider legal indications for abortion. Recognition was becoming widespread that the restrictive laws had in effect denied women adequate medical care to which they should have been entitled.

A prototype of the "reform" approach was the influential 1962 proposal, by the prestigious American Law Institute, in its Model Penal Code, of new legal guidelines for therapeutic abortion. Under the ALI recommendation, abortion by a licensed physician would have been deemed legal if there was "substantial risk that continuance of the pregnancy would gravely impair the physical or mental health of the mother or that the child would be born with grave physical or mental defect." It also proposed allowing abortion in cases of pregnancy resulting from rape, incest, or "other felonious assault," including illicit intercourse with a girl below the age of sixteen (American Law Institute, 1962, pp. 189–190). During the 1960s, several national organizations concerned with the abortion issue were founded. Some of these groups were still oriented toward research and education, others were more activist. But all included among their goals substantial revision of the laws on abortion.

Although the more moderate groups were prepared to settle at least temporarily for "reform"—a widening of the legal indications for abortion and an easing of the procedural restrictions on obtaining terminations—the more militant organizations held out for complete repeal of all abortion statutes (see Humphries, 1977, pp. 217–220). To some extent, this difference reflected the variation in the organizations' membership, with militant feminist groups insisting that nothing short of repeal would be acceptable. This view was mirrored in one of the more radical pronouncements by a professional organization—the socially conscious Group for the Advancement of Psychiatry. Critically evaluating the American Law Institute's reform recommendation (summarized above), this organization stated: "For those convinced, as we are, that the moral issues present an insoluble dilemma that should be left to individual conscience rather than be the subject of a social policy judgment, the ALI proposal disregards the right of a woman to control her own life" (Group for the Advancement of Psychiatry, 1970, p. 39). Recommending that abortion be entirely removed from the domain of the criminal law, the Group asserted: "We believe that a woman should have the right to abort or not, just as she has the right to marry or not" (ibid., p. 49).

Framed by what appears to have been an all-male committee of psychiatrists, this statement is especially noteworthy for its strong and unequivocal assertion of women's rights. It seems to reflect a realization, which was growing at that time, that merely widening the legal "indications" for abortion would not provide women with full freedom and dignity in dealing with unwanted pregnancies. As biologist Garrett Hardin noted (Hardin, 1968), the system in which administrative approval of the grounds for a legal abortion had to be sought placed the "burden of proof" on the woman. *She* had to show the likelihood of fetal abnormality, *prove* that she was raped, *convince* primarily male authorities that carrying the pregnancy to term would impair her health. Only if she could establish herself as an acknowledged exception could she free herself from the system's demand for "compulsory pregnancy" (ibid.).

Active efforts to revise abortion legislation met with considerable success. By the end of the 1960s, twelve states had enacted "reform" statutes roughly patterned after the American Law Institute's "model" proposal (Sarvis and Rodman, 1974, pp. 40–44). By 1970, three states (including New York) had passed "repeal" bills, under which abortion was permitted on the decision of the woman and her physician provided that certain procedural requirements were met (ibid., pp. 44–46). The escalation of reform, and the increased tendency to push for complete abolition of restrictive laws, can be attributed largely to the efforts of the growing women's liberation movement. One of the early organizers of abortion reform activity has asserted:

> It was the surge and fervor of neofeminism that paved the way for the abortion movement. Each was essential to the other, and neither would have advanced without the other. Still, it was the voices of angry women, organizing across the country, that shook legislatures out of their complacency, and produced the first breakthrough for new abortion laws (Lader, 1973, p. 40).

The culmination of the campaign for repeal came with the U.S. Supreme Court decision in the case of *Roe* v. *Wade* (1973). During the first three months of pregnancy, the Court held, a decision to abort reached by the woman and her physician is not subject to state interference. With respect to the second trimester, the state may regulate abortion procedures (e.g., by specifying where abortions may and may not be performed), in order to promote the health of the mother. With respect to the final trimester, the Court declared, states might regulate and even proscribe abortion except when it is necessary to preserve the life or health of the mother (see Sarvis and Rodman, 1974, Ch. 4; Lader, 1973, pp. 244–245; also Jaffe, Lindheim, and Lee, 1981, especially Chs. 1 and 2).

This decision has been a matter of great public controversy ever since it was issued. The decision has led to a greatly heightened politicization of the abortion issue (see Schur, 1980, pp. 45–59; also Jaffe, Lindheim, and Lee, 1981, Chs. 6–14). There has been a sharp polarization of "pro-life" (i.e., favoring restrictive abortion laws) and "pro-choice" (i.e., opposing same) forces—the former including many persons motivated by sincere religious sentiment —and a stepping-up of political organizing and activism on both sides. Since *Roe* v. *Wade* there has been a fluctuating succession of specific judicial rulings and other enactments in various jurisdictions, some enhancing women's abortion rights and some limiting them. In a 1979 review, the New York Civil Liberties Union noted the following abortion-related policy issues on which there was persisting dispute: the basic right to an abortion; public funding of abortions; abortions for minors; husband's consent or notification; requirements of pre-abortion counseling; the performing of abortions in public hospitals (*New York Civil Liberties,* Jan.–Feb. 1979, p. 5).

A major setback for abortion rights occurred in July 1980, when the U.S. Supreme Court upheld the constitutionality of the so-called Hyde Amendment, by which Congress (in 1976) had banned federal Medicaid funding of most abortions (*The New York Times,* July 1, 1980, p. 1). Funding of abortions for low-income women by the various states continues to vary a great deal. As of this writing, the "right-to-life" forces are exhibiting considerable political strength nationally. A variety of measures aimed at over-turning the 1973 Supreme Court ruling has been introduced in the Congress. These include a proposed constitutional amendment banning abortion and a number of proposed "human life" and "family protection" statutes that would produce the same result.

Before attempting an interpretation of this recent trend, we should consider briefly the general situation under legal abortion —as it has existed since the passage of repeal legislation and then more widely following *Roe* v. *Wade.* By 1978, the number of legal abortions had reached 1,374,000; termination of pregnancy "had become the most frequently performed operation on adults in the United States" (Jaffe, Lindheim, and Lee, 1981, p. 7). While this situation has been cited with great alarm by right-to-life advo-cates, they have tended to ignore the enormous number of illegal, and often dangerous, abortions performed prior to "legalization" —estimated figures for which (i.e., 200,000–1,200,000 annually) were presented above. Furthermore, it is a mistake to believe that the Court ruling established a system of "abortion on demand," as critics often describe it.

On the contrary, a recent report states, "the rulings [in *Roe* v. *Wade* and related cases] created a complex decision-making pro-cess for abortion. The pregnant woman, the doctor, and the state all are participants in this process. Particularly striking is the Court's delegation of responsibility for abortion to the medical profession and its institutions" (ibid., p. 9). In fact, the same ob-servers contend, "many women still are denied the option of abor-tion" (ibid., p. 10) primarily because the medical profession has not assumed this responsibility to the extent it should have done. As a result, there have been "great disparities in the availability of abortion services in many parts of the country" (ibid., p. 32). A 1977–1978 survey showed that seven out of ten non-Catholic hospitals in the United States were performing no abortions at all (ibid., pp. 32–33). Hospitals providing abortions—and also the "freestanding" clinics which have been set up to provide the services hospitals have not adequately provided—are heavily concentrated in a limited number of metropolitan areas. And neither type of institution is adequately providing services for low-income women (ibid., pp. 32–41).

Even when there is access to legal abortion facilities, the right to terminate the pregnancy "must still be mediated by a figure of authority—now a physician, rather than a policeman" (Laws, 1979, p. 214). In addition to specific restrictions a state may impose on the performance of abortions, abortion-seeking women may have to contend with the judgmental responses of physicians ruling on their abortion applications. Laws cites an unpublished study (Stewart, 1971, discussed ibid., pp. 215–218), in which obstetricians who were interviewed revealed a tendency to "type" abortion seekers as being "stupid" or "careless," or as having "made a mistake," or as being "promiscuous," and to deny abortions to those in the last category, whom they viewed as "undesirable" patients.

Imposition of other people's definitions of the situation was also noted in Luker's study of abortion clinic clients. She refers to "the disapproval expressed through the psychiatric labeling process: women seeking abortions are viewed negatively as 'having problems,' whereas women who come to contraceptive clinics are seen as prudent and 'future-oriented' people" (Luker, 1978, p. 38). Such responses, Luker further observes, were likely to be affected by the client's marital status, because that aspect of the woman's situation "triggers certain assumptions [regarding the circumstances of becoming pregnant] in the minds of those who put labels on her as she goes through an abortion clinic" (ibid., p. 38). Overall, Luker found, "almost a third of the women going through the Clinic were viewed by the staff as "sick" people. . . . For many women, then, receiving negative social labeling and feeling its consequences were an integral part of getting an abortion" (ibid., p. 40).

Community attitudes and various interpersonal responses outside the abortion setting itself may also convey a sense of stigmatization. In another interview study of abortion seekers in a Midwestern community, Mary Zimmerman found:

None of these women perceived their community in terms of an overall and genuine approval of abortion. . . . for most of this group, abortion was entered into with the view that it represented a form of deviance. For the women involved in abortion to perceive that others in their community disapproved of abortion and for them to have frequently disapproved of abortion themselves implies that their own pregnancy must have constituted, for them, a highly problematic situation (Zimmerman, 1977, p. 72).

The reactions of male partners, friends, parents, and siblings to these women's pregnancies were mixed—eighteen respondents (45 percent) received no negative reactions, but twenty-two (55 percent) did (ibid., pp. 136–138). Likewise, some of the women afterward felt troubled by having had an abortion, while others did not. It is significant, however, that those "who reported no trouble or disruption [of their ordinary activities] after the abortion were nevertheless concerned about stigma and were carefully maintaining secrecy. Troubled women were even more concerned about the morality and appropriateness of what they had done" (ibid., p. 183). Zimmerman found that for the women she interviewed, obtaining an abortion posed a distinct threat to their views of themselves as "moral" persons. However, instead of convincing themselves there was nothing "wrong" in terminating a pregnancy, the dominant tendency among these women was to acknowledge abortion's "deviance," yet to deny that they personally had any other viable choice. Thus, they absolved themselves of personal "responsibility," while not really dismissing the deviance definition itself (ibid., pp. 192–195).

No doubt there are limited social circles and milieux in which the legalization of abortion has led to its being viewed as a routine and merely inconvenient procedure. For much of the population at large, however, a woman's termination of an unwanted pregnancy—whatever the circumstances—continues to place her at least slightly in the "wrong." Women experience shame and guilt when they exercise this option—feelings which, in large measure, are attributable to negative social response. Self-acceptance of the aborting woman may be made even more difficult when anti-abortion campaigners label her and the doctor who terminates her pregnancy as "murderers." Right-to-life activists have been quite successful in their efforts to depict themselves as representing the "moral" side in the abortion controversy. Abortion seekers have, correspondingly, been labeled as selfish persons who are following the dictates of expediency.

In these evaluations, the moral issues posed by unenforceable and harm-increasing laws (Schur, 1965; Lader, 1966; Schur, 1968), and by giving birth to unwanted children (see Hardin, 1968) are scarcely considered. Nor is the fact that the fetus's life is not preserved when the woman ends up getting an illegal abortion. At the same time, the situations and feelings of most abortion-seeking women are misrepresented. As Sarvis and Rodman (1974, pp. 141–146) suggest, a concern has developed over the possibility that a glib "abortion mentality" might take hold. From that standpoint, a certain amount of post-abortal guilt is seen as a desirable safeguard against the emergence of widespread "disrespect for life." Yet there is no evidence at all that most women who terminate pregnancies fail to respect life, or that their behavior is merely "expedient." It is true that the central and common motivation of abortion seekers is "that they do not want the child" (Rossi, 1966). Yet studies show (see Lee, 1969, Ch. 4; Zimmerman, 1977, Ch. 6) that in most instances women do not glibly or unfeelingly choose abortion. On the contrary, obtaining the abortion is usually the outcome of a complex and personally painful decision-making process. After weighing her alternative courses of action, the woman concludes that terminating the pregnancy is the best (or least worse) thing she can do.

In most cases, there are good personal and social reasons for reaching this decision. Women who abort do so in order not to bear children who would be unwanted, "illegitimate," or congenitally abnormal, or for whom they would not be able to provide adequate care. Thus, the abortion decision is not merely self-serving. There is indeed a self-affirmative principle at stake, "the right to bodily self-determination" (Petchesky, 1980; also Gordon, 1977; Gordon, 1979). But linked to it is a claim to abortion rights based on "the social position of women and the socially determined needs which that position generates" (Petchesky, 1980, p. 662). Placing all childrearing responsibility on women—with little support either from specific male partners or through social services provided by the state—implies a further need to preserve women's right to control childbearing.

The stigma attached to abortion reflects the free-floating tendency to "blame" the woman for virtually any result of her sexual activity—and to disregard the male who made her pregnant. Unmarried women have "no business" engaging in such activity at all. Hence they are stigmatized for terminating their pregnancies, but also (as we have seen) if they carry them to term. Married women who seek abortions should have "known better" than to incur unwanted pregnancies, they should have been more "careful" in practicing contraception, and so on. Women who conceived through rape or incest may somehow have "brought" those situations on themselves (see Chapter Four, on victim-blaming in rape). Women who are too young or too poor to care for children adequately, or who already have "too many" children, have "only themselves to blame." Women who are bearing what will be a severely deformed or retarded child should endure nobly and try to "make the best of a bad situation."

These persisting punitive outlooks make it clear that belief in the fetus's "right to life" (however sincerely held) is *not* the only factor underlying current anti-abortion activism. That conclusion is supported by findings in a recent attitude survey of members of one statewide right-to-life organization. The study found considerable evidence that "opposition to abortion reflects a conservative or traditional approach to matters of personal morality" (Granberg, 1982, p. 17). Thus, members of the "pro-life" group held conservative attitudes on premarital and extramarital sex, homosexuality, contraception, easy divorce, and sex education. Consistent with these findings was the fact that the membership was predominantly Roman Catholic (see also Jaffe, Lindheim, and Lee, 1981, Ch. 6). Unfortunately the study does not appear to have examined attitudes toward other "life" issues—such as capital punishment, and war and peace. The fact that pro-life activists have not regularly opposed the taking of life in these other contexts also raises a question as to the real grounds of their position on abortion.

It is significant that, despite the efforts of such activists, public opinion in general continues to support legal abortion. Data collected by the National Opinion Research Center in 1980 showed the following percentages of approval for the circumstances indicated: mother's health, 90 percent; rape, 83 percent; defect in child, 83 percent; family poor, 52 percent; mother unmarried, 48 percent; no more children wanted, 47 percent. Forty-three percent gave approval to availability of legal abortion in all six situations;

only 7 percent approved under none of the circumstances (Jaffe, Lindheim, and Lee, 1981, pp. 100–101). The variation in approval rates for the different circumstances is noteworthy. In particular, it is significant that only a minority approved of abortion for the unmarried woman. Presumably this is a reflection of the same kind of negative judgment that produces the frequent deploring of abortion "on demand."

While it might be noted that many married women are among those obtaining abortions, it has become true in recent years that unmarried females constitute the majority of abortion seekers. Quite apart from the statistics, however, the case of the unmarried woman might be seen as the one which most directly poses the issue of reproductive self-determination. One commentator recently has asserted that the pro-choice movement has avoided meeting head-on "the deepest causes of antiabortion feeling," which she describes as "sexism and sex fear" (Stone, 1982, p. 14). The same writer also states that "instead of taking a challenging, prosex stand, the choice movement pretty much conceded the subject of sex to antisex advocates. Many feminists and choice advocates don't want to champion the sexually free life" (ibid.). Advocating abortion rights as a means of achieving "the sexually free life" could, however, unwittingly lend support to the anti-abortion forces. Such advocacy could be taken as an acknowledgment and even an endorsement of the "hedonism" and "promiscuity" that pro-life activists claim are widespread. Nonetheless, Stone's argument may indeed highlight the kernel of the abortion dispute. Unless freedom from unwanted childbearing is ensured under *all* circumstances, the *principle* of female control over reproduction will not really be upheld.

STIGMATIZING SEXUALITY

In the broadest sense, norms regulating sexuality suffuse all of the topics treated in this book. Catharine MacKinnon, who was quoted earlier on the centrality of sexual objectification, asserts that "sexuality is the linchpin of gender inequality" (MacKinnon, 1982, p. 533). According to MacKinnon's critique, "A woman is a being who identifies and is identified as one whose sexuality exists for someone else, who is socially male. Woman's sexuality is the capacity to arouse desire in that someone." If what is deemed "sexual" about a woman, MacKinnon asks, "is what the male point of view requires for excitement, have male requirements so usurped its terms as to have become them?" This same idea, that the very meaning of sexuality has been appropriated, is reflected in another writer's contention that "female sexuality becomes distorted, swallowed up in a fantasy world of symbol-objects rather than real people. Like the schizophrenic, we are alienated from our own experience and our own powers of initiation" (Phelps, 1979, p. 23). The topic of women and sexuality obviously deserves a book, or a shelf full of books, unto itself. Although we will keep returning to sexuality-related issues below, we can only present here a few major points regarding the deviance labeling females encounter in connection with their sexual activities.

Persisting Ambivalence

As John Gagnon and William Simon have emphasized (Gagnon and Simon, 1973; also Laws and Schwartz, 1977; Miller and Fowlkes, 1980), acts and situations are imbued with sexual meaning through the "sexual scripts" to which people in a given culture are socialized. Even sexual "attraction" and "arousal" are largely determined by such scripting. Patterns and evaluations of sexual behavior can be expected, therefore, to reflect the overall character of male-female relations, along with other aspects of the sociocultural context. The point is well made by Kate Millett (1971, p. 23) when she notes that sexual intercourse "serves as a charged microcosm of the variety of attitudes and values to which culture subscribes. Among other things, it may serve as a model of sexual politics on an individual or personal plane."

In our society, the meanings attached to female sexuality remain highly ambivalent. We already have noted this element of ambivalence at several points. It appears in connection with the general notion of femaleness as a "threat," the mixed messages conveyed through women's visual objectification, the "gentle tyranny" aspect of female subjugation, and the ambivalent views displayed by the medical profession. It also is quite evident in the responses to abortion and unmarried motherhood we have just considered, as well as in the content (seemingly at the same time "erotic" and "hostile") of pornography, to which we return in the next chapter. Some of the impact on women of this tendency toward contradictory evaluations is suggested in the following statement:

> From an early age, we are alienated from ourselves as sexual beings by a male society's ambivalent definition of our sexuality; we are sexy, but we are pure; we are insatiable, but we are frigid; we have beautiful bodies, but we must paint and shave and deodorize them. We are also alienated because we are separated from our own experience by the prevailing male cultural definition of sex—the male fantasy of active man and passive woman (Phelps, 1979, p. 25).

Taboos surrounding menstruation—at least for young girls, "the feeling tone is of shame, secrecy, and even guilt" (Laws and Schwartz, 1977, p. 45)—and the absence of "scripts" for childhood sexuality generally (ibid., pp. 45–50) may contribute to the development of this alienation. Our culture's general ambivalence toward female sexuality is nicely illustrated by the prevailing norms regarding sexual self-presentation or display. It is considered socially desirable for a woman to appear "sexy," and yet she will encounter stigma if her efforts to project that image are viewed as being too "blatant" or too "extreme" (see ibid., pp. 42–45). As we already have seen, women in our society are heavily subject to commercially touted urgings that they make themselves into visual objects. Yet they are expected to achieve what Laws and Schwartz term "a carefully calibrated degree of display and concealment" (ibid., p. 43) in which they hint at, yet do not "flaunt" their physical sexuality. This requirement for women is necessarily depersonalizing. Strategies for projecting acceptable and standardized images of their sexuality become a central preoccupation, leaving little room for autonomous personal behavior.

These contradictions and ambivalences continue to be reflected also in negative evaluations of female sexual behavior. It is unquestionably true that attitudes toward female sexual activity, and also the actual patterns of such activity, have undergone considerable change in recent years. Sociologist Ira Reiss (1980, Ch. 7) has conducted attitude research on premarital sexual standards over the past three decades. His studies have suggested that, beginning in the late 1950s, the traditional double standard—in which premarital intercourse is deemed acceptable for men but not for women—was being displaced as the dominant norm. Reiss labels the standard which by now has largely superseded it "permissiveness with affection." Under this norm, premarital sex is acceptable for the female as well as the male, provided "a stable relationship with love or strong affection is present" (ibid., p. 177). Corresponding to this attitudinal shift have been substantial changes in the premarital sexual behavior of women. Reiss reviews all of the relevant research (ibid., Ch. 7) and concludes that "probably 75 percent of all women and 90 percent of all men are entering marriage nonvirginally in 1980. Females in particular have changed the most in many sexual attitudinal and behavioral areas" (ibid., p. 188).

In one extremely thorough recent study of premarital sexuality (DeLamater and MacCorquodale, 1979), the major findings seem strongly to support Reiss's general conclusion regarding attitudinal change. These researchers report:

> The majority of both men and women accepted intercourse when there was affection or love in the relationship; one-third or more did not require affection and one-sixth or less believed one should abstain from intercourse until after marriage. Our data indicates that the "double standard," in the strict or traditional sense of accepting premarital coitus for men but not women, has disappeared, at least in this population; our interviewees reported almost identical personal ideologies for males and for females (ibid., p. 93).

Interestingly, this study also found more than half the respondents saying that responsibility for using contraception should be shared jointly by both partners (ibid., p. 195). As to sexual behavior itself, the survey found that among college student respondents 75 percent of males and 60 percent of females had engaged in intercourse; among nonstudent respondents in the same age range, the corresponding figures were 79 percent and 72 percent (ibid., p. 59).

Despite these indications of apparent change, it is unlikely that women feel no more constrained than men by current norms of sexuality. Studies such as those just cited usually are limited to a tabulation of respondents' professed attitudes about various hypothetical situations. They do not really tell us much about how individuals directly experience and evaluate the situations in which they themselves come to be involved. Historian Edward Shorter (1975, pp. 15–18) has claimed that the recent sexual revolution has seen a substantial displacement of "instrumental" sexuality, with the rise of more affection-oriented and empathic sexual relationships. However, as we are going to see below—in considering both male sexual aggression and the commoditization of female sexuality—exploitation in male-female sexual interaction has far from disappeared.

Double standards of evaluation seem to maintain a tenacious hold even when there has been an apparent "liberalizing" of overt behavior. Thus Pepper Schwartz's 1973 study of dating behavior at Yale University (see Laws and Schwartz, 1977, pp. 109–112) found that "even though recreational sexual contact was expected in dating, nonetheless women (but not men) tended to be downgraded by such contact" (ibid., p. 110). We have noted already that females more than males may be held accountable (practically and morally) when sexual acts result in unwanted pregnancy. The persisting use of several deviance labels that imply or charge improper or excessive sexuality—"loose," "cheap," "easy lay," "promiscuous," "nymphomaniac," and so on—further limits female sexual autonomy. An extreme case of "blaming" women for their presumed sexuality, even in situations where it is not at all germane, is the victim-blaming claim in rape cases (see the next chapter) that the woman really "was asking for it." In connection with their sexual activity, males evoke few if any negative imputations that can be compared to these diverse prospects of labeling that women seem perpetually to face.

Under the circumstances, and notwithstanding an alleged "sexual revolution," most women continue to have a high awareness that they are vulnerable to being stigmatized for what they do sexually. Certainly it is true that, as Laws and Schwartz point out, "While sexual freedom and experimentation may receive verbal support in our contemporary culture, recreational sex, or sex without affection, is still basically viewed as a male prerogative" (Laws and Schwartz, 1977, p. 135). But a woman frequently may find herself subject to stigma even when a serious sexual relationship is involved. A study by Laurel Richardson (see discussion in Richardson, 1981, pp. 274–277) of single women who had had long-term relationships with married men illustrates this point.

While Richardson found that such relationships did often serve positive functions for single women, especially for those who sought a low-level involvement that would not interfere with their other life goals, she also noted that a persisting double standard invariably colored the relationship.

> Although it is the male who is breaking the monogamy norm, it is the single woman who, should his transgression be known, will be subject to [such labels as] "other woman," "home wrecker," "husband stealer," and/or to accusations that her career success is attributable to "whom she knows—in the biblical sense—not what she knows." Few women are immune to the potential impact, should their relationship be revealed (ibid., p. 276).

At least until recently, the persistence of double standards reflected widespread stereotypes regarding women's sexual drives. Psychoanalytic notions of innate female passivity (see discussion in Chapter Five) encouraged the view that women, by nature, were not sexually active beings. The recent research demonstrating women's strong orgasmic capacity, cited earlier in this book, has —from a scientific standpoint—greatly undermined that outlook. Yet, as we also saw, such findings may be experienced by males as posing a "threat." If that is so, then there may be an impetus to try to sustain some version of the double standard, in order to keep female sexuality under male control.

Several studies of the professional literature on female sexuality have provided evidence of both the early downgrading tendency and the more recent attempt to modify that view—and yet not eliminate it entirely. Diana Scully and Pauline Bart (1973) analyzed the leading gynecology textbooks during a thirty-year period. They found that the negation of female sexuality persisted, in one form or another, throughout the entire period.

> In the last two decades at least one-half of the texts that indexed the topics stated that the male sex drive was stronger than the female's; she was interested in sex for procreation more than for recreation. In addition, they said most women were "frigid" and that the vaginal orgasm was the "mature" response. Gynecologists, our society's official experts on women, think of themselves as the woman's friend. With friends like that, who needs enemies (ibid., p. 287)?

Studies of more widely distributed books of sexual advice

suggest some change in approach over the years, but again with the emphasis on male impulses and needs ultimately preserved. One content analysis of "marriage manuals," undertaken in the mid-1960s (Lewis and Brissett, 1967), noted that the growing interest in sexual technique had introduced a "work ethic" into the domain of sexuality. These books instructed people that sexual behavior is not to be treated lightly. Mastery of the skills that will "produce" good sex involves learning, preparation, scheduling, and control. "The female is particularly cautioned to work at sex, for being naturally sexual seems a trait ascribed only to the male" (ibid., p. 11). Another study included examination of mass-marketed advice books of the late 1960s (Gordon and Shankweiler, 1971). These researchers found that by that time, and especially in popularized books, female sexual desire was being openly acknowledged. Yet it was depicted differently from that of males —women's sexuality was discussed in terms of emotions and romance, rather than as a matter of physical needs or drives. Females now were encouraged sometimes to take the initiative sexually, but this recommendation seems to have been intended less to enhance their freedom than to increase their husbands' pleasure. Thus the new research on female sexuality was accommodated, but in a way that did not totally undermine traditional relations.

Michel Foucault has observed that "we must not think that by saying yes to sex, one says no to power" (Foucault, 1980, p. 157). The new possibilities of female sexual assertiveness do not appear to be producing a basic alteration of male-female power relations. One sees this in emerging patterns of supposedly liberated sexual behavior. In their study of predominantly heterosexual "singles' bars," Natalie Allon and Diane Fishel did not find much evidence of female autonomy. They reported, for example, that whereas men frequently entered the bars alone, "Most women entered with female friends in order to feel more secure" (Allon and Fishel, 1981, p. 116). On the basis of their observations and interviews, the same researchers noted the persistence of highly traditional behavior patterns.

> The people in the singles' bars seem to conform to traditional stereotyped sex roles. Men light women's cigarettes, buy them drinks, offer them bar stools, and so on. Women try to be superfeminine; they

expect the men to light their cigarettes and buy them drinks. The men play to women's egos and vice versa.

The division of sex roles is perhaps even more clearly defined in the bar environment than elsewhere. Most women expect a man to take their phone number or ask them out; most men do not expect a woman to call them or ask them out. When a woman in a dating bar says that she is liberated, she generally means sexually liberated only (ibid., pp. 117–118).

Male control over sexual encounters is also evident in the more radical pattern termed "swinging"—group sex, as it has emerged out of private "co-marital" (or "wife-swapping") relations (Walshok, 1971; Henshel, 1973; Stephenson, 1973). Anne-Marie Henshel, who conducted interviews with twenty-five female "swingers," found that in most cases it had been their husbands who first found out about swinging and suggested participation, and who played the dominant role in connection with their deciding to engage in the behavior. "In the context of decision making," Henshel concluded, "swinging can be viewed as a male institution, and confirmations of the advent of a 'sexual revolution' and of the abolition of the double standard should be reconsidered" (Henshel, 1973, p. 128). Consistent with this finding are those of another researcher, who has noted that "individuals involved in co-marital sexuality sustain highly conventional life styles in all other spheres except the sexual," and that "swingers are rarely political or social reformers" (Walshok, 1971, pp. 491, 494). Recently, swinging has been marketed commercially as a public form of recreation. Informal observation suggests that advertising for "on-premises swing clubs" is aimed primarily at attracting male customers. It is interesting to speculate whether, when "couples" do attend, there is equal motivation to do so and equal participation of the sexes.

Feminists often point out that sexual liberation and female liberation are not always identical. Studies such as those just reviewed indicate some of the basis for this contention. All too often, the purported liberation of female sexuality turns out to be an illusion. Frequently the expectation that women's sexuality is there to please men impedes significant change (see Rowbotham, 1973, pp. 113–115; also Firestone, 1971, pp. 148–155). One writer comments further that "the isolated focus on sexual liberation was seized and manipulated by capitalists in their ever extending search for profits. Sexual pleasure itself, both that produced by human beauty and that from caresses, has become commoditized, while the market produces its own, distorted, sexual needs" (Gordon, 1979, p. 128).

It is the "isolated focus" aspect of this supposed liberation that has been most strongly emphasized by critics. Their argument is similar to that of Herbert Marcuse (1964), who suggested that "repressive desublimation" (in effect, culturally promoted sex preoccupation) serves as an instrument of social control in contemporary society. Thus, Alix Kates Shulman writes: "The renewed search for personal solutions to collective problems is as arid today as it was a decade ago. Personal solutions to sexual problems center on finding the right partner or the right attitude or the right technique—at best chancy, at worst harmful since they obscure the power relations inherent in sexual relations" (Shulman, 1980, p. 603). In a similar vein, a psychiatric specialist points out that "from the feminist point of view, sexual liberation can be a conservative force in society, insofar as it enshrines the status quo as bedrock. . . . The feminist movement must deal not just with personal liberation but also with the institutions that shape desire" (Person, 1980, p. 629).

In summary, women today may be less likely than before to be depicted as the totally passive recipients of male sexuality. Frequently, however, their sexual activity continues to give rise to negative evaluations. The threat of stigmatization limits their freedom of action in the sexual sphere. Furthermore, when women's active sexuality is acknowledged, it may be misleadingly presented as the main path to full female liberation. Women may be encouraged to "turn the tables on" men and treat them as sexual objects. Female sexual self-aggrandizement may, in turn, distract women from the pursuit of real social change as well as lead to personal relationships that are no more genuinely intimate or satisfying than those which exist at present (see Schur, 1976; Ehrenreich and English, 1979, pp. 292–324).

Lesbianism

As we noted earlier, lesbianism threatens heterosexual males with the possibility that they will be rendered sexually superfluous.

Men's "fear of women," the poet Adrienne Rich has suggested, may really be a fear "that women could be indifferent to them altogether, that men could be allowed sexual and emotional—therefore economic—access to women *only* on women's terms, otherwise being left on the periphery of the 'matrix' (Rich, 1980, p. 643). Indeed, in Rich's view, the open acknowledgment of lesbian feelings raises the possibility that "heterosexuality may not be a 'preference' at all but something that has had to be imposed, managed, organized, propagandized, and maintained by force" (ibid., p. 648). We shall return to Rich's argument. Even without adopting such an extreme view, however, one is forced to recognize that lesbians are stigmatized because they violate core requirements of the prevailing gender system.

The very concepts of "feminine" and "masculine," as they are presently understood, are threatened by homosexuality—male as well as female. As Dennis Altman points out, "Being male and female is, above all, defined in terms of the other: men learn that masculinity depends on being able to make it with women, women that fulfillment can only be obtained through being bound to a man" (Altman, 1973, p. 81). Homosexual object-choice and life-style represent a breach of the "heterosexual assumption" (Ponse, 1978, pp. 58–59; Rich, 1980)—the presumed heterosexuality of human actors, around which most interaction and social arrangements are organized. Likewise, homosexuality threatens the "principle of consistency" (Ponse, 1978, pp. 28–30)—the common expectation that people's biological sex, gender identity (self-conception as "female" or "male"), and sexual object-choice and orientation should all neatly fit together.

Beyond these points, there is a sense in which lesbians even more than male homosexuals threaten the gender system. Noting that lesbians try to build a stable home life without men, Sidney Abbott and Barbara Love comment: "It is acceptable for a man to do without women . . . but it is never acceptable for a woman to be without a man. A woman is defined in relationship to men and family. A female without a man and a family is not considered a complete woman" (Abbott and Love, 1972, p. 611). Lesbian feminist Charlotte Bunch describes the lesbian as a person "in revolt."

> In revolt because she defines herself in terms of women and rejects the male definitions of how she should feel, act, look, and live. To be a Lesbian is to love oneself, woman, in a culture that denigrates and

despises women. The Lesbian rejects male sexual/political domination; she defies his world, his social organization, his ideology, and his definition of her as inferior. Lesbianism puts women first while the society declares the male supreme. Lesbianism threatens male supremacy at its core (Bunch, 1972, 1975, p. 29).

This militant proclamation implies conscious defiance of the current order of male-female relations. But either way—whether the lesbian is *unwilling* to play the prescribed "feminine" role or simply finds herself *unable* to do so—the dominant norms are being undermined. Either way, the "natural order" (see Plummer, 1975, pp. 118–121) is threatened. Stigma must be imposed, because "such anomalies have to be reckoned with if the 'natural order' is to retain its credibility" (ibid., p. 120). The implicit threat to the entire system of gender relations has been emphasized by literary historian Lillian Faderman (1981). Noting the widespread existence of "romantic friendships" between women in the eighteenth and nineteenth centuries (see also Smith-Rosenberg, 1975), Faderman observes that if the partners "appeared feminine" and did not demand "masculine privileges" their love relationships were likely to be condoned. "At the base it was not the sexual aspect of lesbianism as much as the attempted usurpation of male prerogative" (ibid., p. 17) that evoked stigmatization.

Faderman suggests that these earlier "romantic friends" escaped being "labeled" (see ibid., pp. 142–143) because at that time women were not yet actively threatening the system of male domination.

> When women's increasing freedom began to threaten to change the world—or at least parts of Europe and America—many who had vested interests in the old order were happy to believe the medical views of lesbians as neurotic and confused and to believe that women who wanted independence usually were lesbians. . . . It is doubtful that any of the theories regarding female homosexuality would have been offered or have enjoyed such currency a hundred years earlier [than the post-World War I period], since independent women presented no significant threat at that time (ibid., p. 332).

Stigmatization of lesbians today takes many forms. To begin with, the very pervasiveness of the "heterosexual assumption" ensures that the lesbian will be ever conscious that she is a norm-violator. In addition to being oppressed by various patterns of "male privilege" which all women confront, she is also subjected to the widespread phenomenon of "heterosexual privilege." Thus, she ends up being treated as doubly deviant, negated both as a woman and as a lesbian. She is likely to feel the impact of these judgments, regardless of whether she has been overtly maligned or patently discriminated against. The culture provides "models of stigma" (Plummer, 1975, pp. 79–80; see also Goffman, 1963, pp. 6–10) that individuals tend to use as a basis for self-evaluation.

As the quotation from Faderman indicates, theories purporting to "explain" lesbianism as a psychological disorder have played a major role in its devaluation (see Simpson, 1977, Ch. 6). Invariably, such theories have been based on clinical data only. Evaluation of psychiatric patients was taken as a basis—along with a psychoanalytically grounded presupposition that homosexuality is "abnormal"—for inferring that lesbianism is necessarily psychopathological. Psychiatrist David Rosen (1974) had a volunteer sample of *nonpatient* lesbians complete the Gough Adjective Check List (a standard indicator of self-conceptions and personal adjustment) and also a more general questionnaire asking about their background, experiences, and outlooks. Based on his own findings, and his review of other nonpatient studies, he concluded that "the majority of female homosexuals are mentally healthy and do not desire to be heterosexual. Female homosexuals have the same or a lower incidence of psychiatric disturbances when compared with matched heterosexual controls. No significant difference in the prevalence of neurotic disorders exists between female homosexuals and heterosexuals" (ibid., p. 65). Even if a high proportion of lesbians were to show signs of psychopathology, the determination of cause and effect would be very difficult. Given the stigma on homosexuality, and the many real life problems lesbians encounter, one might well expect a high incidence of mental illness *as a result.*

Actually, there is little evidence that this has happened. Virginia Brooks (1981) relied in part on questionnaires completed by 675 lesbians in her exploration of the "minority stress" lesbians experience. Respondents ranked aspects of their identities which they felt caused the most stress in their lives, and more than twice as many attributed greater stress to being female than to being lesbian (58.3 percent versus 28.6 percent) (ibid., p. 64). Brooks attributed this finding to the fact that her respondents all were *visible* as females, whereas many had not fully disclosed their homosexuality. But on the basis of her own findings and a review of other studies Brooks develops a further, quite controversial, point. She implies that, given currently dominant definitions of mental health—which place high valuation on stereotypically "masculine" qualities (see discussion of this matter in Chapter Five)—lesbian women may actually surpass heterosexual women with respect to certain beneficial psychological resources. Noting that "androgyny" (essentially, "role breadth and flexibility") may be positively related to self-esteem, Brooks comments that "a role repertoire which includes both instrumental and expressive behaviors and skills optimizes coping resources, and the employment of this repertoire provides opportunities for increasing self-esteem" (ibid., p. 112). Whether by basic inclination or through necessity, lesbian women—in this interpretation—have developed special resources for coping which can significantly offset the stress imposed through social stigmatization.

In 1973, following a heated dispute within the profession, the American Psychiatric Association deleted homosexuality (per se) from the list of psychological disorders in its standard diagnostic manual (see Spector and Kitsuse, 1977, pp. 17–20; Conrad and Schneider, 1980, pp. 204–213; Bayer, 1981). The earlier view, that "conversion" of most homosexuals (female or male) to heterosexuality was both feasible and desirable, is no longer widely held. Many therapists now see as their major goal enhancement of the voluntary patient's well-being *on the basis of her* (or his) *chosen orientation.* As of this writing, it is not clear to what extent devaluation of lesbians will be reduced because of these changes in psychiatric outlooks and practices. Widespread acceptance of lesbianism as falling within the range of "normality"—even by psychiatrists, let alone by the general public—seems at the very least a long-term goal.

In addition to being devalued through lingering psychopathology notions, lesbians regularly face certain other popular conceptions that negate their sexual choice. One particularly common idea is that lesbians really "want to be men." This notion seems to be grounded in the aforementioned "principle of consistency"

—which does not distinguish between sexual orientation and gender identity. It also seems to reflect misguided inferences from the facts that some lesbians—though by no means all—may violate "feminine" appearance norms, and that some—though by no means all—adopt "butch" ("masculine") roles in sexual behavior as well as self-presentation. Actually, as recent empirical research shows, the pattern of contrasting "butch" and "femme" types involved in sexual "role-playing" is not the dominant one among lesbians today.

Deborah Wolf (1980), who conducted a two-year anthropological field study of the lesbian community in the San Francisco Bay area, found such role-playing to be characteristic of an earlier "old gay life" that revolved around gay "bar culture." Even then, during the period prior to lesbian activism and the women's liberation movement, playing set "roles" did not always allow for full expression of lesbian affections.

> Many women who were defined by the community as butches or femmes, and who learned to play out the role, often did not maintain it privately as they adjusted to living with a lover in a long-term relationship. The strain of maintaining such an extreme role in day-to-day life was too great. After all, the women with whom they were relating did not want a man or to be a man, they wanted a love relationship with another woman, and the personal characteristics of the individual transcended arbitrary role delineations (ibid., p. 43).

Contemporary research on lesbians suggests (see Lewis, 1979, pp. 40–42) that femme/butch involvement in role-playing tends to be associated with age—it is infrequent among lesbians under thirty, and practically nonexistent among those in their mid-twenties or younger. Indeed most lesbians today pride themselves on having achieved role-free ways of relating sexually. E. M. Ettore's extensive English study (1980) revealed that those who engage in such role-playing "are usually referred to as 'straight lesbians' by other lesbians" (ibid., p. 62). That is, they are seen as modeling their behavior on the dominant and oppressive heterosexual pattern, rather than demonstrating their freedom from its normative constraints.

Another common conception—to an extent encouraged by psychoanalytic theory—has been that lesbians are afraid of men, or hostile toward them. Available evidence does not support this claim. Many lesbians have previously been married; many others indicate that, at one time or another, they have found men sexually attractive. In the Kinsey Institute's survey of homosexuals' attitudes and behavior (Bell and Weinberg, 1978, pp. 286–287), over four-fifths of the lesbian respondents reported having at some time engaged in heterosexual coitus, and over three-fifths indicated that they had sometimes reached orgasm during such intercourse. Nearly three-quarters of questionnaire respondents in the Ettore study (Ettore, 1980, p. 86) reported having at some time been attracted to a man or to men, and only 27 percent in this sample reported having hostile feelings toward men (ibid., p. 87). In the large questionnaire survey conducted by Brooks (1981, p. 31) respondents were asked to indicate by ranking which aspects of heterosexual relationships they found unattractive. Only 13.9 percent ranked intercourse as the most unattractive feature, whereas 55.2 percent checked "assumption of male dominance," and 26.1 percent cited "women's role expectations."

This point seems to have been supported also in the interview data collected by Barbara Ponse (1978). Respondents who had experienced heterosexual relations "describe a variety of feelings and attitudes with respect to their prior relationships with men" (ibid., p. 176). Some of the disenchantment they voiced did not have to do with the specifically sexual aspects of heterosexual relations. Thus one respondent stated:

> I've had relationships with men and think the negativity of those relationships for me was not because I didn't enjoy sex with men but because I didn't like the other expectations that went along with it, the kind of role playing that happens in relationships with men. The kind of thing where his work should come before mine.... I wasn't prepared to accept that. That was always perfectly clear to me. I knew exactly what a good wife was supposed to do and that it was not my bag (ibid., p. 177).

As we shall see below, socially and psychologically oppressive features of heterosexual relations—as they are presently constituted—may indeed lead some women to consciously choose to live as lesbians. At the same time, however, most lesbians today would disavow any basically negative "explanation" of their sexual or affectional preference. Such preference, they insist, is primarily a matter of their affection for and commitment to women. Nonetheless, it seems that men continue to find comfort in the belief that if a lesbian might only experience sex with *them* (the proverbial claim that all such a woman *really* needs is "one good lay") the same-sex preference would disappear.

In addition to their basic consciousness of themselves as norm-violators, and their awareness of these negative theories and folk beliefs, most lesbians experience some direct stigmatization—informal if not formal. Del Martin and Phyllis Lyon have stated:

> ... the stumbling blocks deliberately and precisely placed in her way by our society provide for her a seemingly never-ending obstacle course. She jumps one hurdle, then another and another, but there are always more hurdles to overcome. These are hazards and pitfalls which the Lesbian must face over and beyond the ordinary trials everyone meets in life. Families, friends, employers, clergymen, doctors, legislators ... continue to put up the blocks, build the fences and set the traps that prevent the Lesbian from taking her place in the human race (Martin and Lyon, 1972, p. 28).

The following similar statement by a male gay activist also applies to the lesbian: "There are few homosexuals who have not felt at some time the various attitudes—sin, crime, illness, curse—with which society brands us" (Altman, 1973, p. 62). Many studies, particularly of male homosexuals, have emphasized that stigmatization may produce the "traits due to victimization" discussed early in this book. Faced with ostracism and derision, homosexuals were described as likely to become defensive, withdrawn, and even self-hating (see Hoffman, 1968; Martin and Lyon, 1972; Altman, 1973; also Adam, 1978, pp. 83–113).

Most recent studies of lesbians depict their situation in a somewhat more favorable, or positive, light. The finding by Brooks, cited above—that her respondents considered their female identity to be more stress-producing than their lesbian identity—is worth recalling in this connection. In some respects, lesbians have not been as heavily stigmatized in our society as have male homosexuals. Open display of affection between females, at least up to a point, is socially accepted and viewed as being "normal." Even two unmarried women living together will not always evoke a negative response. As we have seen, however, the very state of being unmarried may itself give rise to stigma. This underscores the fact that, while lesbians may be reacted to more moderately than gay males, they nonetheless face continuous devaluation on two major counts—their femaleness and then also their "deviant" sexual orientation.

Current research (Ponse, 1978; Lewis, 1979; Wolf, 1980; Ettore, 1980; Brooks, 1981; and see the review by Krieger, 1982) stresses that the collective resources and support of an emerging lesbian subculture—at times incorporating women's liberation activists—are now greatly helping lesbians to cope with the problems and strains of social stigmatization. On the basis of her observations and interviews Ponse (1978; also see Warren, 1974) found that collective solidarity among lesbians afforded opportunities for "destigmatization" and "normalization" of lesbian identity. Wolf's (1980) ethnographic account shows that a substantial network of lesbian-oriented and lesbian-staffed community institutions and projects can provide significant practical assistance, in addition to enhancing morale.

When there are links to radical feminism—as there were in the lesbian community Wolf studied—further possibilities exist for sustaining self-esteem through a strong affirmation of femaleness. In such a context, she notes, a specialized "world view" may develop. Males, heterosexual and bisexual women, and even non-political lesbians, may be held in contempt (ibid., pp. 170–171). As the basis for a virtual lesbian separatism, femaleness may be elevated to close to mystical status. Among the lesbians Wolf studied, "Women are thought to be inherently deeply involved with the rhythms of the natural world. This involvement is personified by the concept of the Mother Goddess as a source of healing, intuitive thinking, and the unity of all sentient beings" (ibid., p. 172). Short of such mystical affirmations—which paradoxically incorporate, once again, a categorical perception of females—the development of a feminist consciousness and active involvement in feminist politics are likely to enhance feelings of self-worth among individual lesbians (see Ettore, 1980; also Lewis, 1979).

Notwithstanding these growing collective resources, outside the self-affirming and supportive subculture lesbians continue to face scorn, harassment, and discrimination. Indeed—in a pattern that would be consistent with what Faderman claims regarding earlier reactions to lesbianism—it may be that lesbians who are collectively involved and committed politically pose the greatest "threat." Such principled opposition to and rejection of the dominant outlooks and patterns, rather than the lesbian's sexual behavior specifically, may be the primary reason for persisting stigmatization.

The situation of lesbian mothers remains particularly difficult. Such women violate the dominant norms defining proper maternity and proper sexuality. In addition, they may be especially condemned for "wanting to have it both ways." It continues to be widely assumed that their influence as parents will have harmful effects on their children, despite the absence of any systematic evidence supporting this claim. People who make that argument gloss over the enormous harm that heterosexual parents can and do produce. (And, in their great concern lest the lesbian's children turn out to be homosexual, they also ignore the fact that most current homosexuals were raised in heterosexual households.) The likelihood is that, as Martin and Lyon put it, lesbians who are mothers "are raising their children well, or raising them poorly or raising them indifferently, just as their heterosexual counterparts do" (Martin and Lyon, 1972, pp. 140–141; see also Richardson, 1981).

Although nowadays particular judges may, in certain circumstances, adopt a relatively unprejudiced and impartial outlook, the overall legal standing of lesbian mothers remains low. "Husbands, by their sole claim to heterosexuality, have been [and, typically, they still are] awarded custody regardless of their suitability as parents. The onus is on the mother, and the label 'Lesbian' is enough to deny her her children" (ibid., p. 141). Furthermore, as Sasha Lewis reports, a lesbian mother never really has a permanent sense of security about her parental rights.

> It is a fear that seemingly has no end. Explains one woman, "Their father ran out on us. I never know when he'll be back, when he'll decide to go to court and grab custody. I never know when some neighbor is going to complain to child welfare authorities, or some teacher is going to complain and some state or county official appear on the scene and take the kids away. It is like living every day with the fear of a death sentence hanging over you" (Lewis, 1979, p. 118).

Self-help groups within the lesbian community (Wolf, 1980, pp. 142–150), and efforts to publicize the plight of the lesbian mother, have provided these women with some assistance and support. However, Wolf reports that not all segments of the lesbian community fully approve of the lesbian mother. Some radical lesbians perceive her as being "in an ambiguous position: because of her association with the father of her children, they are not certain that she is a 'real' lesbian" (ibid., p. 136). Ideological pressure of this sort may cause some lesbian mothers to voluntarily give up custody of their children. But a decision to do so may be viewed as "unnatural" not only by heterosexuals, but also "by some lesbians who, though ideologically in accord with this decision, identify to some extent with the children who are being given up" (ibid., p. 158). Most lesbian mothers try to keep their children, even though they face much difficulty. Presumably, the never-married lesbian who chooses motherhood (and who either selects a man to impregnate her, or obtains artificial insemination) avoids ideological condemnation at the hands of radical feminists. But outside the lesbian community she probably faces even greater stigmatization than does the previously married lesbian mother.

Lesbians who do not encounter the special problems posed by motherhood all experience some situations in which they are explicitly devalued or discriminated against. Their sexual behavior (but not their orientation, per se) is in most jurisdictions technically subject to criminal sanction—although prosecutions of lesbians are infrequent. In many communities, lesbian bars and lesbian activist organizations undergo frequent police harassment. While recent test cases have begun gradually to expand the recognition of gay rights, overall progress in this regard has been slight. As the American Civil Liberties Union's authoritative review of "the rights of gay people" (Boggan, et al., 1975) makes clear, homosexuals are not well or widely protected against discrimination in employment, housing and public accommodations, occupational licensing, or the armed forces. With respect to job and economic opportunities (and perhaps in other spheres as well), lesbians face double discrimination—their chances and rewards suffer to some extent because of their sexual preference, but probably to an even greater extent simply because they are female. (Recall Brooks's point that the latter status is immediately visible, whereas the former is not.)

We have noted that current research depicts lesbians as managing reasonably well despite the difficulties that they face. However it is significant—and a key indicator of persisting stigma—that most lesbians still do not openly disclose their sexual preference to all persons, but instead "pass" as heterosexual in some situations. In the Kinsey Institute homosexuality survey, for example, about two-thirds of the female respondents said that their employers did not know they were homosexual (Bell and Weinberg, 1978, p. 67). Brooks, on the basis of her large sample's questionnaire responses, rated overall disclosure (to others generally) by her respondents as follows: low, 37.5 percent; moderate, 20.6 percent; high, 41.9 percent (Brooks, 1981, p. 96). Clearly specific strategies of concealment/disclosure vary a great deal. Concealment at work is extremely common, as the Kinsey statistics show. One close observer comments that "typically the work world is a straight environment in which the lesbian must keep her gay self hidden." Although the need to pass will vary depending on the circumstances, "the consequences of breaches of secrecy in the world of work are usually seen as grave, potentially reaching far beyond mere disapprobation to include the curtailment of a whole career" (Ponse, 1978, p. 67).

While concealment serves obvious functions for the lesbian, at the same time it imposes considerable psychological strain and potentially undermines her positive self-conceptions. Brooks found high disclosure of lesbian identity (along with high socio-economic status and having lesbian reference groups) to be *inversely* correlated with self-reported stress (Brooks, 1981, p. 102). The persistence of the partial concealment pattern is particularly noteworthy, given the fact that today it is widely condemned by lesbian feminists. Thus, one writer has recently stated that "passing for straight and the leading of a double life are in practice modes of subscribing to the heterosexist norms that it is shameful for women to love women" (Zita, 1981, p. 175). Similarly, Ettore asserts, "the closet [i.e., concealment] makes one unable to challenge publicly society's views. Society wins out. The dominant ideology remains intact and perhaps, it gathers more power" (Ettore, 1980, p. 41). However that may be, until the stigma attaching to lesbianism is significantly reduced so that the situation of the individual lesbian becomes much more secure, we cannot expect the phenomenon of "passing" to disappear.

Several additional points regarding the relations between the gender system and lesbianism deserve mention. One particularly intriguing recent development has been the advent of the "political lesbian." Women adopting this stance proclaim that their lesbianism is "more than a sexual preference, it is a political choice" (Bunch, 1972, 1975, p. 30). Repudiating the oppressive system of male-female relations, and simultaneously asserting their love for women, they advance the principle of the "woman-identified woman." Such a woman is committed to other women "for political, emotional, physical, and economic support" (ibid.; also Radicalesbians, 1970, 1977). A classic document of this radical lesbian movement states that "being 'feminine' and being a whole person are irreconcilable," and insists that women together "must find, reinforce and validate our authentic selves" (Radicalesbians, 1970, 1977, p. 176).

Opinions will no doubt differ regarding the validity of claims by particular lesbians that their lesbianism represents a conscious political choice. But what is especially interesting for our purposes is the fact that, given the present character of male-female relations, it seems perfectly plausible that some women *might*—out of opposition to the system—reach such a conscious decision. As we have seen, most lesbians insist that their orientation primarily reflects positive feelings toward women rather than negative feelings toward men. Nonetheless, it is evident that many women find the context within which heterosexual relations occur to be oppressive. At the same time, we should note that making a "decision" for lesbianism does not fully enable a woman to "opt out" of the oppressiveness imposed by dominant gender arrangements and norms. Unless they are able to live a totally separatist existence, lesbians—whose *femaleness* remains visible—are subject to most of the devaluation and exploitation that all women confront. They may be able to avoid some of the specifically sexual aspects of male domination. But they can still be scorned, discriminated against, harassed, physically attacked, or raped—*on account of being female.* So lesbianism has great limitations if seen as a "solution" to gender oppression, and of course it carries its own stigma as well.

The woman who suddenly, and on political grounds, declares her lesbianism is not always well accepted within the lesbian community. It may be questioned whether she is a "real lesbian," and she may even be labeled a "fad lesbian"—that is, seen as a basically heterosexual woman who seeks approval for what she thinks of as politically correct behavior (see Brooke, 1978, p. 81). On the other hand, women who wish to be militantly feminist may find radical lesbians telling them that "until all women are lesbians there will be no true political revolution" (Johnston, 1974, p. 166). These comments begin to suggest the substantial disagreements that exist within both lesbian and feminist groups, and the difficulties of forming an effective alliance between the two movements.

We cannot explore these matters in any detail here. Among politically active lesbians (we should have in mind that many lesbians are not political at all) there is much dispute regarding social separatism, relations with men, and relations with heterosexual or bisexual women (see discussion in Rich, 1980; Ferguson, 1981; Zita, 1981). Active feminists vary greatly in their personal attitudes toward lesbians, let alone on the issue of whether lesbianism is essential to female liberation. It is not surprising, then, that the lesbian rights movement and the women's liberation movement have at best joined forces on a tenuous basis—in connection with particular issues, for specific demonstrations, and so on. The relationship between lesbian groups and gay male activists has likewise been an uneasy one (Altman, 1973; Lewis, 1979; Ettore, 1980). Various observers have commented on male domination of the gay liberation movement. The gay male's opposition to heterosexual privilege may not always prevent him from displaying remnants of a sexist male upbringing or guarantee his willingness to forego *male* privilege.

Lesbians, gay males, and feminists all oppose the restrictiveness and exploitation built into the present gender system. It remains somewhat unclear just what changes must occur for that oppression to cease. In particular, views differ regarding the precise nature of the relation between heterosexuality and the subordination of females. Many commentators agree that male-female relations, *as they are presently constituted,* oppress women and, in some respects, men. There remains, however, great disagreement over the claim advanced by Rich (1980, p. 633) that "heterosexuality itself" is a "beachhead of male dominance." Some observers cannot conceive of a nonexploitative heterosexuality. Others (who may note that homosexual relations can be exploitative too) believe that—given significant changes in the social and attitudinal context within which they occur—heterosexual relations could become egalitarian and humane. The topic of lesbianism (and homosexuality in general) brings this crucial issue to the forefront. A definitive resolution of it has yet to be provided.

SUGGESTED READINGS

Berger, John, *Ways of Seeing.* New York: British Broadcasting Corporation and Penguin Books, 1972, 1977. Illustrated television talks by a British art critic, which contain insightful comments on the visual objectification of women.

Brooks, Virginia R., *Minority Stress and Lesbian Women.* Lexington, Mass.: D. C. Heath and Co., 1981. A large-sample study of lesbians, emphasizing their resources for coping with "minority stress."

Goffman, Erving, *Gender Advertisements.* New York: Harper Colophon Books, 1979. Pictorial essay analyzing "gender display" in advertisements.

Jaffe, Frederick S., Barbara L. Lindheim, and Philip R. Lee, *Abortion Politics: Private Morality and Public Policy.* New York: McGraw-Hill, 1981. Systematic review and discussion of the abortion controversy.

Laws, Judith Long, *The Second X: Sex Role and Social Role.* New York: Elsevier, 1979. Social psychological text on woman's situation, which stresses the normative evaluation aspect of gender.

Millman, Marcia, *Such a Pretty Face: Being Fat in America.* New York: Norton, 1980. Sociological analysis of the devaluation of fat people. Adopts a deviance perspective; emphasizes collective action to combat stigmatization.

Rothman, Barbara Katz, *In Labor: Women and Power in the Birthplace.* New York: Norton, 1982. Critique of the medicalization of childbirth, by a feminist sociologist.

Rutter, Michael, *Maternal Deprivation Reassessed.* 2nd ed. New York: Penguin Books, 1981. Exhaustive review and critique of the evidence regarding "maternal deprivation."

CHAPTER 4

Victimization of Women: Deviance or Conformity?

As we have just seen, women in our society are subject to deviance labeling in an extremely wide range of situations. Although attempts may be made to rationalize the imposition of stigma in some of these circumstances, collectively the many stigmatizations of women demonstrate the deep-seated devaluation of femaleness itself. In the present chapter, we turn to a counterpart tendency—our culture's disinclination to stigmatize males for offenses committed against women. Thus, our focus here shifts from female behavior to male behavior. And instead of examining the application of deviance labels, we will be noting the failure to effectively "deviantize" offensive male behaviors. The two tendencies—to stigmatize women and to absolve men of responsibility for victimizing women—are closely intertwined. Both reflect the dominance within our system of male power and male privilege.

Recent commentators on offenses against women have begun to recognize that their root causes often may lie in the dominant gender system itself. Basic socialization and ongoing patterns of routine interaction have encouraged males to victimize women, and have imposed on women the victim role. This behavior-causing aspect of the gender system is one of the key points we should keep in mind as we explore the victimization of women. There is, however, a closely related but slightly different focus that equally demands our attention. To understand or to curb the victimization of women, we must not only determine what "causes" these behaviors to occur. We must also consider the social responses their occurrence elicits. These two lines of inquiry tend to merge when

133

we adopt a broad conception of cause—asking not why particular individuals commit these acts, but rather why the behaviors are so prevalent in our society. From that standpoint, we can see that *both* the occurrence of such victimization *and* the failure to effectively stigmatize the male offenders are attributable to dominant gender prescriptions.

There are several factors that help to account for our society's weak response to the victimization of women. The low value placed on womanhood seems to have carried the general implication that women's rights are not really worth recognizing, protecting, and enforcing. This aspect of devaluation is seen more specifically in the frequency with which women's charges that they have been victimized or exploited are discounted or disbelieved. And it is most dramatically evident in the fact that such women often are treated as though *they* were the "deviants." When that happens, yet another link to the gender system may be evident from the apparent or purported bases for victim-blaming. As we shall soon see, in many instances the imputation that she has violated a gender norm is used to "justify" treating the victimized woman as though she were a deviant. Perhaps the most interesting way of interpreting our society's toleration of the victimization of women is in terms of the links between these supposed offenses and patterns of approved behavior. If these male behavior patterns actually incorporate elements—however slight or distorted—of "conformity" to persisting gender norms, then to that extent it is unlikely they will be effectively labeled "deviant."

Discussing the victimization of women as a separate topic is done here primarily for the sake of convenience. Both the overall devaluation of femaleness and the wide array of specific stigmatizations of women could themselves be described as types of victimization. So too could the various forms of economic and employment discrimination that women experience. In this chapter, we are going to consider three major categories of victimization: sexual harassment in the workplace, direct violence against women (rape and woman-battering), and victimization built around the commoditization of female sexuality (prostitution and pornography). As we explore the systemic groundings of these phenomena, it should become very clear that individualized "explanations" of victimizing behavior are inadequate. These male offenses are closely tied to our society's scenarios of *approved male behavior*. The persistence *and the relative tolerance of* such victimization represents, therefore, a price we pay for maintaining a dehumanizing and exploitative gender system.

SEXUAL HARASSMENT

Sexual harassment of working women is nothing new. Since the earliest days of female factory labor, if not before, women employed by men and working under their authority have faced numerous types of sexual blackmail and overt sexual abuse (see Farley, 1978, pp. 56–58; and on related aspects of women's early work situations, Rothman, 1978, pp. 42–60; Hartmann, 1979). Almost totally dependent on men for job security and a semblance of decent working conditions, let alone for advancement in a "career," women perennially have had few options when confronting an employer's or supervisor's (or even a male coworker's) sexual advances or demands. They could submit, they could quit the job (though often with few alternatives), or they could try to stay and resist—with a strong likelihood, if they were not fired outright, of facing various types of retaliation and unpleasantness.

As part of the recent women's liberation movement, an unwillingness any longer to accept such a situation has been growing. Lin Farley (1978, p. 32) suggests that the very concept of "sexual harassment" signals "a new awareness," one that strongly asserts women's longtime "negative perception of male aggression in the workplace." Numerous personal accounts by women of offensive male behavior at work have become available, and organized efforts to oppose sexual harassment have increased greatly. As a result, what Catharine MacKinnon has aptly termed "economically enforced sexual exploitation" (MacKinnon, 1979, p. 25) cannot easily be ignored.

The effort to publicize and take action against sexual harassment received a major boost in April of 1980. The federal Equal Employment Opportunity Commission published amended guidelines (*The New York Times*, April 12, 1980, p. 1; also Neugarten and Shafritz, eds., 1980, pp. 154–157) under which sexual harassment was unequivocally declared to be a violation of Title VII of the U.S. Civil Rights Act, which bans discrimination because of sex. The new regulations state that "unwelcome sexual advances, requests for sexual favors and other verbal or physical conduct of a sexual nature" constitute an offense when submission becomes "either explicitly or implicitly" a condition of employment; when submission or rejection is used as a basis for employment decisions affecting the individual; and even when the conduct "has the purpose or effect of substantially interfering with an individual's work performance or creating an intimidating, hostile, or offensive working environment." The commission at the same time declared that employers have an "affirmative duty" to take "all steps necessary" to prevent sexual harassment and to impose appropriate sanctions when it does occur.

As the broad definition used by the commission begins to suggest, sexual harassment can take many different substantive forms. These include persistent and pointed sexually tinged staring; verbal abuse, including repeated sexual innuendo, reference to the employee's body parts, discussion of her presumed sexual activity, and overt suggestions or requests of specific sex acts by the male; numerous types of overt fondling (unnecessary and uninvited body contact of all kinds); as well as outright attempts at rape. The specific manner in which such behaviors will be "backed up" by male power to hire and fire, promote and demote, reward and punish, also can vary greatly. So too do the specific work contexts within which these acts arise. The documented cases now make clear that sexual harassment can be anticipated in virtually any work situation in which working women are subject to male supervision and authority.

Although it is not clear whether harassment has actually increased in recent years, the large body of evidence that now has emerged—through questionnaire and interview studies, personal accounts, and testimony in legal cases—indicates both the extensiveness and the diverse forms of this phenomenon (see Farley, 1978, Ch. 2; Alliance Against Sexual Coercion, 1981, Appendix A). An upstate New York survey conducted in 1975 by the Working Women United Institute found that of the 155 women questioned, 70 percent reported they had been harassed at least once. In a 1976 *Redbook Magazine* study, with 9,000 readers responding, 88 percent reported having experienced some form of sexual harassment and 92 percent considered the problem serious. A survey of workers at the United Nations, in the same year, disclosed that of the 875 persons polled one-half of the women and 31 percent of the men were either aware of sexual pressures existing within the organization or had directly experienced them (these findings are discussed in Alliance Against Sexual Coercion, 1981, pp. 47–50).

In 1980, the *Harvard Business Review* in conjunction with *Redbook Magazine* conducted a major survey of the *Review's* subscribers. Over 1,800 of these—most of whom occupied lower- to middle-management positions—returned completed questionnaires (Collins and Blodgett, 1981). It is very clear from this study (and consistent with what one might expect on the basis of Kanter's "tokenism" findings, discussed above) that occupying a managerial post does not shield a woman from sexual harassment. Commenting on her experience in a chemical manufacturing concern, one first-level manager reported, "jokes about my anatomy, off-color remarks, sly innuendo in front of customers—in short, turning everything and anything into a sexual reference was an almost daily occurrence" (ibid., p. 77).

By and large, respondents in this study were more likely to have heard of, observed, or directly experienced instances of the less extreme forms of harassment (supervisors continually eyeing woman subordinates up and down, supervisors starting each day with a sexual remark, unnecessary touching of female subordinates, repeated requests for dates following refusal) than of the more extreme forms (such as direct physical advances). Nonetheless, it is significant that a full 10 percent of those responding had heard of or observed in their companies a situation as extreme as the following: "Mr. X asked me to have sex with him. I refused, but now I learn that he's given me a poor evaluation" (one of a number of hypothetical vignettes used in the study, ibid., p. 84).

Female and male respondents in the *Harvard Business Review* study differed considerably in their responses to the general statement that "the amount of sexual harassment at work is greatly exaggerated." Only 32 percent of the women, as compared with 66 percent of the men, agreed or partly agreed with this statement (ibid., p. 81). Reactions on this item also varied according to respondents' management levels. Top managers were more likely to agree or partly agree (63 percent) than either middle managers (52 percent) or lower-level managers (44 percent). This finding accords well with the fact that top managers also reported less direct knowledge or observation than others of specific types of harassment occurring in their companies (ibid., p. 82). With respect to viewing various types of behavior as harassment, there was substantial agreement (regardless of respondents' sex or management level) regarding the extreme situations. Understandably, responses to the descriptions of potentially harassing behaviors that were more indirect or subtle revealed greater variation and uncertainty (ibid., pp. 84–85).

A 1978 study of female students in their senior year at the University of California, Berkeley (Benson and Thomson, 1982), explored the phenomenon of sexual harassment in a different type of setting. The hierarchical relation between teachers and students does not always directly provide a setting for "economically enforced" sexual exploitation. But it certainly carries a strong potential for exploitation, sometimes involving economic elements (e.g., award of fellowships, appointment to assistantships, effect on future career chances, etc.). Of the 269 women in the final Berkeley sample, 59 percent said that sexual harassment occurred occasionally on their campus, and an additional 9 percent thought it occurred frequently. More than a third of the respondents (93 women) reported knowing personally at least one female student who had been harassed, and 80 respondents (29.7 percent) had themselves experienced at least one harassment incident—either at Berkeley or at previously attended colleges (ibid., p. 241). Of sixty-eight specific incidents described in detail, ten involved direct physical advances. Thus one respondent reported: "I needed help with an assignment so I went to the professor's office hours. He was staring at my breasts . . . It made me uncomfortable and confused . . . He reached over, unbuttoned my blouse and started fondling my breasts" (ibid., p. 242). Leering, verbal advances, suggestive "body language," and "emotional come-ons" were more frequently reported than was such extreme behavior. Likewise, sexual bribery tended in most cases to be implicit rather than explicit. Another campus survey, at the University of Rhode Island (Lott, Reilly, and Howard, 1982), similarly found reported incidents of direct "sexual intimidation" to be much less frequent than those involving "sexual insult."

The Berkeley study found that students often were reluctant to complain (even to the professor himself) about harassment, and that when they did so the offensive behavior did not always cease. In situations where the student was highly dependent on a tenured professor (because of graduate school aspirations, being in the same academic field, etc.), it was particularly difficult for her to bring the harassment to a halt. As a result of these experiences, respondents reported trying to avoid situations in which harassment might occur, losing confidence in their academic performance, and becoming disillusioned about male faculty in general (ibid., p. 246). Perhaps because the economic impact may be less direct and because the student need not always be in continuous contact with the offending professor, these consequences are less severe than those often found in other work situations.

In a study conducted by the Working Women's Institute of the harassment experiences of ninety-two women (primarily low-income clerical and service workers who were economically dependent on their jobs), 96 percent reported emotional stress symptoms (nervousness, fear, anger, sleeplessness); 83 percent reported interference with job performance (distraction, avoidance, loss of motivation); 63 percent experienced physical stress symptoms (headaches, nausea, weight change); and 12 percent found it necessary to obtain therapeutic help (Crull, 1980, p. 70; see also Farley, 1978, Ch. 2; Alliance Against Sexual Coercion, 1981, p. 31). Although there are indications that a woman worker's self-esteem may be enhanced if she can openly reject harassment efforts, the practical risks involved in doing so—at least until recently—have usually been very great. Dependence on the job, particularly, has been a deterrent to even reporting harassment incidents. As the Alliance Against Sexual Coercion succinctly states, "To refuse sexual demands from those who control one's livelihood is to endanger that livelihood" (Alliance Against Sexual Coercion, 1981, p. 12). It is not surprising then that "most women are coerced into tolerance" (MacKinnon, 1979, p. 140).

From the standpoint of examining the workings of the gender system, sexual harassment is a particularly interesting phenomenon. As Figure 1 (discussed in more detail on p. 142) indicates, it is grounded in and reinforced by a combination of structural (economic and occupational) factors and cultural-interactional themes and processes (primarily the visual objectification of women). Most discussions of sexual harassment have emphasized the structural and economic aspects (which are depicted on the right side of Figure 1). Women's occupational segregation, employment disadvantage, and resulting economic dependency were referred to briefly earlier in this work. The subordination of

Figure 1. Sexual Harassment at Work

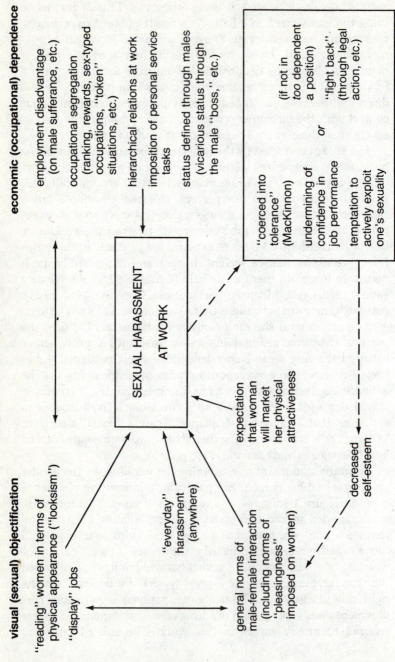

women in and at work unquestionably promotes sexual exploitation in the workplace. Such exploitation, in turn, reinforces women's overall socioeconomic subordination. Employment discrimination and job segregation regularly place working women under male supervision and control, heavily dependent on males for their economic security. Because of these aspects of their economic and occupational situations, most women have neither autonomy in the workplace nor (realistically) the freedom to leave it.

Negative male response to having women in the workplace is also clearly an underlying factor in some if not all cases of harassment. "The emergence of women into the workforce," two commentators suggest, "has upset the entire perceptual framework within which men have been secure for centuries" (Forisha and Heady, 1981, p. 135). The threat posed by women as direct job competitors (see Alliance Against Sexual Coercion, 1981, pp. 12–13) will sometimes trigger harassment. This response may be heightened when a woman worker is seen as having violated a traditional male preserve by making a highly "deviant" occupational choice, as discussed above. In particular, harassment seems common in jobs that previously had been thought to require stereotypically "masculine" qualities—for example, coalmining (see Lane, 1981; also *The New York Times,* April 29, 1982, p. A24, on a major lawsuit by female miners charging harassment), and the military (see *The New York Times,* June 10, 1982, p. A12, for discussion of the Army's efforts to combat sexual harassment).

This seems to suggest that harassment may sometimes implicitly constitute punishment for women's perceived violation of specific gender norms—in these cases, the norms decreeing job segregation according to sex. Likewise, those who subject cocktail waitresses to persistent and overt sexual harassment (for a specific case, see Alliance Against Sexual Coercion, 1981, p. 11) may rationalize their behavior on the ground that such women have become "fair game" by exceeding the limits of "proper" sexual display. It is clear, however, that neither presumed "impropriety" of this sort nor an ultra-"masculine" setting is needed for harassment to occur. This is seen in the general survey data disclosing its occurrence in a wide range of work situations, and also in the specific findings concerning educational institutions (as in the Berkeley study) and large business offices (as in the *Harvard Business Review* study; and see also Korda, 1979) where such conditions do not pertain.

Some observers contend that a generalized perception of threat to male power and control lies behind most harassment in the workplace. It is important, however, to keep in mind that something besides occupational power and control is involved in the harassment phenomenon. MacKinnon's characterization of sexual harassment as "dominance eroticized" begins to suggest this. She writes:

> The sense that emerges from incidents of sexual harassment is less that men mean to arouse or gratify the women's sexual desires, or even their own, and more that they want to know that they can go this far this way any time they wish and get away with it. The fact that they can do this seems itself to be sexually arousing. The practice seems an extension of their desire and belief that the woman is there *for them,* however they may choose to define that (MacKinnon, 1979, p. 162).

Thus harassment seeks to sustain both male workplace power and male power to treat women as sexual objects.

The specifically visual aspect of objectification, which we considered at some length above (and see the left side of Figure 1), is a crucial element in sexual harassment. MacKinnon nicely captures the objectification-harassment link when she comments on reports that leading secretarial schools promise to make the graduate into a pretty "package." "Why has it been so unthinkable," she asks, "so carefully skirted, that such attitudes would be *acted upon,* that, to continue the metaphor, packages are meant to be unwrapped by the purchaser?" (ibid., p. 21). Workplace harassment, then, is not *merely* a result of women's occupational and economic vulnerability. On the contrary, it also reflects the socialized and reinforced tendency of (at least heterosexual) men to literally *see* women primarily as visual sexual objects. From this standpoint, harassment of women workers has as much to do with the "everyday harassment" (see Figure 1) women experience in many diverse contexts as it has to do with other specific features of women's economic and work situations.

Visual objectification and occupational trivialization tend to reinforce one another. Furthermore, the two processes appear in combination in the now-prevalent pattern (also noted in Figure 1) of "display jobs"—work roles in which perceived female attractiveness is treated as being highly salient. Such salience is understandable in certain occupations, such as actress or model (and, with less "respectability," striptease artist or pornography star). Yet the "display job" phenomenon now greatly transcends these standard categories. Women's "looks" continue to be treated as a relevant employment criterion in a wide range of situations, despite the usual denials that this is happening. There appears to be a persisting tendency within our present gender system for many if not most jobs held by women to become, in some degree, display jobs. To the extent this continues to occur, we have further evidence that the objectification and trivialization of women have far from disappeared.

The broken lines in Figure 1 point to some of the likely effects of sexual harassment at work, and to the fact that these in turn can feed back to reinforce the conditions that promote harassment in the first place. As we have noted, various studies show that the harassed worker may feel she has to accept being treated offensively, and that however she responds there is a strong likelihood her self-esteem and job confidence will be seriously impaired. These latter consequences may also follow should a woman choose to take advantage of the fact that the system encourages her to exploit her sexuality for purposes of advancement. And it does need to be acknowledged that female willingness to play the sexual object role gives implicit support to the sexual harassment pattern.

Increasingly, however, women are unwilling to market themselves sexually or to accept sexually offensive behavior by males in the workplace. It is not yet clear to what extent the "new awareness" regarding harassment and the broadened EEOC guidelines are going to enable women effectively to "fight back." MacKinnon's exhaustive analysis (MacKinnon, 1979) has shown that prior to the 1980 regulations the legal record emerging through sexual harassment complaints and lawsuits was a very mixed one. Court decisions reflected uncertainty as to what constituted harassment and as to whether harassment represented—in technical legalistic terms—sex discrimination as proscribed by law. How courts ruled in particular cases depended partly on their responses to various legal "defenses" raised by attorneys for the defendants. Thus it was argued that what goes on between the sexes at work is "personal," that it reflects the "natural attraction" of males and females to each other, which in turn (it was claimed) is grounded in their real biological differences. Employers asserted it would be unfair to hold them responsible for the predictable consequences of these "natural" conditions, and that to do so would also have a chilling effect on amicable work relations between the sexes. Furthermore, it was claimed that since females are in theory equally free to harass males, harassment does not involve sex-based discrimination (all these arguments are analyzed at length by MacKinnon, ibid.).

The last of these arguments seems to have been disposed of by the EEOC's unequivocal proclamation that sexual harassment *does* constitute sex discrimination—although that ruling itself may still undergo testing in the courts. As to the other arguments used to discredit women's harassment claims, it is not certain how they will be received in the future. There now exists a general atmosphere which is somewhat more conducive than before to an effective combatting of harassment. And following the EEOC's statements regarding the "affirmative duty" of employers, large corporations have been issuing policy statements and warning memoranda to employees, holding special training sessions on the topic, and so on (see *The New York Times,* October 24, 1980, p. A20). However, one commentary on the new policies warns that "the government does not share a feminist perspective and analysis of the problem," and points out with reference to workplace implementation that "no mechanisms exist to monitor policy statements or grievance procedures, and there is no means to check the effectiveness of those procedures that do exist" (Alliance Against Sexual Coercion, 1981, pp. 81, 83; but see also Brandenburg, 1982).

As women increasingly move into positions of authority at work, the male power to coerce is bound to recede. The general tendency to visually objectify women is likely to prove more intractable. It seems probable that effective action will increase rapidly against the *most* offensive and blatant forms of sexual harassment, while a reduction in the subtler forms will require a much longer period of time. Borderline behaviors will no doubt persist, yet it is noteworthy that even activists like MacKinnon acknowledge that "few would want every passing glance to be legally actionable sex discrimination" (MacKinnon, 1979, p. 95). The crucial challenge with respect to outlawing sexual harassment is posed in another of the same writer's statements: "Sexism should be no more acceptable as a working condition than racism, verbal forms no less than physical forms" (ibid., p. 210).

RAPE AND WOMAN-BATTERING
Rape

The act of rape and the sociolegal response to rape epitomize many of the gender system–deviance links we are considering in this book. Rape has been described as "the ultimate sexist act" (Russell, 1975, p. 265). According to Kate Millett (1971, p. 44), "In rape, the emotions of aggression, hatred, contempt, and the desire to break or violate personality, take a form consummately appropriate to sexual politics" (Millett, 1971, p. 44). The prospect of being raped presents to women a constant reminder of the extent to which they are devalued and objectified, deprived of personal autonomy. When women are raped, they are indeed treated as "nothing but" objects. Few women in our society are free from the fear of rape, a fear which operates to keep women dependent and under male control. As Susan Brownmiller has pointed out, "The ultimate effect of rape upon the woman's mental and emotional health has been accomplished *even without the act.* For to accept a special burden of self-protection is to reinforce the concept that women must live and move about in fear and can never expect to achieve the personal freedom, independence, and self-assurance of men (Brownmiller, 1976, p. 449; italics in original).

Rape also provides perhaps the best example of a serious male offense against women which is widely deplored but which is in practice not severely condemned or punished. As we are going to see, the criminal justice system—reflecting ambivalent attitudes in the society at large—has been very ineffectual in its response to the rape problem. Its processes have incorporated the widespread tendency to blame women for being raped rather than to respond directly and strongly to the violation itself. Women themselves have to a considerable extent internalized this distorted outlook. As a result, we find a rather thoroughgoing stigma-reversal with respect to rape. Thus, most women who are raped experience not only pain, fear, violation, and outrage—but also *shame.*

The notion that rape victims "brought it upon themselves" is gradually being discredited, as are several other elements of a once dominant rape mythology. Today it is very difficult, for example, to trivialize rape—as was commonly done in earlier times—by underestimating the harm done to rape victims. Testimony by and observation of women who have been raped reveal the occurrence typically of a severe "rape trauma syndrome" (Burgess and Holmstrom, 1974, in Chappell, Geis, and Geis, 1977). This encompasses many diverse traumatic reactions, both short term and long term, some of which are physical in nature and others of which are primarily emotional. The long-term effects of rape can include lingering fear and anxiety, shame (as noted above), and sometimes more specific and severe psychological phobias (ibid., pp. 323–325). Women who have been raped often feel the need to reorganize their lives; frequently they change residences, or jobs, or their friendship networks. One study of five women who had been raped at work disclosed that "one year after the rape, four of the five victims were still not working full time" (Brodsky, 1976, p. 44). A more general analysis by two other specialists emphasizes that "rape and its aftermath seriously affect the victims' ability to continue to perform the normal duties expected of them" (Burgess and Holmstrom, 1976, p. 23). Adolescents frequently drop out of school; housewives and mothers find it difficult to perform routine domestic tasks.

Another rape myth that is rapidly losing credence asserts that women really want to be raped. This theme, which also is central to pornographic depictions of women, represents one of the unfortunate legacies of orthodox psychoanalytic theory (see Chapter Five). A simplistic notion of basic female masochism (an unconscious desire to experience pain) emerged.

> This has given support to the belief that women often enjoy violence during coitus, and therefore might precipitate or actively encourage it. The result of this particular psychoanalytic construction is particularly disastrous for a reading of the rape situation. Victims of sexual assault are interpreted via the intervention of "vulgar" Freudianism as desiring rape and at a subconscious level consenting to sex even when at a conscious level they may say "no" (Edwards, 1981, p. 101).

With the growing availability of detailed data regarding actual rape situations, it has become increasingly clear that such conceptions cannot be applied to rape without great distortion. Far from representing an acting out of female fantasy, rape is "a man's fantasy, a woman's nightmare" (Medea and Thompson, 1974, p. 11). The masochism theory ignores the extremity of the rape violation. It denies the real facts of the rape experience—in which women are used and discarded as depersonalized objects of assault; in which they are totally deprived of their "sexual self-determination" (ibid., p. 14).

Also being displaced through our growing knowledge about actual rapes is the belief that rape is merely the result of psychological disturbance among particular males. Psychologists who study imprisoned rapists are likely to try to find a basis for that claim. Even given their highly skewed samples—which include only a fraction of actual rape-committers, and from which the most "normal" rapists are especially likely to have been excluded —they have not been successful in identifying a clear-cut psychological profile of "the rapist" (see discussion in Pacht, 1976). While some observers might not be willing to state that "the rapist is the man next door" (Medea and Thompson, 1974, p. 36), it is nonetheless now widely recognized that rapes are committed by all kinds of men in all kinds of situations.

At the very least, there is strong support for Brownmiller's assertion: "The typical American rapist is no weirdo, psycho schizophrenic beset by timidity, sexual deprivation, and a domineering wife or mother" (Brownmiller, 1976, p. 191). It would be comforting—to those who uphold present gender norms—if the responsibility for rape could be placed entirely on a small number of "basically different" offenders. There is of course a literal sense in which rape is "caused by" rapists. However, on a broader explanatory level this statement is by itself misleading. It is as short-sighted as it would be to focus exclusively on "sexists" in trying to understand institutionalized sexism. Such individualized approaches have the effect of depoliticizing the phenomena they address. They encourage us to ignore both the cultural *meanings* of the behaviors in question and the overall *context of power relations* within which the behaviors occur.

Brownmiller has claimed further that rape "is nothing more or less than a conscious process of intimidation by which *all men* keep *all women* in a state of fear" (ibid., p. 5; italics in original). While the implication of conscious intent may be questioned, her statement usefully underscores the *generalized effects* of rape (the aforementioned ever-present fear among all women) and the *grounding* of rape *in the broader system of male control.* Sociological interpreters increasingly view rape as an extension and distortion of, rather than a complete departure from, the approved patterns of sexual behavior in our society. According to one study, rape is "the price we must pay for a society based on coercive sexuality" (Clark and Lewis, 1977, p. 29). Two other commentators similarly assert that rape "is not an aberration, a deviation from the norms of sexual and social behavior in this country." Rather, it "is simply at the end of the continuum of male-aggressive, female-passive patterns, and an arbitrary line has been drawn to mark it off from the rest of such relationships" (Medea and Thompson, 1974, p. 11). In line with this continuum notion, the same authors describe as "the little rapes" (ibid., Ch. 5) the persistent harassment of women in everyday interaction (on the general vulnerability of women in public places, see Goffman, 1977).

It would be an exaggeration to say that in our society men are socialized to rape. Nonetheless, many analysts have become convinced that the difference between rape and approved male sexual behavior is essentially one of degree. One writer has even suggested that "our culture can be characterized as a rape culture because the image of heterosexual intercourse is based on a rape model of sexuality" (Herman, 1979, p. 43). Males are taught from an early age to adopt a conquest mentality in their dealings with females. They must act aggressively if they are to "get" sex from women. This outlook is notable for the lack of mutuality it implies. It is upheld in the all-male subculture, within which boasting of sexual exploits remains a staple item of conversation. It is also evident in some of the terminology used by males to describe their sexual activity: "making out," "scoring," and getting women to "put out." While it may be that today some "liberated" men no longer think and talk this way, a great many other men still do (see Beneke, 1982).

Willard Waller's classic discussion of the "rating and dating complex" (Waller, 1937) pointed up the exploitative context within which male-female relations in our society often begin to take shape. He depicted dating among college students as a highly competitive system in which males were prized for their ability to pay (see the next section on "commoditization" of sexuality) and females were sought after for their general popularity and for sexual "thrills." Both sexes were found to make widespread use of impression management techniques. Particularly on the basis of what he discovered regarding the discussions that occurred within "one-sex groups," Waller concluded that the system engendered considerable antagonism between the sexes.

Another early study of college dating behavior (Kirkpatrick and Kanin, 1957) showed that such antagonism may not infrequently be reflected in overt male violence or the threat of violence. In that research, 56 percent of the female respondents indicated they had been offended by forceful attempts at intercourse; 6 percent of the reported incidents involved threats or the infliction of pain. (As a prelude to considering rape statistics, it is noteworthy too that only 6 percent of the offenses were reported to parents or college authorities.) To be sure, most dating does not involve rape or attempted rape. And studies subsequent to Waller's suggested more generally an alternative picture of dating, in which partners were being sought for their pleasing personal qualities rather than for some crasser kind of "exchange value." Findings cited earlier, indicating a partial decline in the double standard of sexuality, might suggest that by and large this alternative picture would be the truer one today.

Nonetheless, it is noteworthy that when one asks present-day college students about the Waller thesis, invariably they find elements of persisting truth in it. And it is highly significant that researchers conducting, in the early 1970s, a follow-up to the male aggression on campus study, found the overall frequency of offending male aggression to have remained relatively unchanged (see Kanin and Parcell, 1981).

In a still more recent survey at the University of Rhode Island, 29.4 percent of the 542 female respondents reported having at some time personally experienced an incident of sexual assault ("forced sexual contact without consent involving touching or penetration")—either on campus or somewhere else (Lott, Reilly, and Howard, 1982, p. 305). Although only about 10 percent of the incidents occurred on dates, the overall data from this study underscore women's general vulnerability to sexual violence. The researchers concluded that "sexual assault is not a rare occurrence and will be experienced at least once by perhaps 25 percent of all women" (ibid., p. 307). The point stressed in an early feminist analysis of rape seems still to pertain: "Men are again and again encouraged to show force and dominance, to disregard the weak refusals of the female, and when persuasion fails, simply to overpower the passive partner with aggression and control. The pressure to be masculine, in fact, is implicitly an underlying factor in much sexual assault" (Melani and Fodaski, 1974, p. 84).

Many writers tend to emphasize that the rape situation is not primarily a sexual one. By depicting rape instead as a crime embodying hostility toward and contempt for women, they quite properly seek to underline the absence of sexual mutuality. At the same time, it is not without significance that male aggression toward women should take this particular form. Although sexual intercourse is occurring against the woman's will, it is nevertheless conceivable that the rapist may believe that what he is "getting" *is* "sex." In this situation, male emotion norms and sexuality norms intersect. Mutuality of feeling is not one of the qualities males are expected to look for in sexual relations. As Diana Russell suggests, "If men were not taught to separate sexual feelings from feelings of warmth and caring, rape would be unthinkable, and fewer men would impose their sexuality on unwilling women in other less extreme ways too" (Russell, 1975, p. 264).

The several references above to men "getting" sex imply another important theme developed in recent discussions of rape— that of women as sexual property. If woman is valued primarily as sexual property, then perhaps it is predictable that men who do not succeed in "getting" women in other ways may turn to rape (see Clark and Lewis, 1977, Ch. 8). Even more pointedly, however, the sexual property notion is central to an understanding of variations in the social response to rape. Thus it has been suggested that the occurrence of rape will be acknowledged when there is "theft of sexual property under the ownership of someone other than the rapist" (ibid., p. 116), and also that "those women who are most clearly dependent upon a male owner/protector will most readily be viewed as meriting protection from rape" (ibid., p. 117).

A woman who does not "qualify" as valuable and protectable sexual property is likely to find her claim that she has been raped disregarded, or else she may be positively blamed for having been raped. Such victim-blaming—which reflects the persistence of a double standard and of the related assumption that all women can be classified as being either "good" or "bad"—maintains considerable strength in public attitudes. It reveals itself even more significantly in the criminal justice system's processing of rape complaints. Recent studies have indicated (see Brownmiller, 1976; Clark and Lewis, 1977) that historically rape has really been a crime against property (theft by one man of another's sexual property), and that this is the latent meaning of the way we continue to respond to it today. The apparent unwillingness within the criminal justice system to vigorously prosecute (or prosecute at all) certain types of rape cases, seems to lend support to this line of analysis.

It should be noted, to begin with, that rape is a grossly under-reported crime. This is due to the trauma the rape victim experiences, the shame she often is made to feel, and also her likely perception that getting involved with the criminal justice system would itself be traumatic and possibly futile. In addition, the victim may find it especially difficult to report being raped by a prior acquaintance or on a date—circumstances she herself may not always recognize as providing the basis for a formal criminal charge (see Sanders, 1980, pp. 48–51). National sample surveys in which citizens are asked about incidents in which they have been victimized indicate that at least half of all the rapes that are committed may never even be brought to the attention of the police (Hindelang and Davis, 1977; Bowker, 1981). An arrest is made in only about 20 to 50 percent of the cases known to the police (the rate varies among different jurisdictions), and successful prosecution culminating in a rape conviction occurs in only a fraction of those instances. Thus, one report referred to "the almost complete immunity rapists in New York City have enjoyed from effective prosecution. In no recent year have more than 8 percent of rape arrests resulted in rape convictions" (Chappell and Singer, 1977, p. 246; also Randall and Rose, 1981, p. 340).

The winnowing process by which rape cases drop out of the criminal justice process is referred to as "unfounding." In order to become a "successful" rape victim (have her claim accepted and acted upon) a woman must: report the offense promptly; display visible emotional trauma and an attitude of cooperation with the police; "convince authorities that she was in no way responsible for her victimization"; and have a complaint that is deemed not only "legitimate" but also "prosecutable" (Randall and Rose, 1981, pp. 346–349). Cases that do not satisfy these criteria are likely to be "unfounded," formally or informally. It is in this process that one finds the tendencies to disbelieve and discredit the rape victim, as well as the related "sexual property" notions, clearly at work.

Noting that "all of the major factors which make a 'bad' case are linked to the victim," Clark and Lewis assert that there are certain categories of women who "can't be raped" (Clark and Lewis, 1977, pp. 91–94). That is to say, these women are not deemed to be credible or acceptable rape victims. Prostitutes, and women who are viewed as being "promiscuous" (or even "excessively" active sexually) are among those whose charges are least likely to be credited. As Clark and Lewis comment, females "who voluntarily give up that which makes them desirable as objects of an exclusive sexual relationship are seen as 'common property,' to be appropriated without penalty for the use, however temporary, of any man who desires their services" (ibid., p. 121). Virtually anything that can be taken as a basis for questioning the rape victim's "respectability"—including drinking habits, psychiatric history, divorce, being on welfare, etc.—may likewise reduce the chances that she will be believed or supported through legal action.

Interestingly, the woman of highest "respectability" (and conformity to gender norms)—the properly married woman—also may be rejected as an acceptable rape victim, *if* the attacker is her husband (see Grosfeld, 1981; Russell, 1982). Rape by someone other than the husband would be seen as a serious offense (in part, theft of *his* "sexual property"). But, by the same token, he cannot be charged with "taking" that which already and legitimately is his. Although it is now undergoing challenge, the law has long upheld this outcome through a formal "marital exemption" to the prohibition against rape. Feminist interpreters have cited the presence of this exemption as a major indicator that a "property" basis underlies rape laws and their administration.

The circumstances within which a rape occurs also may cause the complaint to be unfounded. Rapes that occur on dates are immediately suspect, the assumption apparently being that the woman "led him on," was "asking for it," or in fact had consented to intercourse. Rape victims are especially disbelieved when they have had prior sexual relations with the attacker.

The view of sexuality that has informed the legal process since 1800 is founded on a belief that a woman who once consents to a man's advances will do so again, and by the same token it is believed that it is a man's right to sexual consortium *ad infinitum* with a woman he has "won." In addition, her credibility is immediately affected and it becomes difficult to "organize the text" in any other way except to believe that she consented (Edwards, 1981, p. 66).

Should a woman who is hitchhiking be raped, she may be viewed as having implicitly waived the right to protection under the law. Presumably, she is thought to "deserve whatever she gets" because of her assumed violation of norms of female decorum and dependence. When women are raped on dates or while hitchhiking, the usual legal response conveys the message that *they* should not have allowed the circumstances in which they were attacked to have occurred. It is almost as though, in some circumstances or once personal interaction has reached a certain stage, the man acquires a "right to rape" the woman. This is, of course, simply another way of describing the woman's assumed ineligibility as a valid rape "victim."

The social science concept of victim precipitation (see Amir, 1971) has had an unfortunate effect in reinforcing the already-existing tendency to hold the woman responsible in rape cases. This concept was originally developed in connection with studies of homicide, as a way of focusing on the interaction between victim and offender (hostile argument, the offender's perception of an attack by the eventual victim, etc.) that frequently precedes that offense. To specify preceding, or even "contributing" conditions is, however, a far cry from specifying ultimate "cause" or laying any basis for the imputing of responsibility. It is no doubt true in a very limited sense that if a woman who was raped while hitchhiking had not been doing so she would not have been (in that circumstance) raped. But that is not at all to say that her hitchhiking "caused" her rape—let alone entitled the driver to rape her—or that she was not entitled to hitchhike. Retrospectively, or at the time of the rape, victim precipitation is always an inference drawn from a male perspective. It is a thesis that, at *most,* describes not the woman's behavior but "the rapist's interpretation" of it (Clark and Lewis, 1977, p. 153)—however distorted and unwarranted.

At least until recently, much of the victim-blaming that rape victims encountered was at the hands of the predominantly male police who investigated their complaints. The prospect of undergoing brutal and insensitive questioning in fact deterred many women from lodging such complaints. A French witness before an International Tribunal on Crimes Against Women described the process as follows: "And after the rape, the rape goes on. One is raped morally in the name of justice. The interrogation, the repeating of the minutest details, is very upsetting. The raped woman is forced to prove that she has been raped, and these proofs are then turned back against her" (Russell and Van de Ven, eds., 1976, pp. 112–113).

In the United States, due to the efforts of the women's liberation movement (see Rose, 1977), treatment of the rape victim has improved considerably. Special units aimed at investigating rape complaints and assisting rape victims have been created in many police departments, often staffed partly by female officers (Keefe and O'Reilly, 1976). William Sanders, who recently studied the Sex Crimes Unit of a metropolitan California police department, asserts that investigators there were considerate and supportive in their dealings with rape complainants (Sanders, 1980, Ch. 4). According to Sanders, the exigencies of police work and a practical concern regarding the prospects of obtaining a conviction determine police decisions in rape cases. He concluded that the unit's officers were not judgmental or biased. If they believed the prosecutor would accept a case, and that it was a strong one, they would push ahead with it.

In fairness to both police and prosecutors, it must be stressed that American law traditionally has placed special evidentiary burdens on the prosecution in rape cases, which have made convictions extremely difficult to obtain. These have included independent corroboration of the complainant's claim that she was raped, often a showing that she resisted adequately or was incapable of resisting, and a virtual demonstration that her biography was free of sexual "impropriety" and that she in no way invited or provoked the rape. Under pressure from the women's movement, legislatures have considerably relaxed these special requirements. Thus one commentator could in 1976 already report that "very few jurisdictions now retain special corroboration requirements for forcible rape, and increasingly the permissible scope of defense questioning about the prior sexual behavior of a victim of forcible rape is being circumscribed" (Chappell, 1976, p. 17). Changes in the letter of the law, however, do not always produce immediate changes in established practice. It has been noted, for example, that "even though the written law does not require [corroborative] evidence that supports the victim's charge, the prosecutor may assume (based upon past experience) that a conviction without such evidence is unlikely. Therefore, corroboration requirements are imposed, although they are not legally sanctioned. Similarly, a prosecutor may 'require' evidence of resistance before taking a case to court" (Randall and Rose, 1981, p. 338). And indeed it may remain true, despite changes in formal evidentiary requirements, that juries will be reluctant to convict in rape cases. An experienced prosecutor has been quoted as follows: "Unless her head is bashed in or she's 95 years old or it's some kind of extreme case, jurors just can't believe a woman was raped. There's a suspicion that it was her fault, that she led the guy on, or consented—consent is the hardest thing to disprove. It's just his word against hers" (Chappell, 1976, p. 21). Another study found that judges too may hold victim-blaming attitudes toward rape. The judges who were interviewed appeared ready to infer female consent when presented with hypothetical factual situations that satisfied the legal requirements for rape (Bohmer, 1974, in Chappell, Geis, and Geis, eds., 1977).

Overall it is probably true that pressure from organized women's groups has produced considerable change in responses to rape (for an in-depth study of the responses of police, hospitals, and courts, see Holmstrom and Burgess, 1978). In addition to new police units and legislative reform, rape hotlines and crisis centers have been established in many communities. There has been an improvement in the medical and social services available to rape victims, and perhaps a general atmosphere has been created which will begin to have an impact on people's beliefs about and attitudes toward rape. There is no clear indication, however, that the number of rapes is being appreciably reduced. Citizens' self-reports of victimization (during 1978) led to a government estimate that in that one year 171,145 rapes had occurred nationally (Hindelang, Gottfredson, and Flanagan, eds., 1981, p. 228). The estimated rate of rape offenses known to the police in the same year was 30.8 (per 100,000 inhabitants), up from a rate of 9.6 in 1960 (ibid., p. 290). Government statistics also show that arrests for rape nationally increased 36.8 percent between 1969 and 1978 (ibid., p. 334). The meaning of these several statistics is not entirely clear. Higher arrest rates may primarily reflect increased reporting of rapes to the police and/or changes in the nature and extent of police activity in this area. Or, they may be a sign that—with occasional fluctuations—rape actually has been on the increase over the past several decades, as a good many observers believe.

For rape and the toleration of rape to decline significantly, dramatic changes in gender norms and relations between the sexes are going to be necessary. We have seen that the following are among the elements requiring change: male sexual aggressiveness and a "conquest" mentality as criteria of supposed masculinity; the notion that a woman can be some man's sexual "property"; the related requirement that women place themselves always under male protection, with a failure to do so properly placing them at risk; cultural encouragement of depersonalized sexuality and the objectification of women; and the inducements now offered women to present themselves as sexual objects.

Effecting such changes in well-established patterns is bound to be difficult. It may impose considerable strain on women as well as men. Russell has noted, for example, that many women today display "an ambivalence about being treated as sexual objects" (Russell, 1975, p. 273). They feel depersonalized and degraded by such treatment, and yet they "have internalized male notions of attractiveness, and so in order to feel good about their appearance, they have to pile on makeup, and display their breasts, legs, or behinds" (ibid.). Early in this book we noted that men may find the movement toward women's liberation highly threatening. In this connection, it has been suggested that anti-feminist backlash could produce—or currently could be producing—short-term *increases* in rape. Thus Russell writes: "Rape is the way some men express their hostility to women. More threatened egos may mean more rape. In the short run, the more women who break out of the traditional female role and assert themselves in new ways, the more threatened male egos there are" (ibid., p. 14).

In conclusion, it is clear that rape will not be eliminated through individualized treatment or piecemeal reform. Given its close ties to socially approved scripts, nothing less than a basic alteration in those scripts can "solve" the rape problem. And until females are more highly valued so that their rights are deemed worth upholding, the implicit denial of the problem's seriousness may well persist.

Woman-Battering

Many of the points raised in the discussion of rape also apply to woman-battering. Socialization which encourages male aggressiveness and female passivity is again involved—as is the possibility that the male will be able to enforce his will partly through greater physical strength. The beating of women is extremely widespread, yet we tend to either deny its presence or "explain" it away in individualized or situational terms. As in the case of rape, we profess to deplore such behavior, yet our deep-seated attitudes regarding it appear to be quite ambivalent. Legal reactions toward it have, by and large, been ineffectual. As we are going to see, blame for the battering frequently is placed on the battered woman. Either she "brought it on herself" in some specific way, or else she is held responsible for getting herself into such a situation or for staying there.

Since most (though not all) woman-battering involves the beating of wives by husbands, two additional aspects of woman-battering are extremely important. One is the dominant conception of the marital relation itself. Traditionally, this relation has been viewed as allowing—if not requiring—forceful control over the wife. At the same time, the interaction between husbands and wives has been thought of as occurring within a "private" domain, with the consequence that legal authorities have been reluctant to intervene in "family disputes." The other marriage-related factor of central significance in most woman-battering situations is the woman's position of dependence. She may be highly dependent economically (as well as emotionally, for social standing, etc.) *on the particular man who is doing the battering.* This common circumstance, and not some special psychological characteristic of the wife, is the major reason why battered women often find themselves unable to leave situations in which they are being systematically and brutally victimized.

According to one major study of domestic violence employing data on over 2,000 couples, in the year preceding the interview "3.8 percent of the respondents reported one or more physical attacks which fall under the operational definition of wife-beating. Applying this incidence rate to the approximately 47 million couples in the United States, means that in any one year, approximately 1.8 million wives are beaten by their husbands" (Straus, 1978, p. 445). Like rape and also sexual harassment at work, woman-battering is not at all a recent development. On the contrary, it is a long-standing pattern that only recently has come to public light and been partly recognized as a serious "problem." Historical analysis has shown (Dobash and Dobash, 1978; 1979; 1981) that the control and "chastisement" of wives only gradually gave way in the eighteenth and nineteenth centuries to moderate legal "regulation" (containment within appropriate "limits"); it was not until the late nineteenth century that wife-beating was clearly outlawed. Current attention to the problem of battered wives is almost entirely a result of pressure brought by the women's liberation movement. As one recent account notes, "In less than ten years, wife beating has been transformed from a subject of private shame and misery to an object of public concern" (Tierney, 1982, p. 210).

However, insofar as woman-battering—like sexual harassment and rape—maintains close ties to patterns of social "conformity," it will not effectively be curbed (see the general discussion of "normative" and "deviant" violence, in Ball-Rokeach, 1980). A good point of departure in attempting to understand woman-battering is the following statement by two leading investigators:

> When this methodology [placing the phenomenon in a broad socio-historical context] is applied to the problem of violence against women in the home, it leads to the indisputable conclusion that wife-beating is not, in the strict sense of the words, a "deviant," "aberrant," or "pathological" act. Rather, it is a form of behavior which has existed for centuries as an acceptable, and, indeed, a desirable part of a patriarchal family system within a patriarchal society. . . . (Dobash and Dobash, 1978, p. 426).

As the same writers go on to note, "Contemporary research provides overwhelming evidence that it is women in their position as wives who become the 'appropriate' victims of violence in the home" (ibid.).

These comments begin to indicate why various students of the problem now insist that "explanations" of woman-battering must acknowledge both its current social "normality" and its roots in the patriarchal system. There is no dearth of attempts at framing theories to explain the "causation" of wife-beating. Sociologists have, for example, specified a large and complex web of factors that—in various degrees and combinations—contribute to the occurrence of this behavior (see Gelles, 1972, Ch. 7; Straus, 1978, pp. 449–456; also Martin, 1977, Ch. 4; Gelles, 1979; Pagelow, 1981,

Chs. 1 and 2). These factors include the general norms and values of "a violent society," the socioeconomic status and childhood socialization of the marriage partners and the situational pressures they currently face, role differentiation and authority patterns in the marriage, and so on.

Usually the sociological formulations are geared to understanding the occurrence of woman-battering as a *general* phenomenon within our society. Sometimes there is the danger that the explanatory focus will become too broad. Thus in a preoccupation with the causes of domestic violence (or even, simply, violence) a more specific focus on *wife*-beating may be lost. Most of these theories do, however, see gender norms as an important causal element. And most of them also recognize the significance of the wife's dependent position.

Psychological and psychiatric interpretations are less likely to keep these key aspects of the problem in mind. Often they seem to take as their point of departure—in a way that mirrors persisting attitudes in our society generally—the question of what it is about *these women* that causes them to be beaten. Such interpretations frequently employ concepts like "provocation" and "masochism." Dobash and Dobash point out that "the idea that nagging provokes or causes the violence is not merely a justification provided by the man for his behavior, it is very much a part of our cultural beliefs and is also used by researchers and representatives of social agencies to explain wife beating or to justify their own actions or inactions" (Dobash and Dobash, 1979, p. 133). As these researchers go on to note, provocation can mean virtually anything of which the husband disapproves. It is a retrospective rationalization of male dominance and control.

A similar unwillingness to explore these women's actual social situations is evident in the search for an assumed masochism on their part. The Dobashes emphasize that while the masochism argument may be comforting to other people—who can thereby rationalize ignoring the problem—its use as a purported explanation of woman-battering is misguided. "We have spoken with hundreds of battered women from Britain, the Continent, and North America and we can say unequivocally that not one of them liked being beaten or found it exciting. None of their actions were aimed at eliciting a violent response" (ibid., p. 160). If one must discuss battered women in psychological terms, the concepts "trapped by fear" (Martin, 1977, pp. 77–80) and "learned helpless-ness" (Walker, 1980, Ch. 2) may be more useful. The former is self-explanatory. As regards the latter, Lenore Walker suggests that "repeated batterings, like electrical shocks, diminish the woman's motivation to respond. She becomes passive. Secondly, her cognitive ability to perceive success is changed. She does not believe her response will result in a favorable outcome, whether or not it might" (ibid., pp. 49–50).

These concepts point up the fact that any psychological distur-bances observed among battered women could well be the *result rather than the cause* of the battering. Thus Walker comments:

> Many battered women's coping techniques, acquired to protect them from further violence, have been viewed as evidence of severe person-ality disorders. These women suffer from situationally imposed emo-tional problems caused by their victimization. They do not choose to be battered because of some personality defect; they develop behav-ioral disturbances because they live in violence (ibid., p. 229).

Post-battering disturbance and an inability to leave the situation of victimization may be reinforced by the guilt or shame that prevailing gender norms impose on the beaten woman. "If things go wrong, well-trained wives feel ashamed for having failed their husbands in some way. They may even believe they deserve their beatings" (Martin, 1977, p. 84).

Until recently, psychiatric "help" for battered women had not often involved encouraging them to oppose or leave their victimiz-ers. As several researchers have pointed out (see Dobash and Do-bash, 1979, pp. 190–192; Pagelow, 1981, p. 70), the prescribing of tranquilizers for such women—no doubt well-intended medical-ly—has been extremely common. Noting that conventional (and predominantly male) therapists have not always been highly sen-sitive and supportive in their treatment of battered women—and also that they have "generally emphasized the value of keeping families intact whenever possible"—Walker recommends "that at this time only women psychotherapists treat battered women" (Walker, 1980, p. 230).

Beginning in the early 1970s, an organized movement devel-oped to aid battered women and increase public awareness of the problem of woman-battering (Tierney, 1982). As a result, there is now a better understanding of the battered woman's predicament.

Legislation designed to protect the rights of battered women has been strengthened, and social services available to them have been greatly expanded. Changes in the public perception of the nature of the problem have been especially important. Because of the increased publicity given to the plight of these women, there is a widening recognition of the real reason why they often stay with brutal husbands—namely, the absence of viable alternatives. The battered wife's situation is succinctly described in the following statement: "In order for a woman to get out of the house even if it is only to escape the violence temporarily, she must have some money and a place to stay. In order for her to leave permanently, she must have sufficient funds to support herself and her children and be able to find suitable accommodation" (Dobash and Dobash, 1979, p. 156).

This is not to suggest that battering occurs only in situations of serious economic deprivation. There is much evidence that many middle-class women are beaten too (see Walker, 1980, Ch. 6; Pagelow, 1981, pp. 82–87). Nonetheless, it needs to be kept in mind that a great many women in our society (especially those with children)—regardless of social class—remain dependent on their husbands for economic support. This dependency becomes a key factor in determining a woman's response to victimization by her husband. So too does a woman's continuing commitment to traditional gender notions—for example, that it is a good wife's duty to please the husband, to "try to work things out," and so on. In her recent study of woman-battering, based on questionnaires, interviews, and observations, Mildred Pagelow (1981) sought to determine why battered wives stay with violent husbands and endure repeated ("secondary") battering. With some specific qualifications, her data lent general support to the following hypothesis:

> The fewer the resources, the more negative the institutional response, and the more intense the traditional ideology of women who have been battered, the more likely they are to remain in relationships with the batterers and the less likely they are to perform acts that significantly alter the situation in a positive direction (ibid., p. 46).

Pagelow found that wives with traditional outlooks were particularly unlikely—other things being equal—to leave their victimizers.

In order for a wife to extricate herself from a battering situation, she must *believe that it is right* for her to do so, *feel that she can manage the emotional turmoil* involved, and *know that she will have the resources and support* needed for day-to-day living. Protection from the husband may be a serious problem. By and large, law enforcement authorities have not offered much help in this regard. The police "are *very unlikely* to make an arrest when the offender has used violence against his wife" (Dobash and Dobash, 1979, p. 207) and the judicial response has been equally weak and indifferent (ibid., pp. 217–222; also see Martin, 1977, Ch. 6). Insofar as wife-beating is concerned, Del Martin has noted, "The sanctity of the family home pervades the world of law enforcement. A man's home is his castle, and police, district attorneys, and judges hesitate to interfere with what goes on behind that tightly closed door" (Martin, 1977, p. 88). At the same time civil remedies, such as judicial restraining orders, have not been effectively backed up with the threat of stern enforcement.

As a consequence of the recent women's movement pressure (see Tierney, 1982), specific criminal law provisions regarding wife abuse have now been enacted in most American jurisdictions. Penalties have been increased, procedures for filing charges eased, and civil protections also have been strengthened. It remains to be seen how significantly these measures will overcome the previous legal laxity. The basic response may well persist: "In wife-beating cases, as with rape, the burden of proof is on the victim, who must overcome centuries of male bias to convince a prosecutor of the seriousness of her charge" (Martin, 1977, p. 112).

The most dramatic development in aid of battered wives has been the growth of a substantial network of women's refuges, also called centers, shelters, and "safe houses" (Martin, 1977, Ch. 10; Dobash and Dobash, 1979, Ch. 12; Dobash and Dobash, 1981; Tierney, 1982). Martin describes such refuges as "the only direct, immediate, and satisfactory solution to the problem of wife-abuse" (Martin, 1977, p. 197). First and foremost, the refuge provides a sanctuary for the battered woman and her children. "The refuges constitute a physical and social space where women can escape from violence and live with their children in an atmosphere of mutual support while they make up their minds about their future. They are also places where women come together and have the opportunity to consider their problems and gain strength through discussions of their shared oppression" (Dobash and Dobash, 1981, p. 575). As the Dobashes go on to note, "The general ethos of the refuge is unique" (ibid.). The shelters mark a break with traditional outlooks and modes of providing service. Women are encouraged to find their own way, but are afforded various kinds of assistance *as desired.* An emphasis is placed on self-determination and the achievement of independence, on mutual support rather than "therapy."

The shelter movement has tended to adopt a fairly radical feminist stance, emphasizing the systematic oppression of women in modern society. It is not surprising, therefore, that in conservative circles, shelter activists might be viewed as "troublemakers." According to Pagelow, "Battered women, by making public their dissatisfaction with their private lives, may well appear to be deviants, since they are thereby attacking the myth of the happy family. . . . And shelter movement people, by demanding alternatives for victims that may include separation or divorce, certainly can be viewed as deviants attacking marriage and family" (Pagelow, 1981, pp. 217–218).

On the other hand, some observers believe that the considerable success of the battered women's movement may be causing it to lose its radical thrust. Thus one recent account asserts that public legitimacy and governmental sponsorship have led to a "coopting" and conventionalizing of programs for battered women. The author predicts that this trend will continue, and that "the emphasis on feminist concerns will decline. Influential sponsors, including federal law enforcement and social welfare agencies, have directed the movement away from 'radical' programs that challenge society's patriarchical values and advocate large-scale social change" (Tierney, 1982, p. 216). These programs may be displaced, she believes, by more traditional individualized and "medicalized" approaches.

Whatever outlooks inform programs for helping specific women who have been battered, it remains indisputable that woman-battering—like rape—is a systemic problem, not just an individual one. That this behavior until recently has been ignored and condoned reflects a willingness to allow approved male physical aggression to take a particularly repellent form. It also reflects, again as in the case of rape, an unwillingness to acknowledge victimization when the victims are members of a systematically devalued category.

COMMODITIZATION OF FEMALE SEXUALITY
Prostitution

The buying and selling of female sexuality epitomizes, in a sense, woman's devaluation and objectification. This is not, however, the only sense in which prostitution—in its heterosexual form, to which this discussion is limited—involves the victimization of women. Individual prostitutes are further victimized through the stigmatizing social reactions their activities and their mere presence evoke. It is extremely revealing that prostitution is thought of almost entirely as something that *women* do. It is viewed as a *female* offense. Thus it is the prostitute whose behavior, respectability, and legal status are treated as being problematic. Her male customer, without whom she could not engage in prostitution, is not given a second thought.

The prostitute, then, is routinely responded to as a deviant. Yet a great many "conformists" appear to be dependent on her services. That prostitution is closely linked to approved sexual and social arrangements has long been acknowledged—by social critics and scholars, if not by the general public. Often it has been noted, for example, that the double standard of sexuality is really a "double double" standard. Affording males greater sexual freedom than females implies the dichotomization of women into two classes— the "bad women" with whom men can enjoy this greater freedom, and the "good women" whose reputability is thereby maintained. As we saw earlier, and as the persistence of prostitution itself suggests, the double standard may be declining but it is far from dead.

Some analysts have treated the ownership and "exchange" of female sexuality as being the core element of our entire gender system. Randall Collins thus asserts: "The basic feature of sexual stratification is the institution of sexual property: the relatively permanent claim to exclusive sexual rights over a particular person. With male dominance, the principal form of sexual property is male ownership of females" (Collins, 1971, p. 7; also Rubin, 1975; and for the anthropological groundings of this argument, see Lévi-Strauss, 1949). The prostitute as "common property" may be the counterpoint that is necessary in order to delineate a category of females whose sexual ownership is "exclusive."

From this perspective, "Marriage is fundamentally a socially-enforced contract of sexual property" (Collins, 1971, p. 8), a point suggested, for example, by the "marital exemption" for rape, as mentioned above. A classic statement of the analogy that often is drawn between prostitution and marriage was made by the Marxist theoretician Friedrich Engels. He asserted that bourgeois marriage "turns often enough into crassest prostitution—sometimes of both partners, but far more commonly of the woman, who only differs from the ordinary courtesan in that she does not let out her body on piece-work as a wage-worker, but sells it once and for all into slavery" (Engels, 1884, 1942, p. 63; see also Goldman, 1910, 1972). The same theme is evident in Kingsley Davis's early "functionalist" essay on the sociology of prostitution (1937). As noted in Chapter One, Davis has been faulted by feminist critics for suggesting that prostitution may be inevitable and implying that it serves useful "functions." His emphasis on the interconnectedness of prostitution and "respectable" social patterns was, however, quite sound. He saw prostitution as representing but one point on a continuum of sexual arrangements which also included engagement and marriage. All the patterns, he believed, displayed a crucial common element—the use of sex for "nonsexual" ends.

Prostitutes themselves frequently express the same basic idea. In statements that cannot easily be dismissed as mere "rationalization," they insist they are not selling their sexuality any more than does the married woman—only they are doing it more openly, less hypocritically (see Bryan, 1966; Strong, 1970; Millett, et al., 1973; Jaget, ed., 1980). This assertion calls attention to the close ties between prostitution and the general patterns of socialization regarding sexuality within our society. Leaving aside the question of whether the modern family system in general is grounded in sexual property notions, there seems little doubt that in our particular society both men and women have been systematically trained to view sex as a commodity.

As Laws comments, "The rules for women in courtship delineate an image of woman as commodity. Her power to attract is her 'capital,' which she should invest frugally to assure an adequate future income" (Laws, 1979, p. 179). The common reference to a woman's physical appearance as her "assets" supports this interpretation. So too does the frequent branding of women who overtly display their sexuality as "cheap." What seems to be implied by the use of that term is that such women are *not placing a high enough price* on their sexuality. The general link between socialization to commoditize sexuality and prostitution has been described as follows:

> This demand which fosters prostitution occurs because of the way in which men and women have been taught to view themselves and members of the opposite sex. Men have been socialized to view sex as a commodity that can be purchased for a twenty-dollar bill and quantity of sexual partners has been more highly valued in the male culture than has been the quality of each experience. Women's training has socialized them to supply the other half of this sexual equation. They have been conditioned to view themselves as sexual objects long before junior high school and encouraged to exchange attractiveness (or sexuality) for things like engagement rings or popularity. While the message is that "good girls" subtly exchange sex, women nevertheless view their bodies as salable (James, et al., 1975, p. 43).

Or, as a former prostitute more bluntly has stated, "From the time a girl is old enough to go to school, she begins her education in the basic principles of hustling" (Strong, 1970, p. 290). Although some girls and women today no doubt resist these tendencies, the women's liberation movement has not caused them to disappear. A good illustration of their persistence was provided by an April 1982 newspaper advertisement (*The New York Times,* April 8, 1982, p. A8). The ad issued a "casting call" for girls 12 years old and under to "star" in television commercials for "Goldigger" clothing. That someone today could consider such a label —with its connotation of exchanging sex for financial security— on young girls' clothes to be sales-effective and perhaps even "cute" shows how deep-seated the sexual commoditization mentality must be.

The "cash nexus" of sexuality continues to influence a good deal of male-female interaction. It is still frequently expected that men will pay on "dates" and that they will seek a "return" on that "investment." Striking the "best bargain" in the marriage "market" often involves sexual-financial exchange considerations. The line between the high-priced call girl and the mistress who receives large gifts (let alone the completely "kept" woman) remains extremely hazy. Female "escorts" and "party girls" confuse the picture still further. In a slightly different vein, one writer describes the current use of sexual surrogates in sex therapy as being, in effect, a form of prostitution—since the "patients" pay for their services (Szasz, 1981, pp. 49–61; also James, et al., 1975, p. 52).

Opinions vary considerably as to whether prostitution is, intrinsically or necessarily, exploitative. Some observers seem inclined to view it as just another line of work that women may choose to enter. At least one writer implies that open acceptance of prostitution may be part of sexual liberation (see Adler, 1976, pp. 82–83). However, another sees the prostitute as but an extreme symptom of a much wider "female sexual slavery" (Barry, 1981). The case for considering prostitution to be inherently exploitative or victimizing (a view which the present writer supports) rests on a number of considerations. The prostitute is literally "used." She is also—by virtue of being "bought and paid for"—literally "owned," albeit for restricted purposes and within the limits of a given sexual transaction. She is likely to be evaluated and selected in highly objectified terms. As one French prostitute has described her experience working in a brothel, "I was the thing he came and literally bought. He had judged me like he'd judge cattle at a fairground, and that's revolting, it's sickening, it's terrible for the women. You can't imagine it if you've never been through it yourself" (Jaget, ed., 1980, pp. 75–76). "Servicing" the man is a totally depersonalized, unfeeling act. And despite the fact that prostitutes sometimes may have a certain degree of choice with respect to clients and practices, ultimately their personal preferences (and, by the same token, their dislikes or revulsions) cannot govern their work. Denial of sexual self-determination is central to the daily life experience of most prostitutes.

It is true that some of the more fortunate prostitutes work under relatively favorable conditions. Some may be able to routinize the sexual activity itself in ways that undercut its most oppressive aspects. And without question some prostitutes—comprising a very small proportion of the total—earn a good deal of money. However, to emphasize these relatively favorable possibilities is to give a highly distorted picture of the overall situation of prostitutes. Few prostitutes can completely ignore the intrinsically debasing quality of sex for hire. As one former prostitute has commented, "That's the worst part of it: that what you're selling is your human dignity. Not really so much in bed, but in accepting the agreement—in becoming a bought person" (Millett, et al., 1973, p. 57). Nor is it easy to dismiss the stigma which attaches to prostitution: "It makes a kind of total state out of prostitution so that the whore is always a whore. It's as if—you did it once, you become it" (ibid., p. 65). A French prostitute has made the same point, in these terms: "Being a prostitute is not so much a sexual occupation, it's more a way of being seen as different, being rejected, and even feeling different. The word itself is more important than the activity" (Jaget, ed., 1980, p. 71).

The ultimate test regarding exploitation (or, conversely, self-determination) would seem to be whether women would become prostitutes if they had full access to and were equally remunerated in other more "respectable" types of work. Available evidence strongly suggests that few women would choose a life of prostitution under those circumstances. Although systematic research—taking into account all the various levels of prostitution—shows that not all prostitutes are forced into this work through extreme economic deprivation (see James, 1977, p. 389), it remains true that "all prostitutes are in it for the money" (Millett, et al., 1973, p. 55). Even when prostitution is not the only option a woman has, she may conclude that it is her best available choice.

> To a young woman looking at her options, prostitution may seem the only way she can earn enough money to acquire the material possessions she's been conditioned to want. If she's an attractive woman, she may decide the foremost "talent" or "ability" she has to offer for which she'll be equitably paid is her sexuality. If she is a Third World woman, racial as well as sexual discrimination may further limit her options. If she has children to support, she'll need even more income (James, et al., 1975, p. 4; see also, Rosen, 1982).

For most of its practitioners, prostitution is barely a way of surviving. This point was underscored by Margot St. James, a political organizer of prostitutes (founder of COYOTE, "Call Off Your Old Tired Ethics"), in testimony before the International Tribunal on Crimes Against Women. St. James noted, "Streetwalkers in America are the most oppressed women, the most oppressed workers in the country. They are mostly minority women, and they are discriminated against by the hotels and the parlor [massage parlor] owners, who I call legalized pimps. The parlor owners take at least 60 to 75% of the money, and give the women no benefits and no job security" (Russell and Van de Ven, eds., 1976, p. 180). On the basis of her worldwide survey of prostitution patterns and statistics, Kathleen Barry (1981, p. 83) has concluded, furthermore, that "physical force and fraudulent seduction are important agents causing many females to be prostitutes." Even assuming that that generalization cannot be applied in all cases, the point Barry goes on to make does seem very widely applicable. She asks (and notes that researchers often fail to ask), "Are these women able to change the conditions of their existence?" (ibid., p. 84).

At any rate, it can be argued that studies of prostitution have concentrated excessively on the narrow issue of why particular women become prostitutes. Here again, approaching an endemic social problem in such a way individualizes and depoliticizes it. Such research itself becomes victim-blaming, in the sense that the prostitute is being seen as the cause of prostitution. When this outlook is adopted, the systemic groundings of prostitution are likely to be ignored. Yet the ultimate reason for women turning to prostitution should be no mystery. As Jennifer James and her colleagues boldly state, "The primary cause of women becoming prostitutes is that there has existed a *demand by men* for sexual services which men pay well for and which, overwhelmingly, they have required be filled by women" (James, et al., 1975, p. 43; italics added).

As mentioned above, not all observers agree that prostitution must (under any conditions) be considered *intrinsically* exploitative or oppressive to women. There is, however, widespread agreement that in present-day American society women who become prostitutes are oppressed and indeed victimized *by the social and legal reactions* to them and to their work. Social and legal discrimination against prostitutes ensures their stigmatization, regardless of how they otherwise might feel about the nature of the work itself. The prostitute woman has almost totally borne the brunt of anti-prostitution law enforcement efforts. As one observer of the legal system puts it, "Prostitution is really the only crime in the penal law where two people are doing a thing mutually agreed upon and yet only one, the female partner, is subject to arrest" (Millett, et al., 1973, p. 146).

The treatment of prostitution in the criminal justice system is widely recognized as a major example of the "revolving door" approach. Prostitutes are routinely shuttled in and out of court and jail, without any significant impact on the overall problem. The police chief of one large American city has been quoted as follows: "We can move it around, make it uncomfortable for the girls. My undercover officers make themselves available for solicitation, but this is not very effective. My uniformed officers make it uncomfortable for the customers. We have to react to complaints, but it's only street cosmetics" (quoted in Vorenberg and Vorenberg, 1977, p. 32). As criminal justice observers regularly note, legal policies toward prostitution at best achieve only a containment (Schur, 1980, pp. 110–124) or informal regulation of the problem. One commentator has stated, of the New York situation:

> The actual situation in the city is that prostitution is accepted by everyone—police, judges, [court] clerks, and lawyers. Arrest and prosecution are purely gestures that have to be made to keep up the facade of public morality. The method of dealing with it is simply a form of harassment, not a form of prevention, abolition, or punishment. There is no conviction at any level that prostitution is a crime on anyone's part, only a total and satisfied acceptance of the double standard, excusing the male, accusing the female (Millett, et al., 1973, p. 143; see also Winick and Kinsie, 1972, Ch. 8).

Patronizing a prostitute is technically a crime in many jurisdictions, but actual arrests of male customers are extremely rare. In 1978 New York passed legislation which ostensibly made patrons liable to the same penalties as prostitutes and which required that customers be fingerprinted, photographed, and "booked" on arrest. There is no evidence that this provision has significantly altered actual enforcement practices. Apart from occasional efforts to "crack down" on male pimps, enforcement of anti-prostitution laws remains almost entirely directed against the female prostitutes. Although these enforcement efforts do not really limit prostitution, the negative consequences for individual women who are proceeded against can be considerable. As one researcher notes, "Prostitutes who are arrested repeatedly become enmeshed in a cycle of debt and degradation from which it is difficult to escape. Other employment becomes hard to find, friends and family may be alienated, and the criminal label becomes permanent. Convicted prostitutes either move elsewhere to work, commit other crimes, or continue being recycled through jails as long as they survive" (James, 1977, p. 383).

At all levels—and whether they are being subjected to customers' sexual demands, harassed by the police, or controlled by pimps—prostitutes directly and continuously experience male domination. Thus, Barbara Heyl (1979) notes that even when one analyzes prostitution in business or occupational terms it is revealed as "an extreme case of sex stratification." Police, pimps, businessmen who employ prostitutes, and clients—almost all of whom are male—control, in various ways, the conditions under which the prostitute works. The key controllers and specific types of control tend to vary depending on the prostitute's position in this stratified occupation: she can be a streetwalker; a "middle-range" prostitute working in a house, massage parlor, or hotel; or an independent call girl or "party girl." But few prostitutes maintain substantial autonomy in the conduct of their occupation. Of the supposedly independent call girl with "strong business ties," Heyl comments:

> Her money is her own. But [the businessman] provides the clients and is thus a pimp in the older, "procurer" meaning of the term. He can cut her off when she no longer pleases him; and for each client she sees for him, he gains, perhaps in vast sums of money for his business, while she earns her salary or is simply paid for seeing the one man. The legitimate businessman benefits from prostitution but avoids its stigma, while the prostitute is vulnerable to the penalties—socially and legally—for what she does (ibid., p. 208).

At every level of prostitution, Heyl observes, "all the males win, and only the women pay the costs" (ibid.).

Prostitution has presented feminists with something of a dilemma. On the one hand, the objectification and commoditization of women central to it are anathema to most feminists. Kate Millett has suggested (Millett, et al., 1973, p. 93) that "prostitution is somehow paradigmatic, somehow the very core of the female's social condition. . . . It is not sex the prostitute is really made to sell: it is degradation." Yet women who become prostitutes, it is felt, are the victims and not the perpetrators of the practice. So while most feminists wish to strongly oppose prostitution, they would like to do so without implying disapproval of prostitutes. Several additional factors compound the dilemma. Some activist-prostitutes demand unqualified endorsement of their right to select this line of "work" and they repudiate any feminist stance—including an excessive stress on their victimization—which they believe smacks of pity or condescension. At the same time, among nonprostitutes within the women's liberation movement the degree of commitment to and solidarity with prostitutes as "sisters" working together in a joint effort has been unclear (see Millett, et al., 1973, pp. 9–27; James, et al., 1975, pp. 74–76). Finally, feminist opponents of prostitution wish to avoid seeming in any way to favor, or to give support to those who favor, a general movement toward sexual repression (for historical analysis of antivice campaigns in the Victorian era see Walkowitz, 1980a; 1980b).

Confronting this still unresolved dilemma, contemporary feminists have usually made a two-fold recommendation with respect to prostitution. First, in order to reduce the ongoing sociolegal victimization of prostitute women, they have favored *decriminalization* of prostitution. This means removing from the statute books the legal ban on prostitution (though penalties could still be kept for pimping and for abusive treatment of prostitutes). Such removal is to be distinguished from any form of "legalization"— in which governmental licensing or regulation of prostitutes would imply state approval or at least acceptance of prostitution as a general practice (see the discussion of alternative policies in James, et al., 1975, Ch. 4).

While decriminalization is seen as desirable in the short run, most of its feminist advocates stress that it should not however be viewed as a long-range "solution." They emphasize that the ultimate goal must be to do away with prostitution by eliminating the male demand for it. At one time it was widely assumed that the "sexual liberation" of nonprostitute women might have that effect. However, the persisting strength of prostitution in the face of a considerable relaxation of sexual mores suggests that this is not about to happen. And the apparent general appeal in American society today of no-strings-attached sex exacerbates the problem of eliminating prostitution.

Despite these difficulties, feminists continue to believe that a major reduction in prostitution will be possible if there can be a revamping of the gender system that sustains it. Prostitution, they assert, is "dependent on a repressive sexist socialization that can eventually be changed. Women and men who are free from sexual stereotypes and economic discrimination will be free from commercial sexual exchange" (Russell and Van de Ven, eds., 1976, p. 196). In the meantime, it is argued, decriminalization could at least free prostitute women from much abuse and indignity.

Pornography

An even more complex dilemma is confronted by opponents of pornography. There is no consensus regarding the definition of

pornography. Nor is there widespread agreement on its harmful-
ness, or on the related issues of whether specific harms from it
must be proven, and if so by whom and how. Those favoring its
elimination risk being charged with advocating unconstitutional
censorship. They may also find themselves, in this particular instance, advocating policies also favored (though for different reasons) by organized political movements that are on other issues
anti-feminist.

Feminists, for reasons that will become clear below, often describe pornography as constituting violence against women. Depictions of such violence are central to the content of most
pornographic materials. As we are going to see, however, a direct
link between being exposed to such materials and then engaging
in specific acts of violence has not really been demonstrated. (We
shall also, though, raise the question of whether a demonstration
of such effects should be deemed necessary at all.) In this text, the
discussion of pornography is presented under the heading "commoditization of female sexuality." This aspect of pornography
seems indisputable. The sale and purchase of sexually degrading
depictions of women has become central to what recently was
described as a multibillion-dollar "sex industry" (*The New York
Times,* February 9, 1981, p. B1).

It is the *degradation of women* in such depictions—and *not the
mere depiction of sex*—to which feminists object. This point needs
to be emphasized at the outset, because sometimes pornography
(particularly the legal dilemma it poses) has been discussed without any specific reference to its debasement of females. Analysts
who bypass that core feature usually have adopted the questionable "assumption that the content of pornography is sex and that
the genre is essentially a medium for sexual expression" (Diamond, 1980a, p. 687). The issue then is misleadingly framed in the
following terms: Which expressions and depictions of *sexuality* are
to be allowed, and under what circumstances?

As soon as one considers the actual content of pornographic
materials, it becomes clear that such a conception is inadequate.
Kathleen Barry summarizes this content as follows:

> The most prevalent theme in pornography is one of utter contempt
> for women. In movie after movie women are raped, ejaculated on,
> urinated on, anally penetrated, beaten, and, with the advent of snuff
> films, murdered in an orgy of sexual pleasure. Women are the objects
> of pornography, men its largest consumers, and sexual degradation its

theme. . . . Variations include an escalation of violence and the use of children and animals as "exotic" objects. . . . [in addition] Pornography presents the stereotype of supersexed blacks and kinky homosexuality and feeds it to the predominantly male heterosexual consumer for his private pleasure. Racism and sexism blend with the other characteristics of pornography to provide entertainment based on sexual objectification, violence, and contempt for women. It is the media of misogyny (Barry, 1981, pp. 206–207).

We should note, for the sake of balance, that there does exist as well pornographic material aimed at a homosexual audience (primarily male)—and which does not, for the most part, demean women. We cannot, however, discuss further here this counterpart phenomenon. Although its existence raises some interesting theoretical questions, it should not divert our attention from the omnipresence in our culture of depictions that degrade women. In pornography aimed at heterosexual males woman is presented as a "thing" (see Griffin, 1982, pp. 36–46) to be gaped at, despoiled, violently assaulted, and humiliated; *an object that is there totally for the use of the man.* According to Andrea Dworkin, "The major theme of pornography as a genre is male power, its nature, its magnitude, its use, its meaning" (Dworkin, 1981, p. 24). And in Susan Brownmiller's similar characterization, pornography is "the undiluted essence of anti-female propaganda" (Brownmiller, 1976, p. 443).

The "excitement" or "satisfaction" derived from pornography, and often achieved through the viewer's masturbation, patently lies in "the eye of the beholder" (see Polsky, 1967, Ch. 5; Gagnon and Simon, 1973, Ch. 9). As a consequence, there is a built-in impediment to defining pornography with confidence and precision. Most feminist critics assert the existence of what might be called *a pornographic continuum.* They specify a broad array of depictions that sexually objectify, degrade, and "violate" women. These include the "hardcore" pornographic materials, such as "adults only" films, books and magazines, peep shows, and so on; so-called softcore pornography, such as "men's magazines" of the *Playboy* type (see Lederer and Bat-Ada, 1980; also Michelson, 1975; MacGregor, 1975), and popular song lyrics and phonograph record jackets (see London, 1978); and at the "respectable pornography" end of the continuum some commentators would include many depictions of women used in ordinary commercial advertising.

However, as a basis for making specific control recommendations, the "continuum" approach tends to be unwieldy. It readily evokes the charge that its users advocate indiscriminate censorship and puritanical "repression." For example, one recent commentator has claimed that "consistent overstatement of the problem and underplaying of the repressive potential in suggested solutions characterize much of the literature generated by the anti-pornography crusade" (Elshtain, 1982b, p. 43). More specifically, the same writer criticizes "the erosion of the distinction between soft-core and hard-core and violent pornography" and what she sees as "a moralistic stand" in which pornography opponents are not content to see actual violence punished but attempt as well to "expunge fantasy" (ibid., pp. 46, 47; see also Willis, 1981).

Recognizing the likelihood of such charges, and also the inevitable "line-drawing" problem which the continuum approach exacerbates, feminists have focused most of their activist efforts—as opposed to their general theoretical critiques—on a more narrowly defined category consisting of the *most* offensive types of pornography. This has involved condemning sadistic-masochistic content and also pornographic depictions of children, emphasizing that the core problem is one of violence against women, and claiming that pornography directly produces dramatic social harms. The now classic statement of this last point is Robin Morgan's widely quoted proclamation: "Pornography is the theory, and rape the practice" (Morgan, 1978, p. 169).

As a matter of tactics if for no other reason, it is understandable that anti-pornography activists have been pushed to distinguish between the most blatantly sadistic and hence arguably the most harmful pornography, and other depictions of women that they may consider sexually degrading. This is the approach most likely to gain public acceptance. It is also the one most consistent with the distinction-drawing which lies at the core of legal efforts to frame criteria for outlawing "obscenity." Nevertheless, as we are going to see, an exclusive focus on hardcore pornography and its supposed direct effects has some distinct disadvantages too. Potentially it diverts attention away from the close link between pornography and "respectable" objectification of women. And it begs the question of whether pornography may be harmful quite apart from any dramatic short-term consequences (such as leading to rape)—harmful either because of long-term and subtle effects on other male-female behavior, or simply because of its symbolic reinforcement of pernicious images and values.

In fact, there is no really persuasive evidence that exposure to pornography directly "causes" specific acts of violence against women. Several types of research aimed at determining whether such a causal link exists were reviewed by the national Commission on Obscenity and Pornography (Commission on Obscenity and Pornography, 1970). Included were general attitude surveys, retrospective studies of prior exposure to pornography of convicted sex offenders, experimental laboratory studies testing the direct impact of exposure to erotic material (sexual arousal, hostility, etc.), and attempts at cross-national inference regarding the relation between policies toward pornography and recorded rates of sex crime. The commission concluded that exposure to erotic stimuli did not significantly change "established" behavioral patterns and attitudes, that sex offenders have not had greater exposure to pornography than other adults, and it also cited claims that legal availablity of pornography in Denmark had led to decreases in the occurrence there of sex crimes. It stated, overall, that there was "no evidence to date that exposure to explicit sexual materials plays a significant role in the causation of delinquent or criminal behavior among youth or adults" (Commission on Obscenity and Pornography, 1970, p. 32).

On the basis of these findings, and its more general review of the topic, the commission recommended that "federal, state, and local legislation prohibiting the sale, exhibition, or distribution of sexual materials to consenting adults should be repealed" (ibid., p. 57). It did, however, support legislation to prohibit public display and unsolicited mailed advertising of pornography, and to prevent juveniles from having access to such materials (ibid., pp. 62–70). The commission's approach, and particularly the research it heavily relied on, has been criticized on many specific grounds (see especially Diamond, 1980a, 1980b; Barry, 1981, pp. 233–248; also McCormack, 1978). Almost all of the studies cited by the commission had distinct methodological limitations or flaws. There are not available any "representative" samples of rapists or other sex offenders; furthermore, those who were studied actually had had considerable exposure to pornography—even though it was not significantly greater than that found among other adult males. Further, more refined analysis of the situation in Denmark has led to the conclusion that the early inferences of a decrease in sex crimes there due to the "safety valve" of legal pornography may have been unwarranted (see, for example, discussion in Diamond, 1980a, pp. 696–697; Barry, 1981, pp. 242–244).

Several observers have noted a double standard in the conclusions regarding media impact reached by national commissions investigating violence, on the one hand, and pornography, on the other. Although the National Commission on the Causes and Prevention of Violence (1969) warned that media depictions of violence could reinforce or trigger aggressive behavior, the pornography commission tended to adopt the contrary "catharsis hypothesis"—in which the depictions of offensive behavior are thought to serve as a "safety valve" that makes actual offenses less likely (see McCormack, 1978). McCormack attributes the difference to sexist bias—to lesser concern when only females are being victimized. Another factor is the aforementioned tendency to think of pornography as being primarily about sex (note the pornography commission's reference to "sexual materials" in its legislative recommendation). In this connection, Diamond observes that "the disparate models and conclusions of two major government research reports produced by leading social scientists can only be understood in light of the prevailing liberal ideology of the later 1960s: violence by ordinary citizens in the midst of civil disorders and a purported crime wave was viewed unfavorably, while sex in the midst of the so-called sexual revolution was viewed most favorably. The respective commissions framed their research questions and designs accordingly" (Diamond, 1980a, p. 691).

One of the most telling criticisms of research on pornography, especially experimental laboratory research, is that even when properly designed and conducted it can only test in an artificially constructed setting for fairly dramatic short-term effects (see Gray, 1982). More subtle long-range consequences of routine and repeated exposure to pornographic depictions cannot be examined through such research. A breaking down of inhibitions on giving vent to deep-seated anger or hostility toward women might, for example, be one such long-term effect (Gray, 1982). Even more significant perhaps may be the indirect impact on the way men view and treat women—quite apart from the production of any actual violence.

This suggests a point that sometimes has been overlooked in discussions of pornography's effects. Pressing the pornography-leads-to-rape argument could be improperly taken to imply that if evidence *dis*proves this connection then pornography must be accepted. Preoccupation with the issue of directly caused violence diverts attention from the possibility that the most socially harmful effects of pornography may be on men who do *not* become "sex offenders"—and, to a lesser extent, on all women who must live in a culture permeated by pornographic imagery. It also leads us to neglect the related possibility that the overall social harm caused by softcore materials—what one writer calls "tabletop pornography" (Lederer, 1980, p. 17)—may be as great as, or even greater than, that caused by hardcore depictions.

The general issue of pornography's effects remains perplexing. By and large, the view has been accepted that the opponents of pornography must shoulder the burden of demonstrating that it causes specific social harms. Yet the ultimate impact of pornography may be so diffuse and indirect as to defy that kind of demonstration. Some observers, therefore, in effect, maintain that the mere *presence* of pornography constitutes the harm, and that no additional proof of harmful consequences is necessary. Thus even if it is true, there may be no way to clearly demonstrate that continuous exposure to pornographic depictions *encourages and reinforces* a general conception of women as impersonal "things" (or even, "parts") to be "used" by men as they see fit.

One critic refers to a "conviction that, safety-valve effects on potential crazies aside, pornography as a steady and inescapable diet is generally (if vaguely) harmful to society—this because of the very nature of pornography, its stunting of human affect and moral consequence" (Fremont-Smith, 1980, p. 42). Susan Griffin describes the very process of making woman into an object in pornography as "a humiliation" and "a sadistic act" (Griffin, 1982, p. 47). She goes on to describe the voyeur who consumes pornography in the following terms: "Hidden in the darkness of a theater, anonymous as the man who stares at a public photograph, he is in the position of power. The pornographic nude has become his object. She performs for his pleasure. He owns and masters her. And as much as she exposes herself and makes herself vulnerable, so is he also unexposed and invulnerable" (ibid., p. 48). Pornography, Griffin further contends, is sadism against *all* women. "A woman who enters a neighborhood where pornographic images of the female body are displayed, for instance, is immediately shamed. . . . It is *her* body that is displayed . . . there is nowhere in culture where a woman can evade pornography" (ibid., p. 83).

From the standpoint of sheer objectification and commoditization, there is little reason to believe that softcore or borderline pornography is less harmful than the hardcore versions. According to one analyst, the obscenity of softcore pornography lies in its promotion and reinforcement of "alienated, game-playing, object-related sexuality in our society" (MacGregor, 1975, pp. 178–179). Another researcher has found that "Playboy-genre magazines" condition readers "by text and images to disavow their sentiments of caring, and to abdicate their social responsibility for respect in female male relationships" (Lederer and Bat-Ada, 1980, p. 124). The same researcher notes too that "*Playboy* is selling a way of life, and its way of life is not love and respect for human beings, but love of commodities—and women and children are regarded as commodities" (ibid., p. 131; see also Michelson, 1975). In such media, female sexuality is appropriated (MacKinnon, 1982) commercially and marketed as a commodity for general consumption. This suggests that the link between pornography and the objectified uses of female sexuality in ordinary "respectable" advertising may be very close indeed. It could be that until women's bodies no longer are used *to sell* commodities, the treatment and sale of women's bodies *as* commodities, through pornography, will be bound to persist.

The potential impact of softcore and borderline depictions that objectify and degrade women may be heightened by the very fact of their quasi-respectability. Current trends in the market for pornography suggest a proliferation-escalation-legitimation cycle. Once a form of pornography becomes quite common, it loses its forbidden quality and may no longer excite in the same degree as before. Escalation, in terms of new or more extreme forms, may then be needed to satisfy the growing market. Once those forms have become widespread, the earlier ones—by contrast—may appear "tame," even inoffensive. Softcore materials, then, give rise to hardcore ones; and are in return to some extent "legitimated" by them.

For all the discussion of pornography's effects there has been relatively little attention devoted to its causes. Yet, as Ellen Willis has properly emphasized, "Pornography is a symptom, not a root cause" (Willis, 1981, p. 18). And, as Laura Lederer has commented, "If it doesn't bother people to see women being raped or beaten or killed for sexual stimulation, then something is wrong" (Lederer, 1980, p. 25). The closest approximation to a substantive "defense" of pornography has been the claim by psychoanalytically oriented writers that objectification and sadomasochistic fantasy are "natural" and perhaps even necessary for sexual excitement. Psychoanalyst Robert Stoller is the major exponent of this view:

> One can raise the possibly controversial question whether in humans (especially males) powerful sexual excitement can ever exist without brutality also being present (minimal, repressed, distorted by reaction formation, attenuated, or overt in the most pathological cases) . . . Can anyone provide examples of behavior in sexual excitement in which, in human males at least, disguised hostility in fantasy is not a part of potency? . . . If hostility could be totally lifted out of sexual excitement there would be no perversions, but how much loving sexuality would be possible? (Stoller, 1976, pp. 88–89).

A critic of recent anti-pornography efforts who cites Stoller's work with apparent approval argues, "To hope to create a world in which male—and female—fantasies have been sanitized of any content that might contain violent imagery, however fleetingly, is to embrace a moralistic stance that easily turns repressive" (Elshtain, 1982b, p. 47). Opponents of pornography do not deny that having sexual fantasies is normal, nor even that a certain amount of objectification is likely to be part of this process. They do, however, question whether the types and degrees of fantasy and objectification that pornography promotes or reinforces are inevitable or desirable. They believe, furthermore, that the omnipresent content of pornographic fantasies is beginning to affect the general character of sexual relations in our society.

> . . . when sexual experience with another is determined by fantasy, the social-sexual reality of the other person is replaced by the fantasy. The extent to which fantasy dominates sexual interaction with another is the extent to which the other is an object of sexual pleasure. One of the effects of widespread pornography has been to introduce movies, books, or pictures as the erotic stimulant between two people, thereby reducing the need for people to relate to *each other* (Barry, 1981, p. 213).

Fantasy, then—in the degree and forms that now color our

sexual lives—may not be so much a cause of pornography as an effect. In thinking about causation, it is important to keep in mind that the audience for pornography is overwhelmingly male. One of the most underexamined questions about pornography has been *why men like it* (Rich, 1982, p. 30). According to recent analysis, dislike of and dissatisfaction with real women seem to be an inescapable part of the answer. As Susan Lurie suggests, "Fantasies that give pleasure are formed to combat a disappointing hostile reality" (Lurie, 1980, p. 160). Students of pornography (see, for example, Gagnon and Simon, 1973, pp. 264–265) have noted that imagined sex with fantasized females does not pose for the man the complications that are involved in dealing with "real world" women.

This brings us back to the theme of male ambivalence toward females—the viewing of woman as a threat—which we examined in Chapter Two. According to Susan Griffin, what the male is trying to nullify or annihilate in and through pornography is a consciously denied and hated "part of himself" (Griffin, 1982, p. 20)—the carnality, materiality, and mortality that woman, at some unconscious level, represents. Pornography, Griffin therefore claims, is culture's "act of revenge against nature" (ibid., p. 66; see also Dworkin, 1974; Dinnerstein, 1977). As we saw earlier, woman's liberation from traditional roles and restrictions is especially likely to be perceived by men as threatening. The possibility exists, then—similar to that which we noted in connection with rape—that the current proliferation of pornography may partly reflect anti-feminist backlash.

In addition to deep-seated ambivalence and counterreaction to the recent women's movement, there should be other systemic factors that help explain the appeal of pornography. Earlier, some of this appeal might have been attributed to the culturally induced sexual inhibitions of "respectable" women. However, the recent surge in pornography has accompanied a significant lessening of such inhibitions. One observer attributes this surge to "the breakdown of traditional ties of social cohesion, familial and communal" (Elshtain, 1982b, p. 47) which she charges some feminists with encouraging. To blame feminists even indirectly for causing pornography seems, however, to be a highly distorted form of victim-blaming.

The prevailing gender system, much more than the feminism that criticizes it, encourages pornography. As we have seen, this system is grounded in and sustained by processes of devaluation and objectification. Pornography reflects these pervasive ways of seeing and responding to women. And exposure and habituation to pornographic depictions has a feedback effect, reinforcing those already-powerful tendencies. Pornography is indeed a "symptom" of such outlooks. Although it would be difficult to prove, it may also be a symptom of male dissatisfaction with the depersonalized sexual relationships such a system encourages.

For those who are convinced that pornography is degrading and harmful, the problem remains whether to try to enact their view into law, and if so how. There is a long and confusing history of judicial efforts to delineate criteria of "obscenity" (the relevant legal term), through which to identify materials that would not be protected under the free speech and free press guarantees of the U.S. Constitution's First Amendment. The major ruling in force as of this writing was laid down by the U.S. Supreme Court in the case of *Miller* v. *California* (1973). Under that ruling, material is obscene if (1) the average person applying "contemporary standards" would find that the work, taken as a whole, appeals to the "prurient interest"; (2) it depicts or describes in "a patently offensive way" sexual conduct specifically defined by the applicable state law; and (3) the material, taken as a whole, "lacks serious literary, artistic, political, or scientific value" (for discussion of *Miller,* see Hughes, 1975, pp. 40–57; Kaminer, 1980a and 1980b; also Gordon, 1980, Ch. 11).

As numerous analysts have pointed out, criteria of this sort are very difficult to apply. What the Court is asserting here, essentially, is a state's right to legislate against certain kinds of "offensiveness" (Hughes, 1975), a notoriously slippery concept. The aforementioned criteria still require determining, in specific cases and hopefully in a consistent manner, precisely what content is "patently" offensive and which are the applicable "contemporary community standards." A more recent ruling upholding the constitutionality of a special New York State law against child pornography (*The New York Times,* July 3, 1982, p. 1) has further confused the legal picture. Asserting that the protection of children from sexual abuse and exploitation is "a government objective of surpassing importance," the Supreme Court held that the *Miller* standards would not necessarily have to be met in order for state laws in this specific area to be constitutional.

Although feminists who oppose pornography are convinced that it is "patently offensive," many of them recognize the dangers of proposing government censorship. As one analyst notes, "Most hard-core pornography would probably be found obscene under *Miller* and could therefore be prohibited. But effective, generalized enforcement of obscenity laws is not possible without violating the very basic prohibition of prior restraints" (Kaminer, 1980a, p. 243). However, the fervor of anti-pornography activists has led one civil libertarian to claim that they seek to "expurgate the First Amendment" (Neier, 1980). Feminists who advocate public controls over pornography may be further dismayed to find similar policies being advocated by conservative groups who oppose both "sexual permissiveness" and "women's liberation." These problems have not greatly weakened feminist opposition to pornography (but see Willis, 1981; Orlando, 1982; and *The Village Voice,* January 4, 1983, pp. 10–12, for persisting disagreement within the women's movement regarding the meaning of pornography and the appropriate response to it). They have caused some activists, however, to moderate their specific demands for legislative controls.

A Note on "Victimless" Crimes

Both pornography and prostitution are, on occasion, referred to as "victimless" crimes. Sometimes, this term is used to imply that the "offenses" so designated do not really involve any direct harm being done to anyone. However, the concept has another meaning —one that is very useful sociologically and which, furthermore, is quite consistent with acknowledging the victimization of women. This alternative conception of "victimless crime" is applied to all those situations in which the proscribed offense consists of a "consensual transaction," a willing exchange of goods or services that does not often generate a directly involved complaining "victim" who initiates enforcement activity (see Schur, 1965; Packer, 1968; Morris and Hawkins, 1970; Geis, 1972; Schur and Bedau, 1974; Hughes, 1975). These are, then—to use a less controversial term —"complainantless" crimes.

In such situations, *regardless* of any assessments of victimization outside observers might make, the persons directly involved do not see themselves as being immediately victimized by the desired exchanges. Hence, they do not ordinarily report "violations" to the enforcement authorities. This circumstance has important and largely predictable consequences. Laws that attempt to curb these exchanges cannot be effectively enforced. The half-hearted efforts to do so involve a wasteful deployment of limited police resources. Because of difficulty in obtaining evidence, law enforcers characteristically are driven to use questionable investigative techniques—decoys, informers, surveillance, and the like.

When the proscribed exchanges are economic in character, legal proscription—as we saw in the case of abortion—for the most part simply diverts demand from legal to illegal sources of supply. It also provides the economic incentives that support a black market and drive up prices (see Packer, 1968, Ch. 15). Criminalization may also produce secondary crime; the major example is money-producing crime committed by the drug addict to support his or her habit. Studies show that when demand for the proscribed goods or services is very strong and widespread, laws banning their exchange do not have a really significant deterrent effect. There is, therefore, little apparent "benefit" of the sort that might offset the "costs" of criminalizing the exchanges.

This kind of analysis often is made by those who advance proposals for decriminalization. Many advocates of legal change also stress that victimless crime laws unjustly as well as uselessly create new classes of "criminals": the lesbian, the prostitute, the abortion seeker, and so on. Overall, these change advocates argue, laws attempting to control such consensual transactions frequently do more harm than good. However, one is not obliged—simply by virtue of making an analysis of this sort—to reach a conclusion that *each and every* victimless crime law ought to be repealed. The pros and cons of legislating in each specific area should be examined and weighed carefully. The consensual transaction feature need not, by itself, *determine* the policy recommendation in such situations, but for a comprehensive assessment to be made it does need to be *taken into account.*

Prostitution and pornography illustrate the complexity of these assessments and policy choices. As we have seen, women are the ultimate victims in both situations. The compromise or dual policy recommendation of feminists regarding prostitution takes into account *both* this ultimate victimization *and* the shorter-term harm produced because of the futile attempt to control prostitution through the criminal law. It argues, in effect, that prostitute women are being *victimized by these laws.* At the same time, it acknowledges that legal change is *only* a stopgap measure, that the ultimate victimization will not be eliminated until there are major changes in the overall gender system.

In the case of pornography, feminists understandably have equivocated regarding the role of law. Although they probably have few illusions about the possibility of truly effective legal control, they tend to see legal proscription as serving in this case very important symbolic functions. The "moral statement" made by a legal ban on pornography outweighs, for them, the possible dangers posed by censorship and the low probability of really curbing the purchase of these materials. While recognizing the likelihood of an expanded black market, they may find that preferable to the present situation. Thus Laura Lederer asserts that "it is better to have it underground than to see it flourish as an accepted part of our culture. Feminists must demand that society find the abuse of women both immoral *and* illegal" (Lederer, 1980, p. 29).

This is a perfectly legitimate conclusion—although it should be noted that similar "moralistic" reasoning may lead others to policy recommendations feminists would not find acceptable, on such "victimless crime" issues as abortion and lesbianism. In any case, the likely consequences of legislating against a widely demanded consensual transaction cannot simply be argued away. From the standpoint of a gender-system analysis, victimless crime analysis has at least one decided advantage. As we can see with respect to both pornography and prostitution, it points up the ineffectiveness of trying to use criminal law to curb the *supply* in the face of an overwhelming *demand*. This, in turn, suggests the need ultimately to focus on the root causes of both pornography and prostitution—male demand and the devaluation and objectification of females that give rise to it.

SUGGESTED READINGS

Chappell, Duncan, Robley Geis, and Gilbert Geis, eds., *Forcible Rape: The*

Crime, the Victim, and the Offender. New York: Columbia University Press, 1977. A collection of empirical research reports and interpretive essays, covering various aspects of the rape problem.

James, Jennifer, Jean Withers, Marilyn Haft, and Sara Theiss, *The Politics of Prostitution.* Seattle: Social Research Associates, 1975. An important feminist statement on prostitution and the law.

Lederer, Laura, ed., *Take Back the Night: Women on Pornography.* New York: William Morrow and Co., 1980. A comprehensive collection of essays, covering social, psychological, and legal aspects.

MacKinnon, Catharine A., *Sexual Harassment of Working Women.* New Haven: Yale University Press, 1979. Exhaustive and socially perceptive analysis of the legal principles and cases relating to harassment, by a legal scholar-activist.

Pagelow, Mildred Daley, *Woman Battering: Victims and their Experiences.* Beverly Hills, Calif.: Sage Publications, 1981. A closely reasoned and data-supported study of woman-battering cases and situations.

Russell, Diana E. H. and Nicole Van de Ven, eds., *Crimes Against Women: Proceedings of the International Tribunal.* Millbrae, Calif.: Les Femmes, 1976. Testimony, discussion, and resolutions concerning the victimization of women, from an international conference held in Brussels, Belgium, in March of 1976.

CHAPTER 5

Producing Female Deviance

THE PRODUCTION OF DEVIANCE OUTCOMES

Labeling studies emphasize that deviance is "produced" or "constructed" through social interaction. In line with the orientation sketched at the beginning of this book, sociologists increasingly focus on the definitions and reactions through which stigma is imposed. Deviance is not simply a function of a person's problematic behavior; rather, it emerges as *other people define and react* to a behavior *as being* problematic. The person's sex—much like her or his social class membership and race or ethnicity—may significantly affect what these other people do.

We saw this in the contrast between the deviance outcomes explored in Chapters Two and Three: we noted, on the one hand, an enormously wide range of at least informally labeled "female" offenses; yet we saw, on the other hand, that when males commit even very serious offenses against women, they may not be likely to face significant stigmatization. Our primary focus in those chapters was on the collective definitions (in these cases, gender norms) that are commonly applied in particular kinds of situations. But in considering the victimization of women we also began to observe more directly the role of social control agents and formal processing mechanisms. This is an aspect of deviance-defining that receives central attention in the present chapter. Through the interpretations and classifications they use in dealing with possibly problematic behaviors, social control and "helping" agents—including for example mental health practitioners as well as criminal justice personnel—play an important role in "producing" deviance.

The significance of this role becomes particularly evident when we think about the real meaning of recorded deviance statistics. Such statistics form the quantitative basis for many of our beliefs about various kinds of presumed deviance. From them and from diverse media accounts we derive most of our impressions of the frequencies, trends, and rate variations within the general population in terms of numerous types of stigmatized behavior. With growing methodological sophistication, observers of social control processes have come to recognize that most of these recorded statistics do not accurately or fully depict the "real" distributions of the behaviors in question. What such statistics actually do is enumerate and describe those "cases" or categories of cases that have been identified and, in one way or another, dealt with. In that sense, the social control process—whether it be concerned with law enforcement, corrections, or psychotherapy—can be conceptualized as a "rate-producing process" (Kitsuse and Cicourel, 1963). The statistics reflect the daily work of, and represent the "output" of, the control agents and the organizations within which they often work.

It is not merely in this statistical sense that the work of deviance identifying, classifying, and processing is consequential. These processes also involve converting specific individuals into "cases." For such individuals, the decisions made and procedures applied can be extremely fateful. Recent research shows that, in both the production of statistics and the generation and processing of individual cases, various unstated and unintended factors can exert an influence. When formal processing enters the picture, there is a "bureaucratization of deviance" (Rubington and Weinberg, eds., 1981, p. 130; also Hawkins and Tiedeman, 1975, Chs. 7 and 8; Schur, 1979, Ch. 6). The control agency's work loads, external pressures, interorganizational relations, internal staff relations—and more generally what can be described as the organization's own "needs" (efficiency, support, legitimation, etc.)—all may affect what happens to the processed individual. The individual control agents play an especially pivotal role in this connection. In many areas, such persons have a great deal of discretion in determining whether a particular instance of behavior is to become a "case," and if so how it will be dealt with. Whatever personal or job-related problems and pressures they experience may therefore affect the course of deviance-processing. Similarly,

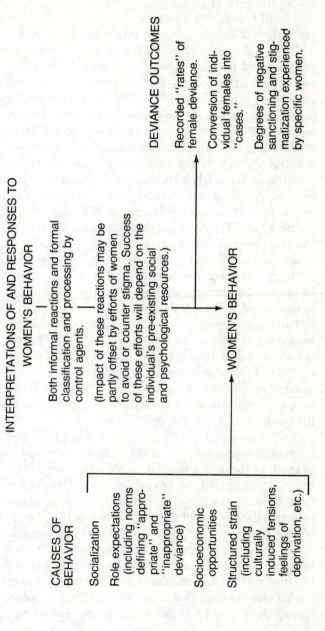

Figure 2. The Production of Female Deviance

CAUSES OF BEHAVIOR

Socialization

Role expectations (including norms defining "appropriate" and "inappropriate" deviance)

Socioeconomic opportunities

Structured strain (including culturally induced tensions, feelings of deprivation, etc.)

WOMEN'S BEHAVIOR

INTERPRETATIONS OF AND RESPONSES TO WOMEN'S BEHAVIOR

Both informal reactions and formal classification and processing by control agents.

(Impact of these reactions may be partly offset by efforts of women to avoid or counter stigma. Success of these efforts will depend on the individual's pre-existing social and psychological resources.)

DEVIANCE OUTCOMES

Recorded "rates" of female deviance.

Conversion of individual females into "cases."

Degrees of negative sanctioning and stigmatization experienced by specific women.

the beliefs and attitudes of these controllers, processors, and helpers are likely to be extremely consequential.

Figure 2 presents a schematic diagram of major elements in the production of female deviance. The same basic ingredients—underlying and precipitating causes of behavior, responses to the behavior and possibly counterresponses, and resulting statistical and individual outcomes—are found in connection with *any* deviance. Thus, if we merely altered the sex designations, the diagram would serve to indicate the processes that result in male deviance. Similarly, the diagram shows the essential factors involved in producing specifically "female offenses" of the sort we considered in Chapter Three. In that discussion, we were concerned primarily with the deviance labels themselves. In the present chapter, however, we are concerned primarily with the differential labeling of behaviors that are ostensibly treated as deviant regardless of the offender's sex. The processes through which this labeling develops and the consequences it has are shown in Figure 2.

In thinking about Figure 2, we should note at the outset that the term "behavior" needs to be given a broad reading. As we saw earlier, women do not really have to engage in specific *acts* in order to be defined and responded to as deviant. Physical appearance—and in a sense perhaps even the mere condition of "being" a woman—can lead to stigmatization. But whatever the "deviantized" act or condition, the interpretation-and-response element is essential. From a sociological as opposed to a merely statistical standpoint, you cannot be "deviant" all by yourself. The deviance outcomes indicated at the right of the chart cannot emerge without the occurrence of other people's responses.

Our main emphasis in this text has been on that necessary element of interpretation and response. But it would be a mistake to think of this element as being the sole "cause" of deviance. A complete analysis of the production of deviance outcomes would have to take into account as well the *behavior-producing* factors shown at the left side of the chart. It should be apparent that these too are significantly shaped by the prevailing gender system.

As research on women has comprehensively shown, female behavior takes the forms it does largely because of the characteristic content of female socialization. This content has regularly included standardized role expectations. As we shall see shortly, among these may be norms defining sex-appropriate and -inappropriate deviance. Such norms may influence other people's interpretations of a woman's behavior. They may also operate as a factor motivating that behavior in the first place. The "opportunity" factor shown at the left side of Figure 2 is another important ingredient of deviance situations. It has a bearing on women's involvement in behaviors widely deemed deviant, in at least two general ways. When women's legitimate economic opportunities are limited, perceived economic deprivation ("structured strain" in Figure 2) may push women to adopt "illicit means" (Merton, 1949; Cloward and Ohlin, 1960). The specific form this takes may in turn be influenced by deviance norms; thus females may be more likely to turn to prostitution than to bank robbery.

As we have already noted in connection with prostitution, the woman's perception of being economically deprived may involve an assessment of *relative* rewards, rather than a feeling of absolute deprivation. Thus, even with increased opportunities for women —perhaps to an extent because of such gains—disapproved behavior due to ˉelt deprivation may persist.

> Partly because of the feminist movement, many women have come to compare their goal achievements with those of men. Where marriage, family, and home have traditionally sufficed as valued objects for most women, occupation, income, and independence have emerged as alternative aspirations. Where the means for achievement have not kept pace with expanding goals, increases in the level of stress and deviance may be expected (Farrell and Swigert, 1982, p. 154).

There is another, rather different sense in which opportunity is a factor in the production of female deviance. One cannot engage in a behavior deemed deviant unless one has the specific opportunity to do so. For our purposes here, a good example of this would be female involvement in white-collar and corporate crime. By definition, a person can only commit such offenses if she or he occupies certain types of occupational roles. Thus the low female rates (at least until now) for such criminality have been an inevitable corollary of the structuring of women's occupational opportunities. This structuring, in turn, can be traced to the prevailing gender conceptions. It might also be suggested—given our system's pervasive devaluation of femaleness—that mental illness (to which we turn in the next section) is a "favored" female deviance precisely because no special opportunity to "commit" it is necessary.

It seems evident that the behavioral causes listed in Figure 2 usually operate together rather than separately. All of these elements shape women's behavior. There is no need for us to emphasize one more than another. When disapproved behavior results from "structured strain," the experiencing of that strain reflects the combined impact of socialization, expectation, and opportunity factors. We should keep in mind, however, that not all behaviors treated as deviant come about because of any such "strain." People engage in some disapproved behaviors primarily because they find them (apart from the stigma aspect) pleasurable. Examples would be marijuana use and lesbianism. Similarly, many if not most of the specifically female "offenses" discussed in Chapter Three do not require any kind of complicated "causal" explanation. As we have seen, the very insistence on such explanations is part and parcel of the "deviantizing" of those behaviors.

It will be recalled from Chapter Three that deviance norms may specify "appropriate and inappropriate deviance" (Schur, 1979, pp. 102–104) for the two sexes. Among those behaviors which ostensibly constitute offenses whether committed by men or by women, some more than others may be viewed as congruent with female gender roles. These are then, relatively speaking, "acceptable" female deviances. Anthony Harris has aptly described such conceptions as deviance "type-scripts." He notes that there are deeply rooted "everyday assumptions about *who does what, including deviance,* in a society" (Harris, 1977, p. 3; italics in original). According to Harris, the "distribution of these background norms about deviance" may provide "the single strongest causal account of the empirical differences in male and female criminality" (ibid.). Such type-scripts may strongly affect the labeling and processing of persons as deviants. Presumably they influence the "typing" (or "typification") that various studies (see Sudnow, 1965; Emerson, 1969; Wiseman, 1970) show is prevalent in the work of social control agencies. And because they are so deeply embedded in the culture, they also become a "motivational" factor leading to the problematic behavior itself (ibid., p. 14). The socialization of women may, in other words, lead them to "choose" those deviances that are considered appropriate to their sex.

This notion of deviance norms or type-scripts helps to explain a major contrast in recorded male-female deviance statistics that receives special attention in this chapter. Whereas officially recorded crime is an overwhelmingly male phenomenon, mental illness statistics indicate high female rates—at least in certain diagnostic categories, such as the neuroses and depressive disorders. As we shall see, it would be a great oversimplification to attribute this difference entirely to "expectation" effects. Nevertheless, the type-script which asserts that mental illness is more appropriately "female" than criminal behavior is a widely held one. It is at least plausible, though difficult to demonstrate conclusively, that it has helped to shape the statistics in question.

We shall return shortly to a general analysis of the labeling and processing of female mental illness and crime. In addition to illuminating the overall rate comparison we have just noted, the type-script concept may help to explain patterns of sex concentration in more specific deviance categories. Its usefulness is quite evident with respect to certain criminal offenses. Harris notes, for example, that "it is (still) type-scripted that it is unlikely or 'impossible' for women to attempt assassination, robbery, or rape" (ibid., p. 12).

More generally, it seems clear that at least until recently all violent, aggressive, and "daring" crimes have been deemed incongruent with femaleness. On the other hand, certain offenses have been highly congruent with the normative prescriptions for females. Thus prostitution fits well with the sexual objectification of women. The perception of shoplifting as an appropriate female offense—whether or not males commit the offense as well—follows from the female's consumer role, and perhaps also from the emphasis on women's personal adornment. (We shall note below recent interpretations which assert that female crime norms may now be changing.)

As regards certain other types of presumed deviance, such as drug addiction, alcoholism, and suicide, the pertinence of deviance type-scripts or norms is a bit less clear. The extent of recorded female involvement in the use of various drugs partly seems to vary depending upon the severity of the stigma which is, in general, attached to their use. Prior to the restrictive legal policy imposed under the federal Harrison Act of 1914, a large proportion of American opiate addicts were female (see Cuskey, Premkumar, and Sigel, 1979; Robins, 1980; also Waldorf, 1973, Ch. 10; Goode, 1978, pp. 248–250). Recent estimates of the sex ratio among heroin addicts have varied a good deal; different studies produce figures ranging from two males for every female to six to one (Waldorf,

1973). But there is no doubt that "since World War II, young drug users have tended to be urban, male, minority group members" (Robins, 1980, p. 218).

Since opiates induce passivity, it might be thought that their use would be deemed "appropriate" for females. On the other hand, the underworld-related distribution network and the typical need of addicts to commit property crimes to support their habits —both of which have emerged as a result of criminalization (Lindesmith, 1965)—may be factors conducive to female-inappropriateness. (It is noteworthy that, among those women who do become fully addicted to heroin, it is common to turn to the "acceptable" deviance of prostitution as a means of financing the purchase of illicit drugs.) One researcher suggests that the very fact that this type of drug use is considered highly criminal is itself relevant to the sex ratio. "Women were deterred by the criminalization of addiction; men were not and became the majority of addicts" (Waldorf, 1973, p. 177). However, the same writer goes on to state that "today when women become addicts they suffer more guilt and remorse [than do males] because it is harder for them to go against society's prescription for femininity and its laws and mores" (ibid.; for a more recent in-depth study of the female addict's problems, see Rosenbaum, 1981).

With respect to marijuana the sex ratio looks very different. Use of this drug, even where technically illegal, is not in practice frequently or heavily penalized. There is less significant underworld involvement in its distribution. Its occasional use as a "recreational" drug taken almost always in ordinary social settings is now quite widely accepted. All these factors may affect its acceptability for females. A leading sociological researcher on marijuana use has noted, "At one time, male marijuana users outnumbered female by at least two to one. Over the years, the sex gap has diminished" (Goode, 1978, p. 208). In 1979, a national survey found the following percentages of respondents reporting that they had "ever used" marijuana or hashish: adults 26 and older— males, 26 percent, females, 14 percent; young adults, 18 to 25— males, 75 percent, females, 61 percent; youths, 12 to 17—males, 34 percent, females, 28 percent (see Hindelang, Gottfredson, and Flanagan, eds., 1981, pp. 286–287).

Without question, the largest proportion of female use of addicting or dependence-producing drugs involves drugs obtained legally, by medical prescription. Some of the relevant data are summarized in the following statement:

> In 1978, the acting director of the National Institute on Drug Abuse told the House Select Committee on Narcotics Abuse and Control that, in the past year, 36 million women had used tranquilizers; 16 million used sedatives (sleeping pills); 12 million used stimulants primarily in the form of diet pills; and almost 12 million women received prescriptions for these drugs from doctors for the first time. Those numbers do not include whole classes of prescribed pain killers, all of which are mood altering and addictive. Nor do they include the billions of doses dispensed to patients directly, without a prescription, in doctors' offices, in military, public, or private hospitals, and in clinics or nursing homes (Nellis, 1981, pp. 1–2).

The same writer suggests that this problem has remained largely hidden because of the stigma attaching to drug use. In another sense, however, this kind of drug-taking (in which, studies show, female usage exceeds that of males) can be seen as constituting a major category of "acceptable" female deviance. The prescribing of such drugs is an integral part of the medicalization of women's life situations, to which we referred above and to which we shall return later in this chapter (with special reference to psychiatry). Whether or not it is so intended, it functions very effectively to "cool" women out, to support a depoliticizing and pathologizing of their dissatisfactions. One analyst observes:

> This drug usage is consistent with medical attitudes toward women. Drug advertisements in medical journals typically present these drugs as appropriate for the solution of 'feminine' problems—anxiety, depression, and so forth. Apparently doctors are more ready to attribute a woman's complaints to psychological causes than they are for men (or perhaps men demand non-psychoactive drugs and treatment). Whatever the explanation, the result is that many women are being given a chemical solution to what is likely a sociological problem (Stoll, 1974, p. 171).

With respect to alcohol addiction, it is very difficult to determine whether the recorded sex ratio indicates a "real" (i.e., behavioral) male-female differential, or whether it simply reflects differentials in the identifying, reporting, and processing of "cases" among males and females. Criteria and reporting procedures for "alcoholism" and "problem drinking" are not widely agreed-upon or uniformly employed. Most observers estimate that male alcoholics continue to outnumber female alcoholics, although there are indications that the gap has been narrowing over the years. In 1966, an expert asserted that "according to the best estimates, there are 3,760,000 men and 710,000 women alcoholics" (Trice, 1966, p. 39). Few specialists believe the current gap is that great, although on the other hand not all would agree with a journalist's recent claim that "at least half of the probably 10 million alcoholics in the country are women" (Nellis, 1981, p. 2).

Studies do continue to show that more men than women drink —in one 1976 national survey, 76 percent of men as opposed to 56 percent of the women (see Goode, 1978, pp. 283–286); also that among persons who do drink, men are heavier drinkers. However, additional findings indicate that the proportion of all women who drink has been growing over the years (ibid; Clinard and Meier, 1979, pp. 337–342; see also Al-Issa, 1980, Ch. 10). Yet arrests of women for public drunkenness remain infrequent. Of 1,117,349 drunkenness arrests reported in 1979, 1,034,412 (or 92.6 percent) were of males (Hindelang, Gottfredson, and Flanagan, eds., 1981, p. 341). As one writer notes, furthermore, "Skid rows are predominantly male settings, partly because women can support themselves whatever their fate (by way of prostitution) while men who fail quickly lose support from family and community" (Stoll, 1974, p. 170).

While social disapproval of women drinking has been on the decline, it seems likely that most people continue to link "hard drinking" to the male subculture. This may well change as collective female activities lose their "demure" emphasis, and also as women increasingly enter new types of work (which may have new drinking patterns associated with them). We can anticipate the acceptance of the "hard-drinking, hard-driving female business executive" and perhaps the female manual worker who drinks with workmates at the close of the day. But whether our society's gender conceptions will change sufficiently that the female "drunken bum" will be an acknowledged type is much less certain.

Although there are almost three times as many suicides among males as among females (see Maris, 1969, pp. 96–100; also Al-Issa, 1980, pp. 123–127), females attempt suicide more frequently—the sex ratio for attempts being virtually the opposite of that for completed suicides. It is sometimes suggested that this discrepancy is due to the fact that women suicide attempters tend to choose less "lethal" or "violent" methods. If that were so, the difference might partly be explained through deviance type-script interpretation—that violent suicide is deemed incongruent with femaleness. It might also be argued that completed suicide requires a kind of decisiveness which our society's gender scripts discourage among females. But even if the difference in success rates is due to motivational factors, the workings of the gender system are probably implicated. According to one researcher, "Female suicides are usually responses to marital problems that manifest themselves relatively early in the female's life. The female suicide is more of a sign of a wish to kill her spouse or children—a retroflexed anger or 'cry for help' in a domestic crisis—than it is a sincere wish to die" (Maris, 1969, p. 97).

WOMEN AND MENTAL ILLNESS
Mental Illness and Social Control

The recognition of "mental illness" always emerges through a process of social interaction (Yarrow, et al., 1955; Sampson, Messinger, and Towne, 1962; Edgerton, 1969; see also the general review by Horwitz, 1982, Ch. 3). Potential "trouble" is progressively elaborated, organized, and crystallized in such a process (Emerson and Messinger, 1977). Whatever psychological distress may actually be present, mental illness *labeling* necessarily involves an *interpretation*. Such interpretations are neither fixed nor uniform. They can change as a situation develops. And they can vary, depending on who is doing the interpreting. The tolerance limits of responding others (see Yarrow, et al., 1955) influence whether a person is viewed as mentally ill, and if so, what actions follow from such a conclusion.

Erving Goffman has suggested (Goffman, 1972, p. 355) that mental illness designating is likely to occur when those persons with whom an individual is regularly interacting conclude that he or she is "not prepared to keep his place." This notion seems particularly germane to the situation of women in our society. Given the numerous restrictions placed on female behavior, women are highly vulnerable to being deemed out of "place." The relative dependence of females—which makes it difficult for them to fend off or ignore such imputations—and male domination of the formal processes of psychiatric diagnosis add further to this vulnerability.

Medical definitions and procedures, as we saw in earlier sections of this book, can function as instruments of social control (Freidson, 1971; Conrad and Schneider, 1980; Ingleby, 1980). Thus, Eliot Freidson has asserted that "medicine is a moral enterprise like law and religion, seeking to uncover and control things that it considers undesirable" (Freidson, 1971, p. 208). Even in the treatment of undoubted organic illness, the patient, in the process of being helped, is also subjected to control. Restrictions are placed on the sick person's activities, and often she or he is not treated as a fully autonomous and capable human being. Furthermore, although sick people ostensibly are not held "responsible" for their illnesses, in fact many illnesses—this is particularly true of "mental" illnesses—evoke stigmatizing reactions.

In connection with his controversial assertion that mental illness is a "myth," psychiatrist Thomas Szasz (1961) has emphasized psychiatry's social control functions. According to Szasz the designation "mental illness" really refers to "problems of living." Unlike physical illnesses, Szasz insists, these problems do not ordinarily have any organic basis. And because such problems involve the relations between human beings, to deal with them is to enter a domain of moral dilemmas and social consequentiality.

Psychiatric diagnosis and treatment necessarily impose control, because they involve classifying people and making various related decisions as to what should be done about them. Given the high prestige and considerable authority of psychiatrists in our culture, these decisions usually represent a largely irresistible imposition of power. One feminist critic, who is also a former mental patient, states: "Disguised as a *medical* process, the social control aspect has been successfully obscured from all concerned (probably including the vast majority of psychiatrists and ancillary personnel, who are comfortably maintained in the fiction that they are engaged in the commendable process of curing disease)" (Chamberlin, 1975, p. 43).

Applying to women a "medical model" of mental illness, in which psychological disturbance is analogized to physical sickness, supports their social devaluation and reinforces an emphasis on supposed biological sex differences. As one psychiatrist-critic comments more generally, "The notion also has a political power, since what is repressed out of the medical model of mental illness is that dimension which considers the person an active social agent defined by what class, community, and history have meant for him" (Kovel, 1980, p. 86). In the medical model, disease is "something going on within a person [rather than in] the entire relationship between the self and the world; and it is to be remedied by individual or particularistic action" (ibid.).

A writer on women and psychiatry similarly comments that "in psychiatric terms what is wrong is identified as what is wrong *with her*" (Smith, 1975a, p. 7). Furthermore, psychiatric ideologies "are part of the ideologies constructed by men from their perspective on the world" (ibid., p. 4). These ideologies, developed and for the most part applied by male therapists, have dominated the socially authorized ways of thinking about women's problems. Women's own responses to their life circumstances have been largely discredited. "Resentment and despair are not treated as valid responses to her situation. The realities of her situation *as she feels them* are not treated as valid" (ibid., p. 7).

In addition to this "appropriation" of their power of self-definition, women have had to confront the stigma and other specific negative consequences of perpetual exposure to being labeled mentally ill. To an extent, this stigma indirectly affects all women. The general tendency to treat women as being emotionally disturbed is always present in the background as a ground for dismissing what a woman says or does and as an implicit "threat" should she seriously step out of line. Notwithstanding well-intended professional justifications, the use of mental illness labels is always to an extent discrediting and stigmatizing. It is one thing to be deemed merely "angry," another to be seen as "mentally ill," and another still to be defined as a "mental patient."

Although the extent of such devaluation varies a good deal, once mental illness concepts enter the picture, a certain amount of it is virtually unavoidable. As Theodore Sarbin has emphasized (Sarbin, 1969, p. 20), "Persons who are labeled mentally ill are not regarded as merely sick, but are regarded as a special class of beings, to be feared or scorned, sometimes to be pitied, but nearly always to be degraded." It may be noted how closely and fully this statement also fits the depiction of our society's devaluation of

femaleness. Regular application to females of mental illness designations builds on, and in turn reinforces, that overall devaluation.

One sociological writer on mental illness recently has stated:
"In contrast to deviants, people who are seen as mentally disturbed are so labeled not when their behavior is seen as morally
wrong but rather when it cannot be attributed to a comprehensible
reason. Observers cannot make sense out of the behavior of the
mentally ill" (Horwitz, 1982, p. 27). As to the first part of this
assertion, it is quite true that persons deemed mentally ill are not
openly "blamed" for their condition any more than females are
blamed for their femaleness. Yet if, as we have suggested, the
imposition of stigma is the hallmark of imputed deviance, then the
absence of conscious blame may not be too socially significant.
The "incomprehensibility" point in Horwitz's statement may apply to cases of severe personal disorientation. However, with respect to the myriad applications of mental illness labels in less
extreme situations—and particularly the diverse labelings of
women we have noted throughout this book—the claim of incomprehensibility is not at all persuasive.

As another commentator points out, "to make a warranted
ascription of insanity [the psychiatrist] has to be sure that *none* of
the ordinary ways of finding conduct intelligible actually works—
and this he cannot do without applying each of them in turn, and
thus invoking subjective judgement" (Ingleby, 1980, p. 31). We saw
in Chapter Three that just about any female behavior which di-
verges from gender prescriptions is likely to be interpreted in
mental illness terms. If a woman is too fat or too thin, if she is too
aggressive or too passive, if she is an unmarried mother or voluntarily childless, if she is heterosexually "promiscuous" or living a
lesbian lifestyle—some psychiatric theory will be put forward to
"explain" the behavior or condition. This is patently *not* because
of unintelligibility. There are perfectly good and "rational" reasons for all these behaviors and conditions. What seems to be
happening instead is a compulsive *effort to find* a "basis" for imputing psychopathology. This is suggested particularly by the fact
that *even in cases of women's victimization,* such imputation may
occur. Examples would be psychological theorizing about why a
woman "allowed herself" to be in a situation in which she was
raped, or why a repeatedly battered wife could not "bring herself"
to leave her husband.

The almost unlimited expandability of psychiatric definitions is one of the major reasons for describing mental illness as a social construction. This expandability rests on the fact that there is no agreed upon definition of mental "health," and also on the fact that imputations of underlying psychopathology can never really be "disproved" (anymore than they can be "proved"). Thus David Ingleby notes that if "there is no explicit definition of what it is that they [psychiatrists] are detecting, then there is no way of demonstrating publicly that they have succeeded in detecting it" (ibid., p. 33). Thomas Scheff's concept of mental illness as "residual deviance" (Scheff, 1966) seems especially useful in thinking about the psychodiagnosis of women. Such diagnosis provides a convenient catchall for devaluing any female behavior that is not easily or sufficiently discredited in other ways. And the very irrefutability of such diagnosis enhances its potency as an instrument of social control.

Female Rates and Diagnoses

Researchers are in general agreement that there has been "a consistently large female involvement with psychiatry in America, an involvement that has been increasing rather dramatically since 1964" (Chesler, 1972, p. 119). Walter Gove and Jeannette Tudor reviewed "community surveys, first admissions to mental hospitals, psychiatric admissions to general hospitals, psychiatric care in outpatient clinics, private outpatient psychiatric care, and the prevalence of mental illness in the practices of general physicians" (Gove and Tudor, 1973, p. 55). On the basis of all these data, they concluded that "more women than men are mentally ill" (ibid., p. 65).

As critics have noted (Dohrenwend and Dohrenwend, 1976; also Smith, 1975b), Gove and Tudor excluded from their definition of mental illness several large diagnostic categories—including "personality disorders" and organic and toxic disturbances. Their findings only relate therefore to neuroses and functional nonorganic psychoses. For these disorders, they consistently found a predominance of females among all persons in treatment. They determined, for example, the following female to male ratios in different patient populations: among first admissions to mental hospitals, 1.46 females to males in the neurosis category, 1.10 for functional psychosis; among psychiatric patients in general hospitals, 1.89 females to males for neurosis, 1.44 for functional psychosis; in psychiatric clinics, 1.73 females to males for neurosis, 1.21 for functional psychosis (Gove and Tudor, 1973, pp. 58–60). Although they did not locate many studies of private outpatient psychiatric care, those that did exist "all found that more women than men are seen by psychiatrists" (ibid., p. 60).

Gove and Tudor accepted such statistics as valid indicators of the "true" prevalence and distribution of mental illness. Hence they concluded that women *really are* mentally ill more often than men. They rejected the possibility that the statistics reflected differential "labeling" of the two sexes. And they likewise dismissed the argument that males' greater reluctance to admit to psychological disturbance (Phillips and Segal, 1969) might account for the difference in rates. The basic explanation of such a difference, they asserted, had to do with women's dissatisfactions and conflicts over their prescribed social roles. Gove and Tudor stated that "there are ample grounds for assuming that women find their position in society to be more frustrating and less rewarding than do men and that this may be a relatively recent development. Let us, then, at this point postulate that, because of the difficulties associated with the feminine role in modern Western societies, more women than men become mentally ill" (Gove and Tudor, 1973, p. 54).

Reviewing both treatment and epidemiological (general population) data Bruce Dohrenwend and Barbara Dohrenwend (1976) were less fully convinced of the "true" predominance of female mental illness. Referring to Gove and Tudor's definition of mental illness as "highly idiosyncratic" (ibid., p. 1448), they make the following overall assessment of sex differences:

(1) There are no consistent sex differences in rates of functional psychoses in general (34 studies) or one of the two major subtypes, schizophrenia (26 studies), in particular; rates of the other subtype, manic-depressive psychosis, are generally higher among women (18 out of 24 studies). (2) Rates of neurosis are consistently higher for women regardless of time and place (28 out of 32 studies). (3) By contrast, rates of personality disorder are consistently higher for men regardless of time and place (22 out of 26 studies). (Dohrenwend and Dohrenwend, 1976, p. 1453; see also, with special reference to rates of depression, Rosenfield, 1980).

Comparing studies done before and after 1950, the Dohrenwends noted that overall rates and those for the various diagnostic categories had all "increased dramatically"—for *both* men and women (ibid., p. 1450). However, they disagreed with Gove and Tudor's argument that heightened female role stress explained the increase over time in women's mental illness rates. Particularly since male rates had gone up too, they attributed changes over time instead to changes in the methods employed by researchers. For example, the more recent epidemiological surveys had used psychiatric screening inventories that focused more heavily on symptoms characteristic of the disorders for which women have the higher rates. Thus, statistical differentials might primarily be "a function of changes in concepts and methods for defining what constitutes a psychiatric case" (ibid., p. 1452).

Even if one is led to question Gove and Tudor's statistical conclusion, their general "explanation" is not without some merit. At least it can be agreed—setting aside, for the moment, the question of formal "mental illness" designation—that the prevailing gender system has produced a great deal of female unhappiness and dissatisfaction. It is not simply by chance that among women in our society "depression" has been a major psychological complaint. The restricted and (for many) unsatisfying nature of women's traditional social roles provides a plausible reason why various kinds of depression might in fact have been very widespread among females.

Jessie Bernard reviewed data from national surveys in which high proportions of married women had judged themselves to be happy. But, she asked, "how happy is the happy housewife? Examination of specific personality and behavioral items reported by women and surveys of mental-health impairment raises doubts. . . . In one study more married than single women were bothered by feelings of depression. . . . Overall, more married than single women were reported to be passive, phobic, and depressed, at least half of the married women falling into one or another of these three categories" (Bernard, 1972, pp. 150–151).

Research by Pauline Bart (1972) revealed that woman's approved motherhood role also can have specific psychological drawbacks. In a study of depressed middle-aged women in mental hospitals, she found that the "empty-nest syndrome"—the experiencing of "role loss" when the youngest child leaves home—was a leading cause of depression. As one might predict, the likelihood of severe depression was greatest among women for whom the motherhood role was an exclusive and all-enveloping one. Bart concluded that "it is the women who assume the traditional feminine role—who are housewives, who stay married to their husbands, who are not overly aggressive, in short who 'buy' the traditional norms—who respond with depression when their children leave" (ibid., p. 184). Woman's traditional role as "other" had, in these cases, a devastating psychological impact: "If one's satisfaction, one's sense of worth comes from other people rather than from one's own accomplishments, one is left with an empty shell in place of a self when such people depart" (ibid., p. 185).

Studies such as these suggest that it is at least plausible that the norms and arrangements which have shaped many women's lives could produce quite a bit of "real" psychological distress. In fact, the general devaluation of femaleness which we considered earlier in this book could itself be expected to have similar effects. However, as we have just noted, being unhappy or dissatisfied and being formally diagnosed as depressed are not the same. The latter involves a specialized evaluation, one that has the effect of "converting" a possibly rational response into a psychopathological one. In the case of depression, such evaluations are not at all clear-cut.

A leading specialist (Weissman, 1980) indicates that depression can be a "normal mood," a "symptom of abnormal mood," or a "syndrome." Even with respect to identifying the second of these, "it is difficult to draw the line between the normal and the pathological. Depressions of mood that are unduly persistent, severe, or inappropriate are usually considered pathological" (ibid., p. 309). It seems evident that—except in the most extreme cases—observers are not always going to agree as to which depressed moods are "unduly persistent, severe, or inappropriate." In considering recent alternatives to conventional psychotherapy, the same writer notes:

> Employment of consciousness-raising groups as an alternative treatment for dealing with female depression rests partially on the premise that the traditional feminine role leads to helplessness and that depression is a state of helplessness. In this view, traditional therapies are seen as encouraging women to adjust to situations in which they are helpless and that are in reality depressing. Helplessness and de-

are helpless and that are in reality depressing. Helplessness and depression can occur by at least two pathways: by real social inequities; or by learned helplessness, which is part of the stereotypical female role (ibid., p. 310).

This statement highlights at least two very important and closely related points. One is the possibility of substituting for a psychopathological interpretation the alternative view that women's situations often "are in reality depressing." Thus, by implication, the depressed feelings are not always irrational. The second point is actually the obverse of this one. It is that the formal clinical diagnosis always represents interpretation, or "labeling." For both aspects—the rational basis of much female unhappiness and the tendency to place formal psychiatric "labels" on women —the overall gender system bears a heavy responsibility. The same is true with respect to a third general factor coloring the relations between women and mental illness. As we shall see further below, our culture has encouraged women to view their own discontent as being pathological and to see themselves as likely candidates for psychotherapy.

A number of these points were brought together by Phyllis Chesler in her provocative and influential book *Women and Madness* (Chesler, 1972). Chesler's major contribution lay in pointing up the dual or mentally-ill-either-way aspect found in the psychiatric diagnosis of women.

> Women who fully act out the conditioned female role are clinically viewed as "neurotic" or "psychotic." When and if they are hospitalized, it is for predominantly female behaviors such as "depression," "suicide attempts," "anxiety neuroses," "paranoia," or "promiscuity." Women who reject or are ambivalent about the female role frighten both themselves and society so much so that their ostracism and self-destructiveness probably begin very early. Such women are also assured of a psychiatric label and, if they are hospitalized, it is for less "female" behaviors (ibid., p. 56).

Thus women are in a double bind as regards the dominant gender prescriptions: they are vulnerable to labeling if they violate them but also if they conform.

The Role of Psychiatry

Chesler did not limit her analysis to those cases in which women were hospitalized. She also discussed the more general tendency to apply mental illness definitions (in either of the "directions" just noted) to women's ongoing everyday behaviors. Particularly noteworthy is her assessment of women's relation to the institution of voluntary individual psychotherapy. Chesler emphasizes the unequal nature of the psychiatrist-patient relationship, which provides women with "one more opportunity to be rewarded for expressing distress and to be 'helped' by being (expertly) dominated" (ibid., p. 108). She draws an analogy between the psychotherapy relationship and that found in traditional middle-class marriage:

> Both . . . isolate women from each other; both emphasize individual rather than collective solutions to woman's unhappiness; both are based on a woman's helplessness and dependence on a stronger male authority figure; both may, in fact, be viewed as reenactments of a little girl's relation to her father in a patriarchal society; both control and oppress women similarly—yet, at the same time, are the two safest (most approved and familiar) havens for middle-class women in a society that offers them few—if any—alternatives (ibid.).

In addition, Chesler points out, both "encourage women to talk—often endlessly—rather than to act" (ibid., p. 109).

As Chesler's comments on the functions of psychotherapy indicate, she—like many other critics—stresses the fact that the practitioners of psychotherapy have been predominantly male. Chesler gives this point a special, and quite controversial, twist. Citing research findings which suggested that sexual relations between male therapists and female patients may occur with some frequency, she treats them as dramatic evidence of the exploitative nature of the therapist-patient relation (ibid., Ch. 5; also Szasz, 1981, pp. 148–151). Interpreting such sexual behavior from a psychodynamic standpoint, she sees it as an acting out of a deep-seated and approved "preference" that women should be drawn sexually to powerful father figures (ibid.).

More recently, another writer has cited opposed research findings which lead her to reject the claim that male therapists often have sex with female patients (Rohrbaugh, 1979, pp. 393–395). However, as she goes on to acknowledge, the likelihood of substantial underreporting suggests that survey data may understate the true frequency of male therapist-female patient sex. She also notes that the concern about the possibility of such behavior has become sufficiently widespread that several professional associations of psychotherapists have issued statements or drafted provisions in their codes of ethics expressing disapproval of it (ibid.). This commentator also claims that "today many women request a female therapist precisely to avoid the power-authority dimension they had previously sought in therapy" (ibid., p. 394).

Whether or not one emphasizes this particular type of direct sexual exploitation, and certainly regardless of whether one accepts Chesler's "incest taboo" interpretation of it, the persisting male domination of psychotherapy remains a fact of great significance. As sociologists have observed, the patient in traditional psychotherapy is almost always in a subordinate and dependent position. There may be a certain amount of subtle "negotiation" between therapist and client in identifying the latter's "problem" and setting ground rules for the therapy (Scheff, 1968). However, as Scheff goes on to point out, the therapist invariably has the upper hand in this negotiation. From his position of greater power, he usually defines the therapeutic situation. He can do this in part "because he is well-trained, secure, and self-confident in his role in the transaction, whereas the client is untutored, anxious, and uncertain about his role" (ibid., p. 6).

This dependency of the client is likely to be especially pronounced when a female is consulting a male therapist. According to Dorothy Smith, "Male psychiatrists *hear* women in treatment, but women do not have the privilege of defining, categorizing, interpreting and assigning value to what they have said" (Smith, 1975a, p. 9). The traditional dependency of females, and their overall deference to males, has supported this hierarchical relation within therapy. Psychiatry, Smith asserts, "relies upon women's lack of authority to speak" (ibid., p. 13). The situation in psychotherapy reflects, furthermore, the general pattern of female subjection or submission to "expert"—and especially, medical—advice and control (Ehrenreich and English, 1973; Ehrenreich and English, 1979). We have noted above various other examples of this pattern. There is a close link between the long-standing "cult of female invalidism" (Ehrenreich and English, 1979, p. 139) and the tendency, cited by Chesler (1972), for many women in our society to make a "career" out of being a psychiatric patient.

The very expectation that females will perpetually have ailments reinforces women's lack of self-confidence and self-sufficiency. It also exacerbates the already-existing inclination of many psychiatrists to err on the side of possible overdiagnosis. Scheff (1966, pp. 105–113) refers to this tendency as a "medical decision rule." The practitioner sees his efforts as being likely to help the prospective patient. Given that view, he can with easy justification prefer to risk imputing too much illness rather than to risk making an error in the opposite direction (ibid.; also Freidson, 1971, pp. 255–261). This preference also reflects the fact that the practitioner has been trained to look for and to "find" illness. And it will be heightened when his expectation of finding medical problems among a particular category of persons—in this case, women—is strong.

At the beginning of this section, we noted the claim that psychiatric ideologies are, essentially, male ideologies. This assertion highlights the specific aspect of male domination of psychotherapy that has been of greatest concern to its critics—namely, psychiatrists' beliefs about, and attitudes toward, women. The major research on this matter is that done by Inge Broverman and her associates (1970; 1972). They administered questionnaires to seventy-nine clinical psychologists, psychiatrists, and psychiatric social workers—forty-six of them male and thirty-three female. The questionnaire listed a series of 122 bipolar items, 33 of which were believed to reflect and tap traditional beliefs about females and males (e.g., not at all aggressive/very aggressive; expresses tender feelings/does not express tender feelings, etc.). For each item, respondents were asked which pole would better describe a "mature, healthy, socially competent" adult. One-third of the respondents completed forms on which the adult's sex was unspecified, one-third completed forms specifying a woman, and the final third completed forms indicating a man.

Both male and female respondents described healthy adults (when sex was unspecified) and healthy males in essentially the same terms. However the depiction of healthy females—given, again, by respondents of both sexes—diverged, in a highly stereotyped direction, from that of healthy adults and healthy males. Healthy females were seen as differing from healthy males (and the generic model for healthy adults) "by being more submissive, less independent, less adventurous, more easily influenced, less aggressive, less competitive, more excitable in minor crises, having their feelings more easily hurt, being more emotional, more conceited about their appearance, less objective, and disliking math and science" (Broverman, et al., 1970, pp. 4–5). As Chesler (1972, p. 67) has noted, these findings clearly indicate "a double standard of mental health." There is one set of criteria for adult males and for adults generally; there is a second set for women. Thus, as another writer suggests, "Should a woman change toward being a healthy adult, she becomes sick as a woman. If she is a healthy woman, she is sick as a person" (Kimball, 1975, p. 123).

A recent commentator (Rohrbaugh, 1979, pp. 424–426) has pointed out that it would be misleading to cite this study as a basis for recommending that women see only female therapists, since clinicians of both sexes displayed the stereotyped views. On the other hand, if such bias is in fact widespread, that is certainly cause for serious concern. One writer (Smith, 1975a, pp. 9–10) has suggested that for females to succeed as traditional clinical practitioners it may be necessary for them to adopt and implement the dominant male perspective. To the extent this is true, it may provide a partial explanation of the similar attitudes found among male and female respondents in the Broverman study.

At least in the past, therapists' outlooks on women have heavily reflected the influence of Freudian psychoanalysis (see Friedan, 1963, Ch. 5; Firestone, 1971, Ch. 3; Millett, 1971, pp. 176–220; Weisstein, 1972; also Stockard and Johnson, 1980, Ch. 9). Seymour Halleck has summarized the effects of Freudianism as follows:

> The writings and teachings of psychiatry have helped to provide a rationale for keeping women in a subservient position. The founders of psychoanalysis saw women as basically masochistic and passive— as needing a certain degree of masculine domination in order to feel comfortable and whole. Many outstanding psychiatrists still refer to women in terms of their needs for passivity, to be companions to men, or to be mothers; little mention is made of their need to be active contributors to the larger society. A woman who enters psychotherapy will usually be exposed to a system of values that emphasizes the virtues of passivity; if she rejects these values her therapist may interpret her attitude as immature (Halleck, 1972, p. 125).

As we shall note below, the influence of Freud's ideas—which, until recently, has been overbearing—is now lessening somewhat in the light of new therapeutic outlooks and in the wake of feminist and other critiques. Actually, the more extreme Freudian conceptions—such as the idea that a woman's divergence from the prescribed female roles suggests "penis envy"—have never been subscribed to fully and literally by all psychoanalysts. Beginning in the 1920s such analysts as Karen Horney and Clara Thompson already were raising many of the points central to the current feminist critique of Freudianism (see the early papers reprinted in Miller, ed., 1973). Nonetheless the general outlook that Halleck describes was rather widely adopted. Woman's supposed "nature" was interpreted in terms of what Naomi Weisstein has called "the fundamentalist myth of sex-organ causality" (Weisstein, 1972, p. 209).

An extreme point in the application of such outlooks was reached in a 1947 book by Ferdinand Lundberg and psychiatrist Marynia Farnham, titled *Modern Woman: The Lost Sex.* Providing in very sketchy form what now would be called a "psychobiography" of the British feminist Mary Wollstonecraft, these writers depicted feminism as being merely a reflection of the deep-seated psychological problems of its leaders. They insisted that "feminism, despite the external validity of its political program and most (not all) of its social program, was at its core a deep illness" (Lundberg and Farnham, 1947, p. 143). The same authors further claimed, "Psychologically, feminism had a single objective: the achievement of maleness by the female, or the nearest possible approach to it. Insofar as it was attained, it spelled only vast individual suffering for men as well as women, and much public disorder" (ibid., p. 167).

Perhaps only the most militant anti-feminists would voice such views today. Nonetheless, the extent to which any departure from prescribed roles still may subject a woman to deviance labeling suggests their continuing indirect force. And the possibility of labeling feminism itself as deviance remains the ultimate reflection of such outlooks. Some feminist writers have come close to the opposite extreme, suggesting in effect that virtually all female mental illness represents protest against the subordination of women. One writer, herself an ex-mental patient, asserts: "Freaking out is a way of rejecting the limited choices offered by society.... Freaking out essentially consists of refusing to perform one's role, and making that choice known in noncriminal, socially unacceptable, and personally unsuccessful ways" (Chamberlin, 1975, p. 42). Given all the evidence regarding psychiatric labeling of women, this last sentence retains considerable validity, even if one rejects the implication that most mental illness is consciously "chosen" protest.

When the early feminist writer Charlotte Perkins Gilman (then Charlotte Perkins Stetson) experienced during the 1880s a severe depression she consulted a leading specialist, Dr. S. Weir Mitchell. "His prescription for her health was that she devote herself to domestic work and to her child, confine herself to, at most, two hours of intellectual work a day, and 'never touch pen, brush or pencil as long as you live' " (Hedges, 1973, p. 47). It is highly significant that Mitchell's views regarding the "illness" and the "cure" were directly opposite to her own. What he saw as the core of the ailment was precisely that which she felt would make her content. Thus she has the main character in her famous story "The Yellow Wallpaper" (based on her own situation and including that incident) assert: "Personally, I believe that congenial work, with excitement and change, would do me good" (Gilman, 1899, 1973, p. 10).

If today the exact prescription might vary a bit, it is still not uncommon for psychiatrists to advise adjustment to approved roles, to emphasize marriage and motherhood as paths to fulfill-ment, and to "interpret" more than to accept a woman's stated priorities and feelings. In particular, as emphasized above, the "real life" grounds for women's feelings of frustration and unhap-piness often may be disregarded. This tendency too can be traced back to Freud and his emphasis on the dynamic unconscious. With respect to diagnosing women, Freud's insight that overt behavior may reflect unconscious process has frequently been carried to an unwise extreme. When this has happened, the rational explana-tions for women's supposed "problems" have been lost to sight.

Prospects for Change

There is reason to anticipate significant change in many of the patterns we have just considered. To begin with, the restrictive life conditions that have produced much real female distress are them-selves undergoing change. One recent longitudinal analysis (Kessler and McCrae, 1981), which drew on data obtained from a number of large-scale surveys, found a trend over time "toward sex parity" (in early studies, females had predominated) in report-ed frequencies of psychophysiological symptoms (such as nervous-ness, tenseness, headaches, nightmares, hands trembling, etc.). Among the possible explanations the researchers mention is the following: "As the role possibilities for women expand, women in many role situations increasingly find it possible to adopt the type of life they would like to have" (ibid., p. 450).

Within psychoanalysis and psychiatry there is a growing diversity of theoretical approaches, as well as a heightened rethinking of basic Freudian concepts as they apply to women (see especially the papers in Miller, ed., 1973; and Heckerman, ed., 1980). This has involved a reviving and extending of the early critiques of narrow Freudianism and discussion of ways in which psychoanalytic ideas and methods may be consistent with feminism (see Mitchell, 1975) or may even facilitate feminist theorizing (Dinnerstein, 1977; Chodorow, 1978). There has also been a proliferation recently of alternative therapies. Various types of "radical" and "humanistic" therapies aim at being nonhierarchical and nonsexist. Women's consciousness-raising groups (Bond and Lieberman, 1980; also Hole and Levine, 1971, pp. 137–142; Sarachild, 1973, 1978; Dreifus, 1973; Mitchell, 1973, pp. 61–63) have provided a basis for undercutting the individual pathology emphasis of traditional psychotherapy. Oriented to the participants' common situation *as women,* these groups have enabled many to redefine as social system deficiencies various conditions and occurrences they earlier might have viewed as personal symptoms. This conversion process has invoked and substantiated the feminist maxim: "the personal is political."

For those women who feel they need psychotherapy as such, consciousness raising has served as a partial model for the emergence of an explicitly *feminist therapy* (Smith and David, eds., 1975, pp. 149–194; Rohrbaugh, 1979, Ch. 21). As one close observer notes, "There is really no one feminist therapy" (Rohrbaugh, 1979, p. 449). While the substantive focal points and specific therapeutic techniques vary, there are some common goals: "to get rid of power and dependence, to share uniquely female experiences with other women, and to change the political and social environment" (ibid., p. 445). Such therapies reflect both the general effort to rid psychiatry of sexist bias and the social action emphasis of the women's liberation movement. Joanna Rohrbaugh suggests that these therapies may, at times, carry the nonhierarchy principle too far. Noting that some feminist therapists seem to view therapy almost as "a special kind of friendship," she insists that therapy ought to be "both caring and businesslike" (ibid., p. 451). Thus she believes, "If the nonreciprocal and working nature of the relationship is ignored or minimized, the client may not be free to concentrate on herself; she may feel that she has to take care of the therapist just when she herself is most needy. The therapist, on the other hand, may become too emotionally involved to be objective and to carry out the confrontations and other work of therapy" (ibid.). Notwithstanding such possible dangers, feminist therapy does represent an important development. The long-range status and impact of this departure from male-dominated and male-oriented therapy remain to be seen.

A number of major social protest movements have helped to bring about these changes that affect women and mental illness. These include the general women's liberation movement, the more specific women's health movement (Ruzek, 1981), the consumer-oriented movement to improve the overall delivery of health care services (Conrad and Kern, eds., 1981), and the movement that has mounted a social critique of psychiatry (Schrag, 1978). While all of these efforts have been having considerable impact, one should not underestimate the persisting strength of psychiatry as a social control mechanism. The typing of women as mental "cases," and the social devaluation this implies, are likely to be with us for some time to come.

WOMEN AND CRIME
Trends and Interpretations

In recent years, there has been much public furor over the supposed upsurge in female crime. Thus, one writer has asserted that recently there has been "a tremendous increase of serious crimes by women" (Deming, 1977). A major influence in creating this impression was Freda Adler's much-publicized book, *Sisters in Crime* (1976). Adler proclaimed the "liberation of the female criminal, whose coming was foretold in song and foreshadowed in unisexual styles of dress and hair and attitude long before it appeared on police blotters" (Adler, 1976, p. 5). According to her, "a new breed of women criminals" (ibid., p. 7) was appearing across the country, there was "an unaccustomed involvement" of women in violent or potentially violent offenses (ibid., p. 22), and women were beginning to enter the "major leagues of crime" (ibid., p. 27).

Adler cited the women's liberation movement as the major cause of these alleged changes.

> . . . what we have described is a gradual but accelerating social revolution in which women are closing many of the gaps, social and criminal, that have separated them from men. The closer they get, the more alike they look and act. . . . The simplest and most accurate way to grasp the essence of women's changing patterns is to discard dated notions of femininity. That is a role that fewer and fewer women are willing to play (ibid., p. 30).

We shall return below to this "explanation," which seems to imply that today women are demanding the "right" to be criminals. First, however, it is necessary to examine Adler's basic claim that female crime is increasing and changing. Many researchers have concluded that this claim was presented in a glib and misleading form.

It is now widely agreed that *only some types* of female criminality have been increasing. A careful statistical appraisal published around the same time as Adler's book indicated such a conclusion:

> . . . the percentage of women arrested for crimes of violence shows neither an upward nor a downward trend. Between 1953 and 1972, the percentages [of females arrested among all arrests for violence offenses] fluctuated from a high point of 13.51 in 1956 to a low of 10.33 in 1968. But the picture for property offenses is markedly different. In 1953, about one out of every twelve arrests was a woman. In 1972, one out of 4.7 persons arrested was a woman. Not only has there been a consistent increase since 1953 in the percentage of women who have been arrested for property offenses; the biggest increases have occurred in the period beginning in 1967 (Simon, 1975, p. 36).

In another comparison, Simon examined the proportions of men and women arrested for serious violent and property offenses among all the men and women who were arrested for any offense. She found, "The proportion of men who have been arrested for violent offenses over the two decades has increased almost four times as much as has the proportion of women. For property offenses, it is the proportion of women who have been arrested that has increased threefold compared to the men" (ibid., p. 38).

Statistical analyses since Simon's have regularly produced the same basic finding: that the overall recorded increase in female crime is almost entirely due to a sizeable increase in female arrests for property crimes. One study examined arrest data for 1934 through 1979 and computed sex differentials in a way that adjusted for shifts over time in the sex distribution of the United States urban population (Steffensmeier and Cobb, 1981). These researchers found a small narrowing of the sex differential for violent crimes—but it is noteworthy that they included negligent manslaughter in their "homicide" category and "assaults besides aggravated assault" in their "assault" category (ibid., pp. 40–41). Their overall conclusion regarding arrest trends was as follows:

> The sex differential has narrowed in most offense categories since the 1930s. The largest narrowing occurred in the 1960s and 1970s. Women made the most significant gains in the petty property crimes of larceny, fraud, and forgery, and in the sex-related crimes of vagrancy and disorderly conduct. They made relatively small gains in traditionally male crimes. Rather, it is larceny which accounts for an increasing proportion of female crime: from about 70 percent (1934–41) to 90 percent (1973–79) of serious crimes, and from about one-sixth to one-third of all female arrests in the 20 categories we examined (ibid., p. 45).

A further dissection of property crime statistics for the period 1960–1978 by one of these same investigators led him to distinguish between "masculine" and other property offenses (Steffensmeier, 1981). The former involve "physical strength, elements of coercion and confrontation with victim, and/or specialized skills" (ibid., pp. 59–60). He concluded that with respect to the "masculine property offenses"—including robbery, burglary, auto theft, arson, vandalism and stolen property—"females have not gained ground on males, nor has there been a shift toward greater commission of these offenses on the part of females" (ibid., p. 60). It was in the aforementioned categories of nonviolent larceny, fraud and—to a lesser extent—forgery, that females showed substantial increases.

These studies of crime trends have been based on officially recorded statistics. As we have noted, such statistics reflect crime-processing as well as actual criminal behavior. Recorded trends and differentials, then, could partly result from variations in such processing (a matter to which we turn below). Researchers sometimes attempt to get around this problem by conducting self-reported behavior studies which do not rely on official statistics but instead obtain data through surveys asking the general population about behaviors they have engaged in. One such study (Feyerherm, 1981) recently obtained self-report data concerning "delinquent" behaviors from over one thousand high school students in a large Northeastern metropolitan area. About half the respondents were male, half female.

This research—like most other self-report studies—found a great deal of "hidden" delinquency. Respondents reported much technically "delinquent" behavior which never had come to the attention of the police or led to their arrest. However, the situation for males and females was not the same. The researcher noted that while there always is a low probability that a delinquent act will result in arrest, that probability is "more than doubled" if the actor is male. That difference, in turn, will be reflected in the male-female differential recorded in the arrest statistics. "In the current study the ratio of male to female delinquency was found to be 1.70 to 1. When examined at the point of arrest, this ratio has increased to 3.88 to 1" (ibid., p. 91).

Among respondents of both sexes, there were high reported frequencies (92.0 percent for males; 78.3 for females) of having engaged in at least one technically illegal type of behavior in the preceding year. There was similarity between males and females as to the most frequently engaged in types of problematic behavior (getting drunk and using marijuana) and the least frequent (fighting with weapons, using force in stealing, breaking and entering, and using heroin). "However, despite these similarities, there remains a substantially greater concentration of female delinquency in the area of substance abuse (including alcohol) and a higher concentration of male offenses in activities involving fighting, property damage, and theft of more valuable items" (ibid., p. 90).

We see in these data an indication that, at least among juveniles, female illegality overall may be considerably greater than is officially recorded. On the other hand, even when one has access to such self-report data, there is little indication that females are becoming violent criminals. As we noted earlier, the only well-established "trend" is an increase in recorded female property crime. And this seems to be accounted for largely by an increase in particular types of nonviolent theft. Police and court practices, discussed below, may have helped to "produce" these trends. On the other hand, Simon's conclusion on this matter still seems warranted. She states that "police behavior alone cannot account for the large increases in larceny, fraud, embezzlement, and forgery by women . . . and the absence of increases in homicide, aggravated assaults, and other violent crimes" (Simon, 1975, p. 47).

Let us assume for the moment that these are "real" behavioral trends and not just artifacts of processing and recording. Many observers accept that assumption. There remains, however, a lack of consensus with respect to interpreting such trends. It will be recalled that Adler—who to some extent glossed over the distinction between violent and property crimes, finding change almost everywhere—attributed increased female criminality to women's liberation. As women overcame previous restrictions, they would "look and act" more like men. This notion, that females are now "behaving" differently, needs to be distinguished from other interpretations based on gender system change.

Since there is little or no evidence that women are now committing the traditionally "masculine" offenses, the idea that current female crime reflects more liberated behavior does not hold up well. With respect to direct "influence" of the women's liberation movement itself on female attitudes and motivations relevant to crime-committing, there is no conclusive evidence available (see Austin, 1982, on temporal sequence of rate changes and the liberation movement). We do not even know, for example, whether many recent female offenders have had direct knowledge of and contact with feminist ideas or groups. We do know that general and gradual change is occurring in attitudes toward women and in women's own outlooks. But it is far from clear to what extent, and in what ways, such change has influenced female criminality.

At any rate, to blame the women's liberation movement, as such, for "causing" increased female crime—as some of its opponents have done—seems rather misleading. It may in fact be the case that relatively few of the current female offenders have been much influenced by feminism. If there has been any significant attitudinal or motivational effect, it probably is of the "relative deprivation" sort we noted at the beginning of this chapter. Another type of general social change, however, may be of greater significance in shaping women's crime patterns. This is the restructuring of female occupational opportunities. The general importance of opportunity in the production of crime was noted in connection with Figure 2 on page 189.

This factor was emphasized by Simon (1975; also Adler, 1976, Ch. 7), although she acknowledged that while women had been moving into the labor force in greater numbers they were still grossly underrepresented in managerial and professional jobs. She concluded, nonetheless, that it was likely that "women are committing those types of crimes that their participation in the labor force provides them with greater opportunities to commit than they have had in the past" (ibid., p. 47). With respect to future trends, furthermore, Simon emphasized that "even if we assume that women's psyche and motivations are no different than men's in their willingness to commit crimes, unless their opportunities expand, it is unlikely that women's crime rates will show a big increase" (ibid., p. 107).

Given women's still limited participation in the higher echelons of the labor force, it is understandable that they continue to show low rates of involvement in major white-collar crimes and other forms of systematic, large-scale "crime as business" (Sparks, 1979). In addition, expansion of opportunities that are not specifically related to women's occupational advancement may affect female crime. Thus, Darrell Steffensmeier has suggested that the increased likelihood of women handling money matters may imply new opportunities for committing forgery and other petty theft (Steffensmeier, 1978). Likewise he argues, "The greater reliance on self-service marketing and the purchasing of credit means that women, being the primary consumers, are faced with expanding opportunities for shoplifting, passing worthless checks, and so on" (Steffensmeier, 1981, p. 63). Yet another interpretation of the property crime increase urges that "we begin to look at the women who make up the arrest statistics and the kinds of crimes they commit from the perspective of *economic marginality* rather than simply 'new opportunities'" (Giordano, Kerbel, and Dudley, 1981, p. 80). These researchers suggest that certain categories of women (those who are young, single, and members of minority groups) may increasingly be in an economically marginal position "at the same time that they are increasingly expected to function independently" (ibid., p. 81).

Not all researchers are fully convinced that the trend seen in the arrest statistics does primarily represent a "real" increase in female property crime. Thus, Steffensmeier and a coresearcher have on balance concluded that "the narrowing of the sex differential reflects changes in law enforcement practices and changes in statistical coverage as much or more than changes in actual behavior" (Steffensmeier and Cobb, 1981, p. 45). Among the specific factors they mention are a decline in sympathetic and "chivalrous" attitudes toward female offenders (see below), outside pressure on the police to engage in even-handed law enforcement, increased professionalism and "more universalistic standards of decision-making" on the part of the police, and changes in the ways statistics are collected and specific offenses defined (ibid., p. 46).

As some of these studies imply, however, the concept of "deviance norms," discussed at the beginning of this chapter, remains pertinent in considering the current production of female crime and crime rates. As we noted there, such norms may influence both women's behavior and the ways in which such behavior is defined and responded to by others. Most consequentially, they may affect the behavior of social control agents. In addition, they play a role in the very "construction" of official crime definitions or categories —through their influence on legislation and judicial decision-making.

Notwithstanding publicized claims that deviance norms (in this case, crime norms) are rapidly changing, the empirical evidence seems to suggest otherwise. We still tend largely to think about specific crimes, and react to them, in terms of sex-appropriateness or inappropriateness. In fact we continue to assume that any reference to "a criminal" refers to a man, while we do not make such an assumption about mental illness designations. And, as we have just seen, with respect to the domain of crime itself the perception of violent offenses as constituting a "masculine" category (normatively as well as statistically) may well be holding firm.

A 1969 research report based on studies of women imprisoned for violent offenses (see Datesman and Scarpitti, eds., 1980, pp. 171–191) found an increase between 1963 and 1968 in the use by such offenders of guns. For the most part, however, the women's behavior conformed to female gender prescriptions. Few of the women had been arrested for robbery and burglary (included here in the definition of violent crimes), and those who had usually played only a "supportive" role in the commission of the offense. Women who had committed homicides and assaults had not violently attacked strangers. Invariably the objects of their violence had been husbands, lovers, and children, and the location of the offenses their own homes. In a recent and quite controversial book, Ann Jones (1981) has described killings by women as "the ultimate act of prepolitical violence," suggesting that often "the same social and legal deprivations that compel some women to feminism push others to homicide" (Jones, 1981, p. 12).

Jones's historical review of celebrated cases involving *Women Who Kill,* the title of her book, shows that the oppression of women—including severe role restrictions, sexual double standards, rape, and woman-battering—often lies behind such offenses. And she emphasizes the especially harsh response that may occur when the believed perpetrator of a killing is female. Jones claims that "homicide is a last resort, and it most often occurs when men simply will not quit" (ibid., p. 298). Although many observers would agree with that statement, Jones pushes her argument still further in a way which seems to imply that *all* homicides by women occur in self-defense or are otherwise justifiable. Thus she contends that "the story of women who kill is the story of women" (ibid., xvi). According to Jones, "Society is afraid of the feminist and the [female] murderer, for each of them, in her own way, tests society's established boundaries" (ibid., p. 13).

Sexuality and Delinquency

Traditionally, the "appropriate" crimes for women have been those that are closely tied to socially approved female behaviors and roles. A major example is shoplifting which, according to Steffensmeier's research cited above, may still constitute a major category of female criminality. In this case, the impact of the deviance norm may be primarily motivational. At the same time, however, the relative "acceptability" of a woman's committing such an offense may—along with other factors—help to determine the absence of stern enforcement in this area.

Women's relation to crime-defining and crime-processing is most dramatically affected by our culture's heavy preoccupation with female sexuality. Indirectly, we see this in the assumption that women involved in robberies must be only "accomplices," that a lover, husband, or some other male must be playing the leading role (see Millman, 1975). We have noted that the criminalizing of abortion, when it has occurred, has at least partly represented an effort to control female sexuality. Prostitution—a major category of female crime—is emblematic of woman's role as sexual object, and at the same time rests on and reinforces a sexual double standard. An unwarranted focus on women's sexuality is frequently apparent in the victim-blaming that occurs in processing rape cases.

The male crime of "statutory" rape also reveals how concern with female sexuality suffuses crime definitions. This offense consists of voluntary sexual intercourse between a male and a female, not his wife, below the "age of consent" (which varies by jurisdiction). As Leo Kanowitz has noted (Kanowitz, 1969, p. 19), courts consistently rule that such a female is incapable of giving meaningful consent. He goes on to point out that "since adult women do not commit the crime of statutory rape when they engage in intercourse with boys of fourteen to twenty-one years, lawmakers presumably believe that, unlike girls, boys of that age are capable of meaningfully consenting to sexual intercourse" (ibid.). The same difference pertains with respect to the offense of "contributing to the delinquency of a minor," which is rarely invoked when the adult is a female and the minor a male.

Sometimes an alleged "protecting" of female sexuality involves applying a double standard that actually punishes women. This is most glaringly evident in the area of juvenile justice. Our system for defining and processing juvenile "delinquency" has certain key features that make such abuse highly likely. These include statutory vagueness in defining the offense; the enormous discretion accorded those administering the system; the allegedly humanitarian goal of "individualized justice" and the claim that the proceedings are in the juvenile's own interests; and the associated use of highly informal court procedures and "indeterminate" sentencing—incarceration for as long as is "needed" (see Platt, 1969; Schur, 1973; Rosenheim, ed., 1976; also Matza, 1964; Emerson, 1969).

Preoccupation with female sexuality has colored the work of juvenile courts from the very beginning. As Anthony Platt notes of the first "child savers," they were not enormously concerned about conventional crimes. Rather, "Their central interest was in the normative behavior of youth—their recreation, leisure, education, outlook on life, attitudes to authority, family relationships, and personal morality" (Platt, 1969, p. 99). Another historical analysis of the early juvenile courts states:

In the Progressive period the abundant literature on delinquency was riddled with stereotypical assumptions about women and, in particular, about immigrant women. These stereotypes laid a basis for more punitive treatment of delinquent girls than delinquent boys. Girls were prosecuted almost exclusively for "immoral" conduct, a very broad category that defined all sexual exploration as fundamentally perverse and predictive of future promiscuity, perhaps even prostitution. But while girls, unlike boys, were almost never accused of violating criminal statutes, they received stiffer legal penalties (Schlossman and Wallach, 1978, p. 68).[1]

A close study of cases that came before the Milwaukee Juvenile Court in the early 1920s revealed "the persistence of Victorian moral attitudes toward children's noncriminal transgressions" (Schlossman, 1977, p. 168). The same researcher cites the case of one girl who "freely admitted to staying out at night with boys on many occasions," and whose investigating probation officer produced "incriminating" photographs and letters.

> Though neither judges nor probation officers were inveterate prudes, they often sought committal for girls (never for boys) solely on the grounds of early sexual activity. Still, in these cases as in others, the ostensible "offense" gave no clear indication what the ultimate disposition would be. Had Deborah not affirmed her right to be sexually active, had her mother not alienated the court by refusing to be contrite, and had the probation staff not turned up the incriminating photos and letters, Deborah, like most girls who appeared in court, might well have been placed on probation (ibid., p. 180).

Generally in these early court cases, boys and girls were treated very differently. Thus, "Significantly higher proportions of girls than boys were incarcerated in reformatories for sentences that could last several years" (Schlossman and Wallach, 1978, p. 72). Dissecting the private lives of alleged female delinquents, and applying an extraordinarily wide definition of "immorality," the courts "did not distinguish between actual delinquency and predelinquency because they saw their mission as the treatment of underlying causes" (ibid., p. 74).

These researchers conclude that "by incarcerating delinquent girls the reformatories removed them from the unregulated sexual

[1]Selections on pp. 221–223 reprinted from Steven Schlossman and Stephanie Wallach, "The Crime of Precocious Sexuality: Female Juvenile Delinquency in the Progressive Era," *Harvard Educational Review,* 48 (Feb. 1978). Copyright © 1978 by President and Fellows of Harvard College.

marketplace of ghetto streets and forced them to save their sexual favors, moral reputations, and health until they were of marriageable age" (ibid., p. 76). The application of vague provisions against "incorrigibility," "ungovernability," and the like was—and still is —abetted by the role of parents in relation to the court. As Meda Chesney-Lind has noted, "The family has always possessed a double standard for evaluating the significance of male and female misbehavior" (Chesney-Lind, 1978a, p. 173). While the defiant behavior of sons may even be approved, that of daughters is reacted to with severity—particularly when parental efforts to "control female sexual experimentation" seem threatened (ibid.).

Virtually all of these points apply equally to the present-day juvenile court. The vast majority of females appearing before the juvenile court are charged with "status offenses"—behaviors that would not be criminal if engaged in by adults. Usually, in the case of females, these involve actual or suspected sexual behavior. Personnel throughout the juvenile justice system assume—notwithstanding considerable evidence to the contrary from various self-report surveys—that female delinquents are, almost by definition, sexual delinquents. This assumption underlies their paternalistic efforts at "protection," efforts which however well intended are in fact stigmatizing and punishing. Reviewing numerous studies of police reactions to juveniles, Chesney-Lind finds evidence of a "relatively harsh police response to the predominantly noncriminal activity of young women" (ibid., p. 180). She also notes the routine subjection of young women placed in juvenile detention to pelvic examinations, regardless of the type of offense they are believed to have committed (ibid., pp. 182–184). She finds too that both probation officers and judges display "a differential standard of evaluating male and female misbehavior. Like good parents, they view female 'acting out' as more significant than its male equivalent and as requiring more drastic intervention" (ibid., p. 186).

As the last point suggests, the dispositions in female delinquency cases may be—at virtually all stages of the juvenile justice process—overly harsh, relative to those received by males (for a recent study that produced mixed findings in this regard, see Teilmann and Landry, 1981). A leading investigator reports:

Data compiled by the National Assessment of Juvenile Corrections as well as by federal agencies and many other students of juvenile justice clearly indicate that females are overrepresented in critical areas of the justice system. One of the most critical pertains to placement in adult jails, lockups, and detention facilities. Females have a greater probability of being detained and held for longer periods than males, even though the overwhelming majority of females are charged with status offenses (Sarri, 1976, p. 76).

Data from the aforementioned National Assessment of Juvenile Corrections also indicate that "females are overrepresented in institutional populations as compared to day treatment centers or group homes" (although 50 percent of institutional females are committed for status offenses), and that "the range of disposition alternatives appears to be more limited for females than for males" (ibid., p. 77). Sarri goes on to note:

> . . . in spite of the fact that juvenile females commit far fewer felonies and misdemeanors, they have extensive contact with the justice system. Females [i.e., committed females] had a mean arrest rate of 4.6 times; an average of 3.8 times in detention, 2.0 times in jail, and 1.3 times in an institution. Foster care and probation are underused in comparison to these more stringent sanctions, with means of 1.5 and 1.4, respectively (ibid., p. 78).

Condemning the system for "institutional sexism," Sarri refers finally to the "overwhelming dominance of male staff in critical decision-making posts." "Although the presence of female staff in leadership positions cannot guarantee a reduction in sexism in juvenile justice, it does appear to be one of the essential preconditions" (ibid., p. 79; see also Flynn, 1982).

Women in the Criminal Justice System

This last comment underlines a major factor in the production of all female crime outcomes. At virtually every level of the criminal justice system, the official agents of control are overwhelmingly male. Current criminology stresses the extent to which every criminal justice outcome is a social and legal production or construction (Quinney, 1970; Hartjen, 1978). The production of "criminals" involves the creation of crime definitions by legislation, and the application of those definitions to particular persons through the various stages of criminal justice processing. At every stage decisions are being made by ordinary, fallible, and sometimes biased, human beings (Frank, 1950; Schur, 1958). To the extent these decision-making processes are dominated by males, women are likely to be disadvantaged.

We have considered already some of the major substantive examples of women being systematically disadvantaged in the criminal justice process. We have seen that such disadvantage may be incurred when the female is a complainant, as well as when she is a perceived offender. Rape and woman-battering victims have met with relatively little success when they have tried to get the criminal justice system to work in their behalf. As we noted, the processing of complaints by predominantly male police, prosecutors, and judges often contributes to such an outcome. (On the other hand, a recent study (LaFree, 1981) found that in one police department establishment of a special sexual offenses unit—which included female detectives—did not significantly alter the rates of arrest and prosecution for sexual assault.) False assumptions about "women who get raped," and unwillingness to intervene in "family disputes" have sometimes undermined support for the victim in such cases. At times, the female complainant has been degraded by those who are supposedly administering justice, just as she was earlier degraded by the criminal offense itself.

Routine and perfunctory harassment of the prostitute provides a major example of the system's treatment of woman as an offender. The very singling out of the female in this situation as an offender, while disregarding the equally culpable male, constitutes a glaring instance of criminal justice inequality. This uneven administering of the law, and indeed the phenomenon of prostitution in general, reveals a persisting sexual double standard. And, as we saw, it also bears a close relation to the broader pattern of objectifying and commoditizing female sexuality.

Both within and without the profession, prostitutes come under continuous male control. Just as it is male outlooks that determine what "services" the prostitute must provide, it is male outlooks that largely determine official response to the prostitute. These outlooks appear to reflect a mixture of desire and contempt —in a way, prototypical of male attitudes toward women generally. Nobody takes anti-prostitution law enforcement seriously. Yet the facade of enforcement is maintained, in part representing a public expression of contempt for the prostitute woman. It seems unlikely these policies would be the same if the administrators of criminal justice included a proportionate share of women. Nor would the laws under which women are deemed the primary "offenders" in prostitution be likely to persist if the sex composition of legislatures were more equal.

The processing of rape and woman-battering complaints and of prostitution offenses—along with the criminalizing of juvenile female sexuality, just discussed—constitutes the most important substantive examples of mistreatment of women in the criminal justice system. If one looks at the system in more procedural terms, examining the various stages in the administration of justice (and without regard for the substantive offenses being dealt with), the evidence of overall mistreatment is not as clear. It does remain true that males make most of the crucial decisions at almost every stage. Yet apart from demonstrating bias in the three specific offense areas noted above, research has not conclusively shown a more general and systematic bias at the several stages of crime-processing.

For example, police attitudes and reactions to females have not been extensively investigated. Since police work has until recently been a bastion of "male culture," we might expect police actions to reflect—in one way or another—sexist bias. The question, however, has rarely been explored directly. Police officers in the field do have a great deal of discretion in handling instances they observe that might be treated as crime "cases." One now-classic study found that superficial cues—such as race, attire, and especially demeanor—significantly affected such field decisions (Piliavin and Briar, 1964) in police encounters with juveniles. A criminologist's recent summary of diverse studies emphasized this possibility:

> It is clear that different segments of the population have different probabilities of having their behavior labeled criminal by the police. Hence they have different probabilities of being formally and socially identified as criminal persons. Although a suspect's behavior is of primary importance in determining his or her chances of being arrested, in most cases the decision to arrest a person is based on factors that have little to do with the degree of a person's behavioral criminality . . . it is not so much what a person does as what kind of person he is (or is seen by the police to be) that affects official labeling (Hartjen, 1978, p. 108).

On the other hand, large-scale observational studies of police-citizen encounters undertaken for the President's Crime Commission suggested that officers by and large employed proper criteria and good professional judgment in making arrest decisions (see Black and Reiss, 1970; Reiss, 1971). In a more recent questionnaire study, police officers and detectives were asked how they would respond to offenses described in hypothetical vignettes. Sex, race, and demeanor of the hypothetical offender were systematically varied in the distribution of questionnaires. The researchers found that "neither sex alone nor race alone directly determined the police officers' responses . . . The major variables in determining how police officers responded were the nature of the offense and the manner in which the offender behaved when confronted by the police" (Moyer and White, 1981, p. 375).

It might be predicted on the basis of the "deviance norms" we considered earlier that—all other things being equal—police reactions to female suspects or offenders would be *less* severe than those evoked by males. In the study of hypothetical responses just cited, this was not found to be the case. Nor did officers react more harshly to females' negative demeanor (which might be viewed as "unladylike") than to males (ibid., pp. 374–375). It should be recalled that in her discussion of national arrest rates and trends Simon concluded that changes in police behavior alone could not account for her findings. She did however acknowledge such change as one possibly contributing factor. Thus she stated that "it is plausible to assume that the police are becoming less 'chivalrous' to women suspects and that women are beginning to receive more 'equal' treatment" (Simon, 1975, p. 47).

This issue of "chivalry" has been much discussed by researchers investigating what happens to women who actually are proceeded against on criminal charges. But because of conflicting evidence, the question remains up in the air. In one of the most frequently cited studies (Nagel and Weitzman, 1971), data on over eleven thousand criminal cases compiled earlier by the American Bar Foundation were reanalyzed for evidence of any systematic biases in the processing of defendants. The authors found that indigent and black defendants received relatively unfavorable treatment (in comparison with white and affluent defendants) at every stage of the criminal justice process. With respect to female defendants, however, a "paternalistic" pattern pertained. The study specifically examined cases of grand larceny and assault. For both types of offenses, female defendants were treated more leniently. They were less likely to be jailed prior to trial, and if convicted more likely to receive probation or a suspended sentence (and hence less likely to be imprisoned). Women were somewhat more likely to be jailed for assault than for larceny. The researchers speculated that this could have been because assault is a more "manly" crime.

A recent study of the influence of gender type-scripts on public attitudes (Phillips and DeFleur, 1982) employed hypothetical vignettes of offenses, with the sex of the offender systematically varied. Respondents were asked to judge the likelihood of various "motivations" for committing the crimes and to indicate what dispositions for the offenders they would recommend. The researchers found (ibid., p. 442) that female offenders were much more likely than male offenders to be perceived as mentally ill or as motivated by a desire to please others (3.7 times as likely, and 4.5 times, respectively). On the other hand, sex of the offender did not significantly influence the disposition recommendations: "Recommended dispositions follow from type of crime [i.e., perceived seriousness of the offense] more reliably than from gender ascription" (ibid., p. 443).

It should also be noted that even where paternalism exists, it does not always imply less stern treatment. Thus, another analyst (Temin, 1973) has emphasized that it may sometimes lead to longer sentences of imprisonment being imposed on women than on men. As her study has noted, there have been a few important court decisions invalidating certain kinds of sex-discriminatory laws governing criminal sentences. Nonetheless, quite a few states have kept on their statute books sentencing provisions under which women are systematically disadvantaged. Such provisions typically stipulate either a mandatory minimum sentence or an "indeterminate" one, when the convicted person is female. They reflect the same kind of protectionist philosophy that we saw at work with respect to the processing of female juveniles. Because specific court rulings on such provisions have varied so much, and since they often have been evaded through revised legislation, researcher Carolyn Temin (ibid.) concluded that a judicial solution to this problem was unlikely. Only through ratification of an Equal Rights Amendment, she asserted, would equality in sentencing be achieved.

Systematic quantitative analysis of the criminal processing of females is hampered because only limited statistics are available.

Thus (unlike the situation with respect to arrest) there are no uniform national statistics as regards convictions and sentencing in the various state courts. Such statistics are available for the federal courts, but these cover only certain offenses, and furthermore federal prosecutions comprise only a small proportion of all crime-processing. Simon (1975) used some federal data, and also data from one state (California), in order to assess the conviction and sentencing of females. Her conclusion was quite equivocal. At the time of her study she believed that women were receiving "some preferential treatment at the bar of justice" (ibid., p. 67). She stated that the eyes of justice "are neither blinded nor fully opened" and that the defendant's sex appeared to be influencing decisions "to some extent" (ibid.).

In addition to limitations imposed by statistical inadequacy, the picture remains clouded because of the undoubted countertendencies in paternalism which we have noted. While some women may be "let off" because of their sex, others are for the same reason sentenced to lengthy imprisonment in the name of "rehabilitation." Furthermore, between arrest and imprisonment lies a sequenced array of decision-making points, at any one of which sexist bias can come into play. Insofar as this specific issue is concerned, investigation of such decision-making has been meager. Decisions by prosecutors, probation officers, judges, and jurors are crucial factors in the production of female crime outcomes.

For each of the substantive examples emphasized above, we have seen already how certain of these decisions become extremely consequential. In rape cases the investigating police, and then even more significantly the prosecutor, make the crucial determination as to whether a complaint will be taken seriously and followed up, or instead "unfounded." The same is true with respect to intervening in woman-battering situations. We also noted the general reluctance of juries to convict rape defendants, and one study showing that even judges may display stereotyped reactions to rape complaints. As regards the treatment of prostitute women, police, prosecutors, and judges all participate in the system of routine harassment and "revolving door justice." In the juvenile justice system's processing of sexual "delinquency," the roles of the probation officer (who investigates the entire situation and makes a recommendation to the court) and the judge are especially crucial.

It is not easy to generalize, however, beyond such specific areas, about the overall extent of sexist bias in the courts. There is little doubt that some bias exists at all levels of the criminal justice system. Even as regards juries—where theoretically the domination of males might be minimal—the problem is a serious one. One writer has noted that "an examination of the literature on the selection of jurors indicates there are many opportunities for sexist stereotypes to be influential in the jury selection process" (Larkin, 1981, pp. 12–13). Furthermore, "Even before voir dire begins, sexism may play a part in limiting the number of women available for jury duty. State laws permitting women to be excused . . . have meant women in general tend to be underrepresented in jury pools" (ibid., p. 13).

In addition, early studies of mock jury deliberations (see Strodtbeck and Mann, 1956) found that women are less likely than men to play an active role in jury deliberations. Even if this has been due to their "token" position (as suggested by Kanter, 1977a) rather than to inculcated passivity, the result still may be that women's interests and perspectives are inadequately represented. It should be recognized too that all jurors are engaged in a process of evaluating the evidence presented and the courtroom behavior of participants in order to "reconstruct" the crime (Schur, 1958). Any stereotypes regarding women, held by jurors of either sex, may influence their perceptions and responses and, ultimately, their decisions. The same is true with respect to judges. We cannot assume that the judge is never affected by other than legal considerations. Indeed, the possibility of sexist bias is considered so great that a major project has been instituted aimed at "educating" judges (through published curricula, workshops, etc.) regarding woman's situation and women's rights (see Wikler, 1980).

Almost all students of women and crime agree that further research is needed on the question of bias in crime-processing. On the basis of her review of all the available evidence, one specialist concludes as follows:

> What may be happening is judicial enforcement of sex-role expectations as well as, and sometimes in place of, the law, with court personnel overlooking female criminal misconduct of the woman who conforms to female sex-role expectations, but responding harshly to women who deviate from sexual and behavioral components of the female sex role (Chesney-Lind, 1978b).

Finally, it should be emphasized that *every* instance in which there is reliance on false assumptions about femaleness and women's roles ultimately disadvantages women. This is true of decisions which result in lessened penalties for specific women as well as those which result in harsher penalties. Under a nonsexist administration of justice, women would not receive "special" treatment of either sort.

SUGGESTED READINGS

Adler, Freda and Rita James Simon, eds., *The Criminology of Deviant Women.* Boston: Houghton Mifflin Co., 1979. A wide-ranging collection of articles on women and crime.

Bowker, Lee H., ed., *Women and Crime in America.* New York: Macmillan, 1981. A useful anthology which emphasizes the treatment of women in the criminal justice system.

Chesler, Phyllis, *Women and Madness.* New York: Avon Books, 1972. A path-breaking feminist critique of psychiatric diagnosis and treatment.

Hawkins, Richard and Gary Tiedeman, *The Creation of Deviance.* Columbus, Ohio: Charles E. Merrill Pub. Co., 1975. A systematic view of the social production of deviance outcomes.

Miller, Jean Baker, ed., *Psychoanalysis and Women.* New York: Penguin Books, 1973. A selection of early and current papers, reassessing narrow Freudian conceptions.

Smith, Dorothy E. and Sara J. David, eds., *Women Look at Psychiatry.* Vancouver: Press Gang Publishers, 1975. A feminist critique by Canadian writers. Includes academic analyses and personal accounts.

PART III

Implications

CHAPTER 6

Summary and Conclusion

Today, virtually all of the deviance labels that have been placed on women are under heavy attack. As we have seen, however, the numerous specific instances of labeling are grounded in a deep-seated tendency to devalue the very condition of womanhood itself. Although a great deal of change is now occurring, this basic devaluation—which has been so extremely strong in the past—will not disappear overnight. In many areas, the stigmatization of females already has lessened. Yet until women collectively have acquired an equal share in the power to develop and impose labels, the controlling of women through an imputation of spoiled identity will persist.

To recognize this is not to ignore the real changes that are taking place. Nor is it to adopt a defeatist stance. The persisting inclination to label women deviant is, quite simply, a deplorable fact of social life. It must be faced up to, if it is to be eliminated. To assume from the dramatic changes that are evident in certain highly limited social circles—feminist, radical, "liberated," and so on—that the problem is over, is naive and unwarranted.

The data and interpretations reviewed and developed in this book may prove useful both for academic purposes and in connection with active efforts to promote social change. They offer a theoretical framework and factual resources from which to analyze, and also to challenge, the stigmatization of females. It is important for both academics and activists to recognize the pervasiveness and systematic character of such stigmatization. Activists have been somewhat more inclined to appreciate this, whereas academics often have undertaken separate analyses of supposedly distinct "problems" in a way that has blurred crucial interconnections. And the dedication of academics to supposedly distinct fields of specialization often has had similar effects.

ACADEMIC IMPLICATIONS

Such dedication helps to account for the past failure of specialists on deviance and specialists in the study of women to identify and explore the area of common interest to both "fields." It is not necessary to treat the facts and ideas presented in this text as belonging to one or the other specialty. On the contrary materials of the sort considered here should engage both specialties and encourage collaboration or cross-fertilization between them. In addition there are, from each of the two specific standpoints, gains to be had from addressing this topic of mutual concern.

For the student of deviance, a focus on the "deviantizing" of women serves to confirm the value of recently emerging concepts and emphases. It also suggests the need to broaden still further certain definitions and modes of analysis. In studying this topic, we throw light on a prime example of the general process of stigmatization or devaluation. As noted in Chapter One, this has become the central focal point in recent analyses of deviance. The case of women, furthermore, illustrates the analytic need to go beyond narrow conceptions of deviance. Many sociologists, for example, now insist that it is actual stigmatization, and not always presumed moral blameworthiness, that is the real indicator of imputed deviance.

Certainly some of the deviance labeling of women is for behavior that is seen as morally wrong and for which women are held "responsible." On the other hand, we have seen that women incur a certain amount of stigma merely by "being" women—an outcome to which the "blame" and "responsibility" notions do not seem relevant. As this outcome shows too, women don't even have to engage in "behavior" in order to face devaluation. We saw a specific example of this—and of the general point that no "act" is needed for deviance-defining to occur—in the labeling of women for violation of physical appearance norms.

In addition, studies of women's ascribed deviance point up the significance of informal, as well as formal, deviance labeling. Most recent research on deviance has been concerned primarily with official and public labeling. Although those types of labeling are extremely consequential, so too is informal deviance-defining in everyday life. As we noted earlier, the recent emphasis in sociology on interaction process, and the associated turn toward qualitative field research, are at least consistent with a focus on informal deviance-defining. Once the stigmatizing of women is viewed as falling within the domain of deviance studies, a good opportunity is provided to consider many specific examples of deviance and control in routine interaction. A good many female "offenses" do not appear in the statute books. These involve rules that are not enforced through specialized and formal procedures, but through many people's quite ordinary and totally unofficial interpersonal responses. These are, nonetheless, perceived "violations" that lead to stigma and punishment, however informal.

Another key theme in recent deviance sociology underscored by the deviance labeling of women is the need to place a heavy focus on the reaction process and the reactors or labelers themselves. Current theorizing emphasizes that what other people— that is, other than the "offending" actor—do largely determines deviance outcomes. In this connection, it is of major significance that it usually has been men who have been in a position to define situations that might occasion the use of deviance labels. Labeling outcomes, and indeed the emergence of specific labels in the first place, are in large measure functions of social power. The experience of women sharply illustrates the central importance of control over the power to label.

Furthermore, recent analysts of deviance see perceptions of threat as the major factor that lies behind concerted efforts to impose categorical stigma. Thus they seek to determine what stake the deviance-definers have in such an outcome. The large body of theorizing about woman as a perceived threat is highly pertinent in this connection. Men appear to benefit psychologically, as well as socially and economically, from the devaluation of women. Hence, the labeling of women offers a good illustration, too, of the role of interests in deviance-defining.

While recent deviance sociology has focused primarily on labeling processes and effects, this should not imply a total lack of interest in other aspects of causation. Such traditional concepts as structured strain, opportunity, and socialization remain useful—as we have seen—in accounting for the occurrence of the behaviors which are deemed deviant. As we also have noted, such behaviors are not intrinsically deviant. They acquire their "deviantness" through processes of social definition, of interpretation. However, in many of the instances considered in this text, both the "causal" and the "labeling" factors can be traced back to the prevailing gender system. Both arise out of and are shaped by its norms, expectations, priorities, and institutionalized arrangements.

Thus, emphasis on the unpredictable course of interaction in specific instances should not obscure the systemic groundings of prevailing definitions of deviance. As mentioned earlier many sociologists, including feminist scholars, have tended to dismiss the "functionalist" perspective out of hand. Yet, the gamut of deviance labels generated by the currently dominant gender norms illustrates well functionalism's central (and largely unobjectionable) theme of connectedness and mutual interdependence among various social patterns and ideas. Tracing the specific deviance-related patterns involving women to the overall gender system involves using this basic functionalist insight. To do so in no way implies the inevitability of the current patterns. Nor is an acknowledgment of such functional ties tantamount to asserting that the pattern "functions" positively for everyone in the society. The system focus does, however, involve recognizing that each specific pattern draws indirect "support" from the others with which it is linked. This is precisely why so many of the specific issues of women's deviance or of deviance against women can only be meaningfully addressed in terms of the broader gender system context.

For those engaged in women's studies, the deviance and control perspective provides yet another useful way to describe and analyze woman's situation. It is very consistent with those analyses that emphasize woman's "otherness," the denial of full human status and identity, and the tendency to respond to women in depersonalized, categorical, terms. Some women's studies specialists may object to the negative connotations of "deviance" terminology. On the other hand, this is perhaps one of the sharpest ways of underscoring the systematic and categorical devaluation of females. And the general conception of deviance as a "social construction"—developed by those in power and employed as a means of social control—makes clear that women's currently perceived deviances are all subject to conscious efforts at change.

A deviance-oriented analysis also has the value, as we have seen, of revealing the close relation between the widespread labeling of women and the failure to adequately stigmatize and punish male offenses against women. It is because women are so routinely treated as deviants that their victimization by men cannot be significantly "deviantized." What this all amounts to really is a monopolization by males of the power to sustain moral judgments and to make assessments of personal character. This monopoly is rooted in control of positions of social, economic, and political power—but in another sense it goes beyond those more frequently cited types of control.

Thinking in deviance and control terms may help one to focus on a level or dimension of implicit social control that has not always been adequately emphasized in women's studies. This was referred to in Chapter One, in terms of the reproduction of gender in ordinary interaction. The recent stigma-emphasizing work on deviance gives central attention to routine processes of interpersonal perception and response. The dominant ways of reacting to women are, to be sure, ultimately grounded in misconceptions about women's "nature," and in basic socialization processes. At the same time, direct perception and response in everyday interaction seems almost to take on a life of its own. At the very least, it is a potent reinforcer of deep-rooted myths and stereotypes. The objectification of females—including specifically visual objectification—has received considerable emphasis in this book. For the women's studies specialist, such objectification processes should be viewed as equal in importance to women's position in the labor market, patterns of childhood socialization, and the existence of economic and social discrimination against women. The objectification process is not a separable entity. On the contrary, as we have begun to see, it is closely intertwined with most other aspects of woman's situation. But it has not always received the direct attention it deserves.

IMPLICATIONS FOR SOCIAL CHANGE

The same point should be of considerable importance also to those actively involved in promoting social change. Feminists may need to recognize that the routine objectification of females—a response that has become for most men virtually a matter of habit—constitutes a major obstacle that must be surmounted. Objectification may contribute to women's persisting subordination almost as much as it results from that condition. How men are to be made to "see" women differently is not entirely clear. Ultimately, socialization to a view of females as inferior encourages seeing them and treating them as "things." On the other hand, the significance of these basic perceptions and responses suggests that feminists may wish to coordinate and strengthen their existing critique of "male culture." In particular, the prevailing visual imagery of women— as perpetuated not only in pornography but also in respectable advertising—may have to be a central feminist target, along with the somewhat less controversial targets of social and economic discrimination.

Equality of opportunity and the achievement of a single standard of sexual behavior will not necessarily eliminate such objectification. Analysis of the pervasive "deviantizing" of women makes clear that the "normalizing" of femaleness must itself be a major feminist goal. Activists must therefore directly concern themselves with trying to undermine the reproduction of sexism as it occurs in routine male-female interaction. It also seems evident that for women to achieve an "equal opportunity to objectify" men cannot be seen as a meaningful long-term gain. While such a situation might be preferable to the present one, it would uphold one of the most unpalatable features of the current system. This underscores the fact that a broader depersonalization tendency in modern society is oppressive in its own right.

A focus on basic processes of devaluation encourages one to recognize the similarities or linkages between various instances of stigmatization. We saw this in two ways. First, we noted the very close analogy between the response to women and responses to other stigmatized sectors of the population such as racial and ethnic minorities, the poor, and the physically disabled. Second, we observed that the various specific "women's issues" that involved some kind of stigmatization are actually connected. They are all parts of a broader devaluation pattern, and in addition we can trace some more specific lines of connection among them. From the standpoint of organizing collective efforts to achieve social change, this multiplicity of stigmatizations may be a hindrance as much as a help.

If all women saw themselves as having common goals, a large constituency favoring change could be marshalled. This is not, however, easily accomplished. In fact, we know that the women's movement has faced a serious problem with respect to collective organization and solidarity. Varying priorities and mixed loyalties have impaired unified action. Middle-class white women, minority women, and working-class women have not always agreed on social priorities. Similarly, the women's movement has suffered from disagreement between heterosexual women and lesbian women, and between prostitute women and nonprostitute women. A focus on the overall devaluation pattern might encourage a greater recognition of common problems and goals, although there is certainly no guarantee that such recognition will follow.

Making use of a stigma focus in studies of women underscores another point that already has been of great concern to feminists. This is the insidious effect that categorical devaluation can have on women's self-conceptions. Such possible consequences as impaired self-esteem and induced passivity were noted above. Here again we can see the importance of the "normalization" goal. Until femaleness in general is seen as ordinary and "normal," individual women are going to encounter difficulty in maintaining positive conceptions of themselves. On the other hand, induced impairment of female self-images is not inevitable. In this connection, each socioeconomic gain achieved by women in general potentially helps every woman, psychologically as well as practically. At the same time, various group programs that offer collective support and that define situations and problems in women's own terms can also help a great deal. Thus consciousness-raising groups, assertiveness training for women, and women's medical self-help programs have all been helping women to surmount devaluation.

The ultimate social action implication of contemporary deviance analysis is that prevailing patterns of deviance-defining can be changed. Those patterns which—at a given time and place—prevail do so primarily because of the social power that upholds them. Stigma does not inhere in behaviors or types of persons. Since it is imposed, it can be deposed. A deviance analysis of the situation of women, therefore, is a call to action as much as it is a call to face facts realistically. We are already seeing considerable change in many of the norms that restrict and oppress women.

Their legitimacy (moral power) is being undermined, and the social power that imposes them is weakening. Yet the devaluation of females persists. Analyzing the ways in which deviance definitions still are used to control women should help motivate and support the work that remains to be done.

REFERENCES

Abbott, Sidney and Barbara Love
 1972 *Sappho Was a Right-On Woman.* New York: Stein and Day.
Adam, Barry D.
 1978 *The Survival of Domination.* New York: Elsevier.
Adams, Karen L. and Norma C. Ware
 1979 "Sexism and the English Language," in Jo Freeman, ed., *Women: A Feminist Perspective.* 2nd ed., Palo Alto, Ca.: Mayfield Pub. Co.
Addelson, Kathryn Pyne
 1981 "Words and Lives," *Signs,* 7 (Autumn), 187–199.
Adler, Freda
 1976 *Sisters in Crime.* New York: McGraw-Hill.
Adler, Freda and Rita James Simon, eds.
 1979 *The Criminology of Deviant Women.* Boston: Houghton Mifflin.
Al-Issa, Ihsan
 1980 *The Psychopathology of Women.* Englewood Cliffs, N.J.: Prentice-Hall.
Alliance Against Sexual Coercion
 1981 *Fighting Sexual Harassment.* Boston: Alyson Publications.
Allon, Natalie
 1975 "Latent Social Services in Group Dieting," *Social Problems,* 23 (Oct.), 59–68.
 1982 "The Stigma of Overweight in Everyday Life," in Benjamin B. Wolman, ed., *Psychological Aspects of Obesity.* New York: Van Nostrand Reinhold.
Allon, Natalie and Diane Fishel
 1981 "Singles' Bars as Examples of Urban Courting Patterns," in Peter Stein, ed., *Single Life.* New York: St. Martin's Press.
Allport, Gordon W.
 1958 *The Nature of Prejudice.* Garden City, N.Y.: Doubleday Anchor Books.
Altman, Dennis
 1973 *Homosexual: Oppression and Liberation.* New York: Avon Books.
American Law Institute
 1962 *Model Penal Code.* Proposed official draft. Philadelphia: American Law Institute.
Amir, Menachem
 1971 *Patterns in Forcible Rape.* Chicago: University of Chicago Press.
Arms, Suzanne
 1977 *Immaculate Deception: A New Look at Women and Childbirth.* New York: Bantam Books.

Austin, Roy L.
  1982 "Women's Liberation and Increases in Minor, Major, and Oc-
       cupational Offenses," *Criminology,* 20 (Nov.), 407–430.
Balkan, Sheila, Ronald J. Berger, and Janet Schmidt
  1980 *Crime and Deviance in America: A Critical Approach.* Belmont,
       Ca.: Wadsworth Pub. Co.
Ball-Rokeach, S. J.
  1980 "Normative and Deviant Violence from a Conflict Perspec-
       tive," *Social Problems,* 28 (Oct.), 45–59.
Barker-Benfield, G. J.
  1977 *Horrors of the Half-Known Life: Male Attitudes Toward Women
       and Sexuality in Nineteenth-Century America.* New York: Harper
       Colophon Books.
Barry, Kathleen
  1981 *Female Sexual Slavery.* New York: Avon Books.
Bart, Pauline B.
  1972 "Depression in Middle-Aged Women," in Vivian Gornick and
       Barbara K. Moran, eds., *Woman in Sexist Society.* New York:
       Signet Books.
Bayer, Ronald
  1981 *Homosexuality and American Psychiatry.* New York: Basic
       Books.
Becker, Howard S.
  1963 *Outsiders.* New York: Free Press.
Bell, Alan P. and Martin S. Weinberg
  1978 *Homosexualities: A Study of Diversity Among Men and Women.*
       New York: Simon and Schuster.
Beneke, Timothy
  1982 *Men on Rape.* New York: St. Martin's Press.
Benson, Donna J. and Gregg E. Thomson
  1982 "Sexual Harassment on a University Campus," *Social Problems,*
       29 (Feb.), 236–251.
Berger, Bennett M., Bruce M. Hackett, and R. Mervyn Millar
  1974 "Child-Rearing Practices in the Communal Family," in Arlene
       Skolnick and Jerome H. Skolnick, eds., *Intimacy, Family and
       Society.* Boston: Little, Brown.
Berger, John
  1977 *Ways of Seeing.* New York: Penguin Books.
Bernard, Jessie
  1972 "The Paradox of the Happy Marriage," in Vivian Gornick and
       Barbara K. Moran, eds., *Woman in Sexist Society.* New York:
       Signet Books.

1973   "My Four Revolutions," in Joan Huber, ed., *Changing Women in a Changing Society.* Chicago: University of Chicago Press.

1975   *The Future of Motherhood.* New York: Penguin Books.

Bettelheim, Bruno

1970   *Children of the Dream.* New York: Avon Books.

Black, Donald J. and Albert J. Reiss, Jr.

1970   "Police Control of Juveniles," *American Sociological Review,* 35 (Feb.), 63–77.

Boggan, E. Carrington, et al.

1975   *The Rights of Gay People.* New York: Avon Books.

Bohmer, Carol

1974/   "Judicial Attitudes Toward Rape Victims," in Duncan Chap-
1977   pell, Robley Geis, and Gilbert Geis, eds., *Forcible Rape.* New York: Columbia University Press.

Bond, Gary R. and Morton A. Lieberman

1980   "The Role and Function of Women's Consciousness Raising," in Carol Landau Heckerman, ed., *The Evolving Female.* New York: Human Sciences Press.

Boskind-Lodahl, Marlene

1976   "Cinderella's Stepsisters: A Feminist Perspective on Anorexia Nervosa and Bulimia," *Signs,* 2 (Winter), 120–146.

Bowker, Lee H.

1978   *Women, Crime, and the Criminal Justice System.* Lexington, Mass.: D. C. Heath.

Bowker, Lee H., ed.

1981   *Women and Crime in America.* New York: Macmillan.

Brandenburg, Judith Berman

1982   "Sexual Harassment in the University: Guidelines for Establishing a Grievance Procedure," *Signs,* 8 (Winter), 320–336.

Brodsky, Carroll M.

1976   "Rape at Work," in Marcia L. Walker and Stanley L. Brodsky, eds., *Sexual Assault.* Lexington, Mass.: D. C. Heath.

Brody, Jane E.

1981   "An Eating Disorder of Binges and Purges Reported Widespread," *The New York Times,* Oct. 20, p. C1.

Brooke

1978   "The Retreat to Cultural Feminism," in Redstockings, *Feminist Revolution.* New York: Random House.

Brooks, Virginia

1981   *Minority Stress and Lesbian Women.* Lexington, Mass.: D. C Heath.

Broverman, I. K., et al.

1970   "Sex-Role Stereotypes and Clinical Judgments of Mental

Health," *Journal of Consulting and Clinical Psychology,* 34, 1–7.

1972   "Sex-Role Stereotypes: A Current Appraisal," *Journal of Social Issues,* 28, 59–78.

Brownmiller, Susan

1976   *Against Our Will.* New York: Bantam Books.

Bruch, Hilde

1973   *Eating Disorders: Obesity, Anorexia Nervosa, and the Person Within.* New York: Basic Books.

1978   *The Golden Cage: The Enigma of Anorexia Nervosa.* Cambridge: Harvard University Press.

Bryan, James H.

1966   "Occupational Ideologies and Individual Attitudes of Call Girls," *Social Problems,* 13 (Spring), 441–450.

Bunch, Charlotte

1972/   "Lesbians in Revolt," *The Furies,* Jan. 1972, as reprinted in
1975   Nancy Myron and Charlotte Bunch, eds., *Lesbianism and the Women's Movement.* Baltimore: Diana Press.

Burgess, Ann Wolbert and Lynda Lytle Holmstrom

1974/   "Rape Trauma Syndrome," in Duncan Chappell, Robley Geis,
1977   and Gilbert Geis, eds., *Forcible Rape.* New York: Columbia University Press.

1976   "Rape: Its Effect on Task Performance at Varying Stages in the Life Cycle," in Marcia J. Walker and Stanley L. Brodsky, eds., *Sexual Assault.* Lexington, Mass.: D. C. Heath.

Cagan, Elizabeth

1978   "The Selling of the Women's Movement," *Social Policy* (May–June), 4–12.

Calderone, Mary Steichen, ed.

1958   *Abortion in the United States.* New York: Hoeber-Harper.

Campling, Jo, ed.

1981   *Images of Ourselves: Women with Disabilities Talking.* London: Routledge and Kegan Paul.

Carver, Cynthia

1981   "The Deliverers: A Woman Doctor's Reflections on Medical Socialization," in Shelly Romalis, ed., *Childbirth: Alternatives to Medical Control.* Austin: University of Texas Press.

Chafetz, Janet Saltzman

1974   *Masculine, Feminine, or Human?* Itasca, Ill.: F. E. Peacock.

Chamberlin, Judy

1975   "Women's Oppression and Psychiatric Oppression," in Dorothy E. Smith and Sara J. David, eds., *Women Look at Psychiatry.* Vancouver: Press Gang Publishers.

Chappell, Duncan
1976 "Forcible Rape and the Criminal Justice System," in Marcia J. Walker and Stanley L. Brodsky, eds., *Sexual Assault.* Lexington, Mass.: D. C. Heath.
Chappell, Duncan, Robley Geis, and Gilbert Geis, eds.
1977 *Forcible Rape.* New York: Columbia University Press.
Chappell, Duncan and Susan Singer
1977 "Rape in New York City," in Duncan Chappell, Robley Geis, and Gilbert Geis, eds., *Forcible Rape.* New York: Columbia University Press.
Chesler, Phyllis
1972 *Women and Madness.* New York: Avon Books.
Chesney-Lind, Meda
1978a "Young Women in the Arms of the Law," in Lee H. Bowker, *Women, Crime, and the Criminal Justice System.* Lexington, Mass.: D. C. Heath.
1978b "Chivalry Reexamined: Women and the Criminal Justice System," in Lee H. Bowker, *Women, Crime, and the Criminal Justice System.* Lexington, Mass.: D. C. Heath.
Chodorow, Nancy
1978 *The Reproduction of Mothering.* Berkeley: University of California Press.
Cicourel, Aaron V.
1968 *The Social Organization of Juvenile Justice.* New York: Wiley.
Clark, Lorenne and Debra Lewis
1977 *Rape: The Price of Coercive Sexuality.* Toronto: Women's Press.
Clinard, Marshall B. and Robert F. Meier
1979 *Sociology of Deviant Behavior.* 5th ed., New York: Holt, Rinehart and Winston.
Cloward, Richard and Lloyd E. Ohlin
1960 *Delinquency and Opportunity.* Glencoe, Ill.: Free Press.
Cohen, Albert K.
1974 *The Elasticity of Evil.* Oxford: Basil Blackwell.
Cole, Charles L.
1977 "Cohabitation in Social Context," in Roger W. Libby and Robert N. Whitehurst, eds., *Marriage and Alternatives.* Glenview, Ill.: Scott, Foresman.
Collins, Eliza G. C. and Timothy B. Blodgett
1981 "Sexual Harassment: Some See It, Some Won't," *Harvard Business Review,* March–April, 77–95.

Collins, Randall
  1971 "A Conflict Theory of Sexual Stratification," *Social Problems,* 19 (Summer), 3–19.
Commission on Obscenity and Pornography
  1970 *Report.* New York: Bantam Books.
Connell, Noreen and Cassandra Wilson, eds.
  1974 *Rape: The First Sourcebook for Women.* New York: New American Library.
Conrad, Peter and Rochelle Kern, eds.
  1981 *The Sociology of Health and Illness.* New York: St. Martin's Press.
Conrad, Peter and Joseph W. Schneider
  1980 *Deviance and Medicalization.* St. Louis: C. V. Mosby.
Coser, Rose Laub and Gerald Rokoff
  1971 "Women in the Occupational World: Social Disruption and Conflict," *Social Problems,* 18 (Spring), 535–554.
Crisp, A. H.
  1980 *Anorexia Nervosa: Let Me Be.* London: Academic Press.
Crites, Laura, ed.
  1976 *The Female Offender.* Lexington, Mass.: D. C. Heath.
Crull, Peggy
  1980 "The Impact of Sexual Harassment on the Job," in Dail A. Neugarten and Jay M. Shafritz, eds., *Sexuality in Organizations.* Oak Park, Ill.: Moore Pub. Co.
Cuskey, Walter R., T. Premkumar, and Lois Sigel
  1979 "Survey of Opiate Addiction Among Females in the United States Between 1850 and 1970," in Freda Adler and Rita James Simon, eds., *The Criminology of Deviant Women.* Boston: Houghton Mifflin.
Daly, Mary
  1974 *Beyond God the Father.* Boston: Beacon Press.
  1978 *Gyn/Ecology.* Boston: Beacon Press.
Datesman, Susan K. and Frank R. Scarpitti, eds.
  1980 *Women, Crime and Justice.* New York: Oxford University Press.
David, Deborah S. and Robert Brannon, eds.
  1976 *The Forty-Nine Percent Majority: The Male Sex Role.* Reading, Mass.: Addison-Wesley.
Davis, Fred
  1963 *Passage Through Crisis.* Indianapolis, Ind.: Bobbs-Merrill.
Davis, Kingsley
  1937 "The Sociology of Prostitution," *American Sociological Review,* 2 (Oct.), 746–755.
de Beauvoir, Simone
  1953 *The Second Sex.* New York: Knopf.

De Lamater, John and Patricia MacCorquodale

    1979   *Premarital Sexuality.* Madison, Wis.: University of Wisconsin Press.

Deming, Richard

    1977   *Women: The New Criminals.* Nashville: Thomas Nelson.

Densmore, Dana

    1972   "On the Temptation to Be a Beautiful Object," in Constantina Saphilios-Rothschild, ed., *Toward a Sociology of Women.* Lexington, Mass.: Xerox College Publishing.

Diamond, Irene

    1980a "Pornography and Repression: A Reconsideration," *Signs,* 5 (Summer), 686–701.

    1980b "Pornography and Repression," in Laura Lederer, ed., *Take Back the Night.* New York: William Morrow.

Dinnerstein, Dorothy

    1977   *The Mermaid and the Minotaur: Sexual Arrangements and Human Malaise.* New York: Harper Colophon Books.

Dobash, R. Emerson and Russell P. Dobash

    1978   "Wives: The 'Appropriate' Victims of Marital Violence," *Victimology,* 2 (1977–78), 426–441.

    1979   *Violence Against Wives: A Case Against the Patriarchy.* New York: Free Press.

Dobash, Russell P. and R. Emerson Dobash

    1981   "Community Response to Violence Against Wives," *Social Problems,* 28 (June), 563–581.

Dohrenwend, Bruce P. and Barbara Snell Dohrenwend

    1976   "Sex Differences and Psychiatric Disorders," *American Journal of Sociology,* 81 (May), 1447–1472.

Douglas, Jack D., ed.

    1970   *Deviance and Respectability.* New York: Basic Books.

    1972   *Research on Deviance.* New York: Random House.

Douglas, Mary

    1966   *Purity and Danger.* New York: Praeger.

Dreifus, Claudia

    1973   *Woman's Fate: Raps from a Feminist Consciousness-Raising Group.* New York: Bantam Books.

Dworkin, Andrea

    1974   *Woman Hating.* New York: E. P. Dutton.

    1981   *Pornography: Men Possessing Women.* New York: Perigee Books.

Dye, Nancy Schrom

    1980   "History of Childbirth in America," *Signs,* 6 (Autumn), 97–108.

Edelman, Murray
   1977   *Political Language.* New York: Academic Press.
Edgerton, Robert B.
   1967   *The Cloak of Competence.* Berkeley: University of California Press.
   1969   "On the 'Recognition' of Mental Illness," in Stanley C. Plog and Robert B. Edgerton, eds., *Changing Perspectives in Mental Illness.* New York: Holt, Rinehart and Winston.
Edwards, Susan S. M.
   1981   *Female Sexuality and the Law.* Oxford: Martin Robertson.
Ehrenreich, Barbara and Deirdre English
   1973   *Complaints and Disorders: the Sexual Politics of Sickness.* Old Westbury, N.Y.: The Feminist Press.
   1979   *For Her Own Good: 150 Years of the Experts' Advice to Women.* Garden City, N.Y.: Doubleday Anchor Books.
Eisenstein, Zillah R., ed.
   1979   *Capitalist Patriarchy and the Case for Socialist Feminism.* New York: Monthly Review Press.
   1982   "The Sexual Politics of the New Right," *Signs,* 7 (Spring), 567–588.
Elshtain, Jean Bethke
   1982a   "Feminist Discourse and Its Discontents," *Signs,* 7 (Spring), 603–621.
   1982b   "The Victim Syndrome: A Troubling Turn in Feminism," *The Progressive,* June, 40–47.
Emerson, Joan P.
   1970   "Behavior in Public Places: Sustaining Definitions of Reality in Gynecological Examinations," in Hans Peter Dreitzel, ed., *Recent Sociology, No. 2.* New York: Macmillan.
Emerson, Robert M.
   1969   *Judging Delinquents.* Chicago: Aldine.
Emerson, Robert M. and Sheldon L. Messinger
   1977   "The Micro-Politics of Trouble," *Social Problems,* 25 (Dec.), 121–134.
Engels, Friedrich
   1884/   *The Origin of the Family, Private Property, and the State.* New
   1942   York: International Publishers.
England, Paula
   1979   "Women and Occupational Prestige," *Sign ,* 5 (Winter), 252–265.
Epstein, Cynthia Fuchs
   1971   *Woman's Place.* Berkeley: University of California Press.
Erikson, Kai T.
   1962   "Notes on the Sociology of Deviance," *Social Problems,* 9 (Spring), 307–314.

1966 *Wayward Puritans.* New York: Wiley.

Ettore, E. M.
1980 *Lesbians, Women and Society.* London: Routledge and Kegan Paul.

Faderman, Lillian
1981 *Surpassing the Love of Men.* New York: William Morrow.

Fanon, Franz
1952, 1968 *Black Skin, White Masks.* New York: Grove Press.

Farley, Lin
1978 *Sexual Shakedown.* New York: Warner Books.

Farrell, Ronald A. and Victoria L. Swigert
1982 *Deviance and Social Control.* Glenview, Ill.: Scott, Foresman.

Farrell, Warren
1975 *The Liberated Man.* New York: Random House.

Fasteau, Marc
1974 *The Male Machine.* New York: McGraw-Hill.

Feinbloom, Deborah Heller
1976 *Transvestites and Transsexuals.* New York: Delta Books.

Ferguson, Ann
1981 "Patriarchy, Sexual Identity, and the Sexual Revolution," *Signs,* 7 (Autumn), 158–172.

Feyerherm, William
1981 "Gender Differences in Delinquency," in Lee H. Bowker, ed., *Women and Crime in America.* New York: Macmillan.

Firestone, Shulamith
1971 *The Dialectic of Sex.* New York: Bantam Books.

Fishman, Pamela M.
1978 "Interaction: The Work Women Do," *Social Problems,* 25 (April), 397–406.

Flynn, Edith E.
1982 "Women as Criminal Justice Professionals," in Nicole Hahn Rafter and Elizabeth A. Stanko, eds., *Judge, Lawyer, Victim, Thief: Women, Gender Roles, and Criminal Justice.* Boston: Northeastern University Press.

Forisha, Barbara and Judith Heady
1981 "The Battle of the Sexes," in Barbara L. Forisha and Barbara H. Goldman, eds., *Outsiders on the Inside: Women and Organizations.* Englewood Cliffs, N.J.: Prentice-Hall.

Foucault, Michel
1977 *Discipline and Punish.* New York: Pantheon Books.
1980 *The History of Sexuality. Vol. I: An Introduction.* New York: Vintage Books.

Frank, Jerome
  1950   *Courts on Trial.* Princeton: Princeton University Press.
Fransella, Fay and Kay Frost
  1977   *On Being a Woman.* London: Tavistock.
Freeman, Jo, ed.
  1979   *Women: A Feminist Perspective.* Palo Alto, Ca.: Mayfield Pub.
         Co.
Freidson, Eliot
  1965   "Disability as Social Deviance," in Marvin B. Sussman, ed.,
         Sociology and Rehabilitation. Washington: American Sociologi-
         cal Association.
  1971   *Profession of Medicine.* New York: Dodd, Mead.
Fremont-Smith, Eliot
  1980   "Pornography's Progress," *The Village Voice,* Oct. 15–21, 43–46.
Friedan, Betty
  1963   *The Feminine Mystique.* New York: W. W. Norton.
Gagnon, John H. and William Simon
  1973   *Sexual Conduct.* Chicago: Aldine.
Garfinkel, Harold
  1956   "Conditions of Successful Degradation Ceremonies," *American
         Journal of Sociology,* 61 (March), 420–424.
  1964   "Studies of the Routine Grounds of Everyday Activities," *So-
         cial Problems,* 11 (Winter), 225–250.
Garrison, Howard H.
  1979   "Gender Differences in the Career Aspirations of Recent Co-
         horts of High School Seniors," *Social Problems,* 27 (Dec.), 170–
         185.
Geis, Gilbert
  1972   *Not the Law's Business?* National Institute of Mental Health.
         Crime and Delinquency Monograph Series. Washington: U.S.
         Government Printing Office.
Gelles, Richard
  1972   *The Violent Home.* Beverly Hills, Ca.: Sage Publications.
  1979   *Family Violence.* Beverly Hills, Ca.: Sage Publications.
Gerson, Kathleen
  1981   *Hard Choices: How Women Decide About Work, Career, and
         Motherhood.* Unpublished Ph.D. dissertation, University of
         California at Berkeley.
Gill, Derek
  1977   *Illegitimacy, Sexuality and the Status of Women.* Oxford: Basil
         Blackwell.
Gilman, Charlotte Perkins
  1899/ *The Yellow Wallpaper.* Old Westbury, N.Y.: Feminist

1973   Press.

Giordano, Peggy C., Sandra Kerbel, and Sandra Dudley

1981   "The Economics of Female Criminality," in Lee H. Bowker, ed., *Women and Crime in America.* New York: Macmillan.

Glueck, Sheldon and Eleanor Glueck

1934   *Five Hundred Delinquent Women.* New York: Knopf.

Goffman, Erving

1956   "The Nature of Deference and Demeanor," *American Anthropologist,* 58 (June), 473–502.

1959   *The Presentation of Self in Everyday Life.* Garden City, N.Y.: Doubleday Anchor Books.

1961a *Asylums.* Garden City, N.Y.; Doubleday Anchor Books.

1961b *Encounters.* Indianapolis, Ind.: Bobbs-Merrill.

1963   *Stigma.* Englewood Cliffs, N.J.: Prentice-Hall.

1972   *Relations in Public.* New York: Harper Colophon Books.

1977   "The Arrangement Between the Sexes," *Theory and Society,* 4 (Fall), 301–332.

1979   *Gender Advertisements.* New York: Harper Colophon Books.

Goldberg, Philip

1968   "Are Women Prejudiced Against Women?" *Transaction,* 5 (April), 28–30.

Goldman, Emma

1910, 1972   "The Traffic in Women," in Miriam Schneir, ed., *Feminism: The Essential Historical Writings.* New York: Vintage Books.

Goode, Erich

1978   *Deviant Behavior.* Englewood Cliffs, N.J.: Prentice-Hall.

Goode, William J.

1982   *The Family.* 2nd ed., Englewood Cliffs, N.J.: Prentice-Hall.

Gordon, George N.

1980   *Erotic Communications.* New York: Hastings House.

Gordon, Linda

1977   *Woman's Body, Woman's Right.* New York: Penguin Books.

1979   "The Struggle for Reproductive Freedom," in Zillah R. Eisenstein, ed., *Capitalist Patriarchy and the Case for Socialist Feminism.* New York: Monthly Review Press.

Gordon, Michael and Penelope J. Shankweiler

1971   "Different Equals Less: Female Sexuality in Recent Marriage Manuals," *Journal of Marriage and the Family* (August), 459–465.

Gordon, Suzanne

1983   "Dressed for Success: The New Corporate Feminism," *The Nation,* February 5, 129, 143–147.

Gornick, Vivian and Barbara K. Moran, eds.
1972   *Woman in Sexist Society.* New York: Signet Books.

Gould, Meredith and Rochelle Kern-Daniels
1977   "Toward a Sociological Theory of Sex and Gender," *The American Sociologist,* 12 (Nov.), 182–189.

Gouldner, Alvin W.
1968   "The Sociologist as Partisan," *The American Sociologist,* 3 (May), 106–116.

Gove, Walter R., ed.
1980   *The Labelling of Deviance.* 2nd ed., Beverly Hills, Ca.: Sage Publications.

Gove, Walter R. and Jeannette F. Tudor
1973   "Adult Sex Roles and Mental Illness," *American Journal of Sociology,* 78 (Jan.), 50–69.

Graham, Hilary and Ann Oakley
1981   "Competing Ideologies of Reproduction," in Helen Roberts, ed., *Women, Health and Reproduction.* London: Routledge and Kegan Paul.

Granberg, Donald
1982   "Family Size Preferences and Sexual Permissiveness as Factors Differentiating Abortion Activists," *Social Psychology Quarterly,* 45 (March), 15–23.

Gray, Susan H.
1982   "Exposure to Pornography and Aggression Toward Women," *Social Problems,* 29 (April), 387–398.

Greer, Germaine
1972   *The Female Eunuch.* New York: Bantam Books.

Grier, William H. and Price M. Cobbs
1968   *Black Rage.* New York: Basic Books.

Griffin, Susan
1982   *Pornography and Silence.* New York: Harper Colophon Books.

Grosfeld, Sharon
1981   *A Sociological Study of Marital Rape.* Unpublished M.A. thesis, Dept. of Sociology, New York University.

Group for the Advancement of Psychiatry
1970   *The Right to Abortion: A Psychiatric View.* New York: Scribner's.

Gusfield, Joseph R.
1966   *Symbolic Crusade.* Urbana, Ill.: Illinois University Press.
1967   "Moral Passage: The Symbolic Process in Public Designations of Deviance," *Social Problems,* 15 (Fall), 175–188.
1981   *The Culture of Public Problems.* Chicago: University of Chicago Press.

Hacker, Helen Mayer
   1951   "Women as a Minority Group," *Social Forces,* 30 (Oct.), 60–69.
Halleck, Seymour L.
   1972   *The Politics of Therapy.* New York: Perennial Library.
Hardin, Garrett
   1968   "Abortion—or Compulsory Pregnancy," *Journal of Marriage and the Family,* May, 246–251.
Harris, Anthony R.
   1977   "Sex and Theories of Deviance," *American Sociological Review,* 42 (Feb.), 3–16.
Hartjen, Clayton A.
   1978   *Crime and Criminalization.* 2nd ed., New York: Holt, Rinehart and Winston/Praeger.
Hartley, Shirley Foster
   1975   *Illegitimacy.* Berkeley: University of California Press.
Hartmann, Heidi
   1979   "Capitalism, Patriarchy, and Job Segregation by Sex," in Zillah R. Eisenstein, ed., *Capitalist Patriarchy and the Case for Socialist Feminism.* New York: Monthly Review Press.
Haskell, Molly
   1982   "Hers," *The New York Times,* Feb. 4, p. C2.
Hawkins, Richard and Gary Tiedeman
   1975   *The Creation of Deviance.* Columbus, Ohio: Charles E. Merrill.
Heckerman, Carol Landau, ed.
   1980   *The Evolving Female: Women in Psychosocial Context.* New York: Human Sciences Press.
Hedges, Elaine R.
   1973   "Afterword," to C. P. Gilman, *The Yellow Wallpaper.* Old Westbury, N.Y.: Feminist Press.
Henley, Nancy M.
   1977   *Body Politics: Power, Sex, and Nonverbal Communication.* Englewood Cliffs, N.J.: Prentice-Hall.
Henley, Nancy and Jo Freeman
   1979   "The Sexual Politics of Interpersonal Behavior," in Jo Freeman, ed., *Women: A Feminist Perspective.* 2nd ed., Palo Alto, Ca.: Mayfield Pub. Co.
Henshel, Anne-Marie
   1973   "Swinging: A Study in Decision-Making in Marriage," in Joan Huber, ed., *Changing Women in a Changing Society.* Chicago: University of Chicago Press.
Herman, Dianne
   1979   "The Rape Culture," in Jo Freeman, ed., *Women: A Feminist Perspective.* 2nd ed., Palo Alto, Ca.: Mayfield Pub. Co.

Heyl, Barbara
> 1979 "Prostitution: An Extreme Case of Sex Stratification," in Freda Adler and Rita James Simon, eds., *The Criminology of Deviant Women*. Boston: Houghton Mifflin.

Higgins, Paul C.
> 1980 *Outsiders in a Hearing World*. Beverly Hills, Ca.: Sage Pubs.

Higgins, Paul C. and Richard R. Butler
> 1982 *Understanding Deviance*. New York: McGraw-Hill.

Hindelang, Michael J. and Bruce J. Davis
> 1977 "Forcible Rape in the United States: A Statistical Profile," in Duncan Chappell, Robley Geis, and Gilbert Geis, eds., *Forcible Rape*. New York: Columbia University Press.

Hindelang, Michael J., Michael R. Gottfredson, and Timothy J. Flanagan, eds.
> 1981 *Sourcebook of Criminal Justice Statistics—1980*. U.S. Department of Justice. Washington: U.S. Government Printing Office.

Hochschild, Arlie Russell
> 1973 "A Review of Sex Role Research," in Joan Huber, ed., *Changing Women in a Changing Society*. Chicago: University of Chicago Press.
> 1979 "Emotion Work, Feeling Rules, and Social Structure," *American Journal of Sociology*, 85 (Nov.), 551–575.

Hoffman, Martin
> 1968 *The Gay World*. New York: Basic Books.

Hoge, Warren
> 1980 "Doctor Vanity: The Jet Set's Man in Rio," *The New York Times*, June 8, 44–70.

Hole, Judith and Ellen Levine
> 1971 *Rebirth of Feminism*. New York: Quadrangle/The New York Times Book Co.

Hollingworth, Leta S.
> 1916 "Social Devices for Impelling Women to Bear and Rear Children," *American Journal of Sociology*, 22 (July), 19–29.

Holmstrom, Lynda Lytle and Ann Wolbert Burgess
> 1978 *The Victim of Rape: Institutional Reactions*. New York: Wiley.

Horner, M. S.
> 1968 *Sex Differences in Achievement Motivation and Performance in Competitive and Non-Competitive Situations*. Unpublished Ph.D. dissertation, University of Michigan.

Horowitz, Irving Louis and Martin Liebowitz
> 1968 "Social Deviance and Political Marginality," *Social Problems*, 15 (Winter), 280–296.

Horwitz, Allan V.
  1982 *The Social Control of Mental Illness.* New York: Academic Press.
Huber, Joan, ed.
  1973 *Changing Women in a Changing Society.* Chicago: University of Chicago Press.
Hughes, Everett C.
  1945 "Dilemmas and Contradictions of Status," *American Journal of Sociology,* 50 (March), 353–359.
Hughes, Graham
  1975 *The Conscience of the Courts.* Garden City, N.Y.: Anchor Press-/Doubleday.
Humphries, Drew
  1977 "The Movement to Legalize Abortion: A Historical Account," in David F. Greenberg, ed., *Corrections and Punishment.* Beverly Hills, Ca.: Sage Publications.
Illich, Ivan
  1976 *Medical Nemesis.* New York: Pantheon Books.
Ingleby, David
  1980 "Understanding 'Mental Illness,' " in David Ingleby, ed., *Critical Psychiatry.* New York: Pantheon Books.
Ingleby, David, ed.
  1980 *Critical Psychiatry.* New York: Pantheon Books.
Jaffe, Frederick S., Barbara L. Lindheim, and Philip R. Lee
  1981 *Abortion Politics: Private Morality and Public Policy.* New York: McGraw-Hill.
Jaget, Claude, ed.
  1980 *Prostitutes: Our Life.* Bristol, Eng.: Falling Wall Press.
Jaggar, Alison M. and Paula Rothenberg Struhl, eds.
  1978 *Feminist Frameworks.* New York: McGraw-Hill.
James, Jennifer
  1977 "Prostitutes and Prostitution," in Edward Sagarin and Fred Montanino, eds., *Deviants.* Morristown, N.J.: General Learning Press.
James, Jennifer, et al.
  1975 *The Politics of Prostitution.* Seattle: Social Research Assocs.
Janeway, Elizabeth
  1980 *Powers of the Weak.* New York: Knopf.
Janssen-Jurreit, Marielouise
  1982 *Sexism: The Male Monopoly on History and Thought.* New York: Farrar, Straus, and Giroux.
Johnston, Jill
  1974 *Lesbian Nation: The Feminist Solution.* New York: Touchstone Books.

Jones, Ann
1981 *Women Who Kill.* New York: Fawcett Books.

Jones, E. E., et al.
forth- *Social Stigma: The Psychology of Marked Relations.* San Fran-
coming cisco: W. H. Freeman.

Kagan, Jerome, Richard B. Kearsley, and Philip R. Zelazo
1978 *Infancy: Its Place in Human Development.* Cambridge: Harvard
University Press.

Kaminer, Wendy
1980a "Pornography and the First Amendment," in Laura Lederer,
ed., *Take Back the Night.* New York: William Morrow.
1980b "A Woman's Guide to Pornography and the Law," *The Nation,* June 21, 754–756.

Kanin, Eugene J. and Stanley R. Parcell
1981 "Sexual Aggression: A Second Look at the Offended Female,"
in Lee H. Bowker, ed., *Women and Crime in America.* New
York: Macmillan.

Kanowitz, Leo
1969 *Women and the Law.* Albuquerque: University of New Mexico
Press.

Kanter, Rosabeth Moss
1977a "Some Effects of Proportions on Group Life: Skewed Sex
Ratios and Responses to Token Women," *American Journal of
Sociology,* 82 (March), 965–990.
1977b *Men and Women of the Corporation.* New York: Basic Books.

Kardiner, Abram and Lionel Ovesey
1951 *The Mark of Oppression.* New York: W. W. Norton.

Kasinitz, Philip
1981 "The Image of the 'New Woman' in Advertising," unpublished
paper, New York University, Department of Sociology.

Katz, Irwin
1981 *Stigma: A Social Psychological Analysis.* Hillsdale, N.J.: Lawrence Erlbaum Assocs.

Katz, Jack
1975 "Essences as Moral Identities," *American Journal of Sociology,* 80
(May), 1369–1390.

Keefe, Mary C. and Henry T. O'Reilly
1976 "Changing Perspectives in Sex Crimes Investigations," in
Marcia J. Walker and Stanley L. Brodsky, eds., *Sexual Assault.*
Lexington, Mass.: D. C. Heath.

Kessler, Ronald C. and James A. McCrae, Jr.
1981 "Trends in the Relationship Between Sex and Psychological
Distress, 1957–1976," *American Sociological Review,* 46 (Aug.),
443–452.

Kimball, Meredith
   1975   "Women, Sex Role Stereotypes, and Mental Health," in Doro-
          thy E. Smith and Sara J. David, eds., *Women Look at Psychiatry.*
          Vancouver: Press Gang Publishers.
Kirkpatrick, Clifford and Eugene Kanin
   1957   "Male Sex Aggression on a University Campus," *American So-
          ciological Review,* 22 (Feb.), 52–58.
Kitsuse, John I.
   1962   "Societal Reactions to Deviant Behavior," *Social Problems,* 9
          (Winter), 247–256.
Kitsuse, John I. and Aaron V. Cicourel
   1963   "A Note on the Use of Official Statistics," *Social Problems,* 11
          (Fall), 131–139.
Klein, Dorie
   1973   "The Etiology of Female Crime," *Issues in Criminology,* 8 (Fall),
          3–30.
Komarovsky, Mirra
   1946   "Cultural Contradictions and Sex Roles," *American Journal of
          Sociology,* 52 (Nov.), 182–189.
   1976   *Dilemmas of Masculinity.* New York: W. W. Norton.
Korda, Michael
   1979   *Male Chauvinism! How It Works.* New York: Ballantine
          Books.
Kovel, Joel
   1980   "The American Mental Health Industry," in David Ingleby,
          ed., *Critical Psychiatry.* New York: Pantheon Books.
Krieger, Susan
   1982   "Lesbian Identity and Community," *Signs,* 8 (Autumn), 91–
          108.
Kunzle, David
   1977   "Dress Reform as Antifeminism," *Signs,* 2 (Spring), 570–579.
Lader, Lawrence
   1966   *Abortion.* Indianapolis: Bobbs-Merrill.
   1973   *Abortion II: Making the Revolution.* Boston: Beacon Press.
Ladner, Joyce A.
   1972   *Tomorrow's Tomorrow: The Black Woman.* Garden City, N.Y.:
          Doubleday Anchor Books.
LaFree, Gary D.
   1981   "Official Reactions to Social Problems: Police Decisions in Sex-
          ual Assault Cases," *Social Problems,* 28 (June), 582–594.
Lakoff, Robin
   1975   *Language and Woman's Place.* New York: Harper Colophon
          Books.

Lane, Raymond M.
1981 "A Man's World: An Update on Sexual Harassment," *The Village Voice,* Dec. 16–22, pp. 1, 15–23.

Larkin, Nancy
1981 "Women in Court: An Examination of Sexism in the Legal Process." Unpublished paper, New York University, Department of Sociology.

Lasch, Christopher
1979 *The Culture of Narcissism.* New York: Warner Books.

Laslett, Barbara and Carol A. B. Warren
1975 "Losing Weight: The Organizational Promotion of Behavior Change," *Social Problems,* 23 (Oct.), 69–80.

Lauderdale, Pat
1976 "Deviance and Moral Boundaries," *American Sociological Review,* 41 (Aug.), 660–676.

Lauer, Robert H. and Jeannette C. Lauer
1981 *Fashion Power.* Englewood Cliffs, N.J.: Prentice-Hall.

Laws, Judith Long
1979 *The Second X: Sex Role and Social Role.* New York: Elsevier.

Laws, Judith Long and Pepper Schwartz
1977 *Sexual Scripts: The Social Construction of Female Sexuality.* Hinsdale, Ill.: The Dryden Press.

Lederer, Laura, ed.
1980 *Take Back the Night: Women on Pornography.* New York: William Morrow.

Lederer, Laura and Judith Bat-Ada
1980 "Playboy Isn't Playing," in Laura Lederer, ed., *Take Back the Night.* New York: William Morrow.

Lee, Nancy Howell
1969 *The Search for an Abortionist.* Chicago: University of Chicago Press.

Lemert, Edwin M.
1951 *Social Pathology.* New York: McGraw-Hill.

Leonard, Eileen B.
1982 *Women, Crime and Society.* New York: Longman.

Levenson, H., B. Burford, B. Bonno, and L. Davis
1975 "Are Women Still Prejudiced Against Women?" *Journal of Psychology,* 89, 67–71.

Lévi-Strauss, Claude
1949/ *The Elementary Structures of Kinship.* Boston: Beacon
1969 Press.

Lewis, Lionel S. and Dennis Brissett
1967 "Sex as Work: A Study of Avocational Counseling," *Social Problems,* 15 (Summer) 8–18.

Lewis, Robert A., ed.
1981   *Men in Difficult Times.* Englewood Cliffs, N.J.: Prentice-Hall.
Lewis, Sasha G.
1979   *Sunday's Women: Lesbian Life Today.* Boston: Beacon Press.
Lindesmith, Alfred R.
1965   *The Addict and the Law.* Bloomington: Indiana University Press.
Lippman, Walter
1922   *Public Opinion.* New York: Macmillan.
Lofland, John
1969   *Deviance and Identity.* Englewood Cliffs, N.J.: Prentice-Hall.
Lombroso, Cesare and William Ferrero
1895   *The Female Offender.* London: Fisher Unwin.
London, Julia
1978   "Images of Violence Against Women," *Victimology,* 2 (1977–78), 510–524.
Lott, Bernice, Mary Ellen Reilly, and Dale R. Howard
1982   "Sexual Assault and Harassment: A Campus Community Case Study," *Signs,* 8 (Winter), 296–319.
Luker, Kristin
1978   *Taking Chances: Abortion and the Decision Not to Contracept.* Berkeley: University of California Press.
Lundberg, Ferdinand and Marynia F. Farnham
1947   *Modern Woman: The Lost Sex.* New York: Harper and Bros.
Lurie, Susan
1980   "Pornography and the Dread of Women," in Laura Lederer, ed., *Take Back the Night.* New York: William Morrow.
Lydon, Susan
1970   "The Politics of Orgasm," in Robin Morgan, ed., *Sisterhood Is Powerful.* New York: Vintage Books.
McCormack, Thelma
1978   "Machismo in Media Research," *Social Problems,* 25 (June), 544–555.
MacGregor, John
1975   "The Modern Machiavellians: The Pornography of Sexual Game-Playing," in Ray C. Rist, ed., *The Pornography Controversy.* New Brunswick, N.J.: Transaction Books.
MacKinnon, Catharine A.
1979   *Sexual Harassment of Working Women.* New Haven: Yale University Press.
1982   "Feminism, Marxism, Method, and the State: An Agenda for Theory," *Signs,* 7 (Spring), 515–544.
Macklin, Eleanor D.
1978   "Nonmarital Heterosexual Cohabitation," *Marriage and Family Review,* 1 (March–April), 1–12.

Maddox, George L., Kurt W. Back, and Veronica R. Liederman
    1968   "Overweight as Social Deviance and Disability," *Journal of Health and Social Behavior,* 9 (Dec.), 287–298.

Marcuse, Herbert
    1964   *One-Dimensional Man.* Boston: Beacon Press.

Maris, Ronald W.
    1969   *Social Forces in Urban Suicide.* Homewood, Ill.: Dorsey Press.

Martin, Del
    1977   *Battered Wives.* New York: Pocket Books.

Martin, Del and Phyllis Lyon
    1972   *Lesbian/Woman.* New York: Bantam Books.

Masters, William H. and Virginia E. Johnson
    1966   *Human Sexual Response.* Boston: Little, Brown.

Matza, David
    1964   *Delinquency and Drift.* New York: Wiley.
    1969   *Becoming Deviant.* Englewood Cliffs, N.J.: Prentice-Hall.

May, Robert
    1980   *Sex and Fantasy.* New York: W. W. Norton.

Medea, Andra and Kathleen Thompson
    1974   *Against Rape.* New York: Farrar, Straus and Giroux.

Melani, Lilia and Linda Fodaski
    1974   "The Psychology of the Rapist and His Victim," in Noreen Connell and Cassandra Wilson, eds., *Rape: The First Sourcebook for Women.* New York: New American Library.

Mercer, Jane R.
    1973   *Labelling the Mentally Retarded.* Berkeley: University of California Press.

Merkin, Donald H.
    1976   *Pregnancy as Disease: The Pill in Society.* Port Washington, N.Y.: Kennikat Press.

Merton, Robert K.
    1949   'Social Structure and Anomie," in Merton, *Social Theory and Social Structure.* Glencoe, Ill.: Free Press.

Michelson, Peter
    1975   "The Pleasures of Commodity, or How to Make the World Safe for Pornography," in Ray C. Rist, ed., *The Pornography Controversy.* New Brunswick, N.J.: Transaction Books.

Miller, Jean Baker, ed.
    1973   *Psychoanalysis and Women.* New York: Penguin Books.

Miller, Patricia Y. and Martha R. Fowlkes
    1980   "Social and Behavioral Constructions of Female Sexuality," *Signs,* 5 (Summer), 783–800.

Miller v. *California,* 413 U.S. 15 (1973).

Millett, Kate
  1971   *Sexual Politics.* New York: Avon Books.
Millett, Kate, et al.
  1973   *The Prostitution Papers.* New York: Avon Books.
Millman, Marcia
  1975   "She Did It All for Love: A Feminist View of the Sociology of
         Deviance," in Marcia Millman and Rosabeth Moss Kanter,
         eds., *Another Voice.* Garden City, N.Y.: Doubleday Anchor
         Books.
  1980   *Such a Pretty Face: Being Fat in America.* New York: W. W.
         Norton.
Millman, Marcia and Rosabeth Moss Kanter, eds.
  1975   *Another Voice: Feminist Perspectives on Social Life and Social
         Science.* Garden City, N.Y.: Doubleday Anchor Books.
Mitchell, Juliet
  1973   *Woman's Estate.* New York: Vintage Books.
  1975   *Psychoanalysis and Feminism.* New York: Vintage Books.
Mohr, James C.
  1979   *Abortion in America: The Origins and Evolution of National Policy,
         1800–1900.* New York: Oxford University Press.
Morgan, Marabel
  1975   *The Total Woman.* New York: Pocket Books.
Morgan, Robin
  1978   *Going Too Far: The Personal Chronicle of a Feminist.* New York:
         Vintage Books.
Morgan, Robin, ed.
  1970   *Sisterhood Is Powerful.* New York: Vintage Books.
Morris, Norval and Gordon Hawkins
  1970   *The Honest Politician's Guide to Crime Control.* Chicago: Univer-
         sity of Chicago Press.
Moyer, Imogene L. and Garland F. White
  1981   "Police Processing of Female Offenders," in Lee H. Bowker,
         ed., *Women and Crime in America.* New York: Macmillan.
Myron, Nancy and Charlotte Bunch, eds.
  1975   *Lesbianism and the Women's Movement.* Baltimore: Diana Press.
Nagel, Stuart S. and Lenore J. Weitzman
  1971   "Women as Litigants," *The Hastings Law Journal,* 23 (Nov.),
         171–198.
Neier, Aryeh
  1980   "Victim Censorship: Expurgating the First Amendment," *The
         Nation,* June 21, pp. 737, 751–754.
Nellis, Muriel
  1981   *The Female Fix.* New York: Penguin Books.

Neugarten, Dail A. and Jay M. Shafritz, eds.
1980 *Sexuality in Organizations.* Oak Park, Ill.: Moore Pub. Co.

Oakley, Ann
1976 *Woman's Work.* New York: Vintage Books.
1981 *Subject Women.* New York: Pantheon Books.

Orbach, Susie
1979 *Fat Is a Feminist Issue.* New York: Berkley Books.

Orlando, Lisa
1982 "Bad Girls and 'Good' Politics," *Voice Literary Supplement,* Dec., pp. 16–19.

Pacht, Asher R.
1976 "The Rapist in Treatment," in Marcia J. Walker and Stanley L. Brodsky, eds., *Sexual Assault.* Lexington, Mass.: D. C. Heath.

Packer, Herbert L.
1968 *The Limits of the Criminal Sanction.* Stanford, Ca.: Stanford University Press.

Pagelow, Mildred Daley
1981 *Woman-Battering: Victims and Their Experiences.* Beverly Hills, Ca.: Sage Publications.

Palmer, R. L.
1980 *Anorexia Nervosa.* New York: Penguin Books.

Person, Ethel Spector
1980 "Sexuality as the Mainstay of Identity: Psychoanalytic Perspectives," *Signs,* 5 (Summer), 605–630.

Petchesky, Rosalind Pollack
1980 "Reproductive Freedom: Beyond 'A Woman's Right to Choose,'" *Signs,* 5 (Summer), 661–685.

Pfuhl, Erdwin H., Jr.
1980 *The Deviance Process.* New York: D. Van Nostrand.

Phelps, Linda
1979 "Female Sexual Alienation," in Jo Freeman, ed., *Women: A Feminist Perspective.* 2nd ed., Palo Alto, Ca.: Mayfield Pub. Co.

Phillips, Derek L. and Bernard F. Segal
1969 "Sexual Status and Psychiatric Symptoms," *American Sociological Review,* 34 (Feb.), 58–72.

Phillips, Dretha M. and Lois B. DeFleur
1982 "Gender Ascription and the Stereotyping of Deviants," *Criminology,* 20 (Nov.), 431–443.

Piliavin, Irving and Scott Briar
1964 "Police Encounters with Juveniles," *American Journal of Sociology,* 70 (Sept.), 206–214.

Piven, Frances Fox
1981 "Deviant Behavior and the Remaking of the World," *Social Problems,* 28 (June), 489–507.

Platt, Anthony M.

    1969   *The Child Savers.* Chicago: University of Chicago Press.

Pleck, Joseph H. and Jack Sawyer, eds.

    1974   *Men and Masculinity.* Englewood Cliffs, N.J.: Prentice-Hall.

Plummer, Kenneth

    1975   *Sexual Stigma.* London: Routledge and Kegan Paul.

Pollak, Otto

    1950   *The Criminality of Women.* Philadelphia: University of Pennsylvania Press.

Polsky, Ned

    1967   *Hustlers, Beats, and Others.* Chicago: Aldine.

Ponse, Barbara

    1978   *Identities in the Lesbian World.* Westport, Conn.: Greenwood Press.

Quinney, Richard

    1970   *The Social Reality of Crime.* Boston: Little, Brown.

    1980   *Class, State, and Crime.* 2nd ed., New York: Longman.

Radicalesbians

    1970/   "The Woman-Identified Woman," in Karla Jay and Allen

    1977   Young, eds., *Out of the Closets.* New York: Jove/HBJ Books.

Rafter, Nicole Hahn and Elizabeth A. Stanko, eds.

    1982   *Judge, Lawyer, Victim, Thief: Women, Gender Roles, and Criminal Justice.* Boston: Northeastern University Press.

Rains, Prudence Mors

    1971   *Becoming an Unwed Mother.* Chicago: Aldine.

Randall, Susan C. and Vicki McNickle Rose

    1981   "Barriers to Becoming a 'Successful' Rape Victim," in Lee H. Bowker, ed., *Women and Crime in America.* New York: Macmillan.

Raymond, Janice G.

    1979   *The Transsexual Empire: The Making of the She-Male.* Boston: Beacon Press.

Redstockings

    1978   *Feminist Revolution.* New York: Random House.

Reiss, Albert J., Jr.

    1971   *The Police and the Public.* New Haven: Yale University Press.

Reiss, Ira L.

    1980   *Family Systems in America.* 3rd. ed., New York: Holt, Rinehart and Winston.

Rich, Adrienne

    1980   "Compulsory Heterosexuality and Lesbian Existence," *Signs,* 5 (Summer), 631–660.

Rich, B. Ruby

    1982   "Anti-Porn: Soft Issue, Hard World," *The Village Voice,* July 20, pp. 1, 16–19.

Richardson, Laurel Walum
1981   *The Dynamics of Sex and Gender.* 2nd ed., Boston: Houghton Mifflin.

Richardson, Stephen A., et al.
1961   "Cultural Uniformity in Reaction to Physical Disabilities," *American Sociological Review,* 26 (April), 241–247.

Roberts, Helen
1981   "Male Hegemony in Family Planning," in Helen Roberts, ed., *Women, Health, and Reproduction.* London: Routledge & Kegan Paul.

Roberts, Helen, ed.
1981   *Women, Health, and Reproduction.* London: Routledge & Kegan Paul.

Roberts, Helene E.
1971   "The Exquisite Slave: The Role of Clothes in the Making of the Victorian Woman," *Signs,* 2 (Spring), 554–569.

Robins, Lee N.
1980   "The Natural History of Drug Abuse," in *Theories of Drug Abuse.* National Institute on Drug Abuse. Research Monograph Series. Washington: U.S. Government Printing Office.

Roe v. *Wade,* 410 U.S. 113 (1973).

Rohrbaugh, Joanna Bunker
1979   *Women: Psychology's Puzzle.* New York: Basic Books.

Romalis, Shelly
1981   "Natural Childbirth and the Reluctant Physician," in Shelly Romalis, ed., *Childbirth: Alternatives to Medical Control.* Austin: University of Texas Press.

Romalis, Shelly, ed.
1981   *Childbirth: Alternatives to Medical Control.* Austin: University of Texas Press.

Rosaldo, Michelle Zimbalist and Louise Lamphere, eds.
1974   *Women, Culture, and Society.* Stanford: Stanford University Press.

Rose, Vicki McNickle
1977   "Rape as a Social Problem: A Byproduct of the Feminist Movement," *Social Problems,* 25 (Oct.), 75–89.

Rosen, David H.
1974   *Lesbianism: A Study of Female Homosexuality.* Springfield, Ill.: Charles C. Thomas.

Rosen, Ruth
1982   *The Lost Sisterhood: Prostitution in America, 1900–1918.* Baltimore: The Johns Hopkins University Press.

Rosenbaum, Marsha
1981   *Women on Heroin.* New Brunswick, N.J.: Rutgers University Press.
Rosenberg, M. Michael, Robert A. Stebbins, and Alan Turowetz, eds.
1982   *The Sociology of Deviance.* New York: St. Martin's Press.
Rosenfield, Sarah
1980   "Sex Differences in Depression: Do Women Always Have Higher Rates?" *Journal of Health and Social Behavior,* 21 (March), 33–42.
Rosenhan, D. L.
1973   "On Being Sane in Insane Places," *Science,* 179 (Jan. 19), 250–258.
Rosenheim, Margaret K., ed.
1976   *Pursuing Justice for the Child.* Chicago: University of Chicago Press.
Rossi, Alice S.
1966   "Abortion Laws and Their Victims," *Transaction* (Sept.–Oct.).
1980   "Life-Span Theories and Women's Lives," *Signs,* 6 (Autumn), 4–32.
Rothman, Barbara Katz
1979   *Two Models of Maternity Care.* Unpublished Ph.D. dissertation, New York University.
1981   "Awake and Aware, or False Consciousness: The Cooption of Childbirth Reform in America," in Shelly Romalis, ed., *Childbirth.* Austin: University of Texas Press.
1982   *In Labor: Women and Power in the Birthplace.* New York: W. W. Norton.
Rothman, Sheila M.
1978   *Woman's Proper Place.* New York: Basic Books.
Rowbotham, Sheila
1973   *Woman's Consciousness, Man's World.* Baltimore: Penguin Books.
Rubin, Gayle
1975   "The Traffic in Women: Notes on the 'Political Economy' of Sex," in Rayna R. Reiter, ed., *Toward an Anthropology of Women.* New York: Monthly Review Press.
Rubington, Earl and Martin S. Weinberg, eds.
1981   *Deviance: The Interactionist Perspective.* 4th ed., New York: Macmillan.
Russell, Diana E. H.
1975   *The Politics of Rape.* New York: Stein and Day.
1982   *Rape in Marriage.* New York: Macmillan.
Russell, Diana E. H. and Nicole Van de Ven, eds.
1976   *Crimes Against Women.* Proceedings of the International Tribunal. Millbrae, Ca.: Les Femmes.

Rutter, Michael
  1981   *Maternal Deprivation Reassessed.* 2nd ed., New York: Penguin Books.
Ruzek, Sheryl L.
  1981   "The Women's Self-Help Health Movement," in Peter Conrad and Rochelle Kern, eds., *The Sociology of Health and Illness.* New York: St. Martin's Press.
Ryan, William
  1972   *Blaming the Victim.* New York: Vintage Books.
Safilios-Rothschild, Constantina
  1972   *Toward a Sociology of Women.* Lexington, Mass.: Xerox College Publishing.
Sagarin, Edward
  1975   *Deviants and Deviance.* New York: Praeger.
Sampson, Harold, Sheldon L. Messinger, and Robert D. Towne
  1962   "Family Processes and Becoming a Mental Patient," *American Journal of Sociology,* 68 (July), 88–96.
Sanders, William B.
  1980   *Rape and Woman's Identity.* Beverly Hills, Ca.: Sage Publications.
Sarachild, Kathie
  1973, 1978   "Consciousness Raising: A Radical Weapon," in Redstockings, *Feminist Revolution.* New York: Random House.
Sarbin, Theodore R.
  1969   "The Scientific Status of the Mental Illness Metaphor," in Stanley C. Plog and Robert B. Edgerton, eds., *Changing Perspectives in Mental Illness.* New York: Holt, Rinehart and Winston.
Sargent, Lydia, ed.
  1981   *Women and Revolution.* Boston: South End Press.
Sarri, Rosemary
  1976   "Juvenile Law: How It Penalizes Females," in Laura Crites, ed., *The Female Offender.* Lexington, Mass.: D. C. Heath.
Sarvis, Betty and Hyman Rodman
  1974   *The Abortion Controversy.* 2nd ed., New York: Columbia University Press.
Scheff, Thomas J.
  1966   *Being Mentally Ill.* Chicago: Aldine.
  1968   "Negotiating Reality," *Social Problems,* 16 (Summer), 3–17.
Schlossman, Steven L.
  1977   *Love and the American Delinquent.* Chicago: University of Chicago Press.

Schlossman, Steven and Stephanie Wallach
  1978 "The Crime of Precocious Sexuality: Female Juvenile Delin-
        quency in the Progressive Era," *Harvard Educational Review,* 48
        (Feb.), 65–94.
Schrag, Peter
  1978 *Mind Control.* New York: Pantheon Books.
Schur, Edwin M.
  1955 "Abortion and the Social System," *Social Problems,* 3 (Oct.),
        94–99.
  1958 "Scientific Method and the Criminal Trial Decision," *Social
        Research,* 25 (Summer), 173–190.
  1965 *Crimes Without Victims.* Englewood Cliffs, N.J.: Prentice-Hall.
  1968 "Abortion," *The Annals of the American Academy of Political and
        Social Science,* 376 (March), 136–147.
  1971 *Labeling Deviant Behavior.* New York: Harper and Row.
  1973 *Radical Nonintervention.* Englewood Cliffs, N.J.: Prentice-
        Hall.
  1976 *The Awareness Trap.* New York: Quadrangle/The New York
        Times Book Co.
  1979 *Interpreting Deviance.* New York: Harper and Row.
  1980 *The Politics of Deviance.* Englewood Cliffs, N.J.: Prentice-Hall.
Schur, Edwin M. and Hugo Adam Bedau
  1974 *Victimless Crimes: Two Sides of a Controversy.* Englewood Cliffs,
        N.J.: Prentice-Hall.
Schwendinger, Herman and Julia Schwendinger
  1975 "Defenders of Order or Guardians of Human Rights?" in Ian
        Taylor, Paul Walton, and Jock Young, eds., *Critical Criminology.*
        London: Routledge and Kegan Paul.
Scott, Robert A.
  1969 *The Making of Blind Men.* New York: Russell Sage Founda-
        tion.
Scully, Diana and Pauline Bart
  1973 "A Funny Thing Happened on the Way to the Orifice: Women
        in Gynecology Textbooks," in Joan Huber, ed., *Changing
        Women in a Changing Society.* Chicago: University of Chicago
        Press.
Shaw, Nancy Stoller
  1974 *Forced Labor.* New York: Pergamon Press.
Sherfey, Mary Jane
  1973 *The Nature and Evolution of Female Sexuality.* New York: Vintage
        Books.
Shorter, Edward
  1975 *The Making of the Modern Family.* New York: Basic Books.

Shulman, Alix Kates
   1972   "Organs and Orgasms," in Vivian Gornick and Barbara
          K. Moran, eds., *Woman in Sexist Society*. New York: Signet
          Books.
   1980   "Sex and Power: Sexual Bases of Radical Feminism," *Signs*, 5
          (Summer), 590–604.
Simon, Rita James
   1975   *Women and Crime*. Lexington, Mass.: D. C. Heath.
Simpson, Ruth
   1977   *From the Closet to the Courts*. New York: Penguin Books.
Skolnick, Arlene
   1978   *The Intimate Environment*. 2nd ed., Boston: Little, Brown.
Smart, Carol
   1978   *Women, Crime and Criminology*. London: Routledge and Kegan
          Paul.
Smith, Dorothy E.
   1975a "Women and Psychiatry," in Dorothy E. Smith and Sara J.
          David, eds., *Women Look at Psychiatry*. Vancouver: Press Gang
          Publishers.
   1975b "The Statistics on Mental Illness," in Dorothy E. Smith and
          Sara J. David, eds., *Women Look at Psychiatry*. Vancouver:
          Press Gang Publishers.
Smith, Dorothy E. and Sara J. David, eds.
   1975   *Women Look at Psychiatry*. Vancouver: Press Gang Publishers.
Smith-Rosenberg, Carroll
   1975   "The Female World of Love and Ritual," *Signs*, 1 (Autumn),
          1–29.
Snyder, M. and S. Uranowitz
   1978   "Reconstructing the Past: Some Cognitive Consequences of
          Person Perception," *Journal of Personality and Social Psychology*,
          36, No. 9, 941–950.
Sours, John A.
   1980   *Starving to Death in a Sea of Objects: The Anorexia Nervosa Syn-
          drome*. New York: Jason Aronson.
Sparks, Richard F.
   1979   " 'Crime as Business' and the Female Offender," in Freda Adler
          and Rita James Simon, eds., *The Criminology of Deviant Women*.
          Boston: Houghton Mifflin.
Spector, Malcolm and John I. Kitsuse
   1977   *Constructing Social Problems*. Menlo Park, Ca.: Cummings Pub.
          Co.
Spence, Janet T. and Robert L. Helmreich
   1978   *Masculinity and Femininity*. Austin: University of Texas Press.

Stannard, Una
    1972   "The Mask of Beauty," in Vivian Gornick and Barbara K. Moran, eds., *Woman in Sexist Society*. New York: Signet Books.

Steffensmeier, Darrell J.
    1978   "Crime and the Contemporary Woman," *Social Forces*, 57 (Dec.), 566–584.
    1981   "Patterns of Female Property Crime, 1960–1978: A Postscript," in Lee H. Bowker, ed., *Women and Crime in America*. New York: Macmillan.

Steffensmeier, Darrell J. and Michael J. Cobb
    1981   "Sex Differences in Urban Arrest Patterns, 1934–1979," *Social Problems*, 29 (Oct.), 37-50.

Stein, Peter J.
    1981   "Understanding Single Adulthood," in Peter J. Stein, ed., *Single Life*. New York: St. Martin's Press.

Stephenson, Richard M.
    1973   "Involvement in Deviance," *Social Problems*, 21 (Fall), 173–190.

Stewart, Phyllis
    1971   "Female Promiscuity: A Factor in Providing Abortion Service." Paper presented at annual meeting of American Sociological Association.

Stockard, Jean and Miriam M. Johnson
    1980   *Sex Roles*. Englewood Cliffs, N.J.: Prentice-Hall.

Stoll, Clarice Stasz
    1974   *Female and Male*. Dubuque, Iowa: Wm. C. Brown.

Stoller, Robert J.
    1976   *Perversion*. New York: Delta Books.

Stone, Gregory P.
    1962   "Appearance and the Self," in Arnold M. Rose, ed., *Human Behavior and Social Processes*. Boston: Houghton Mifflin.

Stone, Laurie
    1982   "Confronting the New Puritans," *The Village Voice*, July 6, pp. 1, 10–14.

Straus, Murray A.
    1978   "Wife Beating: How Common and Why?" *Victimology*, 2 (1977–78), 443–457.

Strodtbeck, Fred L., Rita M. James, and Charles Hawkins
    1957   "Social Status in Jury Deliberations," *American Sociological Review*, 22 (Dec.), 713.

Strodtbeck, Fred L. and R. D. Mann
    1956   "Sex Role Differentiation in Jury Deliberations," *Sociometry*, 19 (March), 3–11.

Strong, Ellen
    1970   "The Hooker," in Robin Morgan, ed., *Sisterhood Is Powerful.* New York: Vintage Books.

Suchar, Charles S.
    1978   *Social Deviance.* New York: Holt, Rinehart and Winston.

Sudnow, David
    1965   "Normal Crimes," *Social Problems,* 12 (Winter), 255–276.

Szasz, Thomas S.
    1961   *The Myth of Mental Illness.* New York: Hoeber-Harper.
    1981   *Sex by Prescription.* New York: Penguin Books.

Taylor, Ian, Paul Walton, and Jock Young
    1974   *The New Criminology.* New York: Harper Torchbooks.

Teilmann, Katherine S. and Pierre H. Landry, Jr.
    1981   "Gender Bias in Juvenile Justice," *Journal of Research in Crime and Delinquency,* 18 (Jan.), 47–80.

Temin, Carolyn Engel
    1973   "Discriminatory Sentencing of Women Offenders," *American Criminal Law Review,* II (Winter), 358–372.

Thio, Alex
    1973   "Class Bias in the Sociology of Deviance," *The American Sociologist,* 8 (Feb.), 1–12.

Thomas, W. I.
    1923   *The Unadjusted Girl.* Boston: Little, Brown.

Thorne, Barrie and Nancy Henley, eds.
    1975   *Language and Sex.* Rowley, Mass.: Newbury House.

Tierney, Kathleen J.
    1982   "The Battered Women Movement and the Creation of the Wife Beating Problem," *Social Problems,* 29 (Feb.), 207–220.

Tresemer, David
    1975   "Assumptions Made About Gender Roles," in Marcia Millman and Rosabeth Moss Kanter, eds., *Another Voice.* Garden City, N.Y.: Doubleday Anchor Books.

Trice, Harrison M.
    1966   *Alcoholism in America.* New York: McGraw-Hill.

Veblen, Thorstein
    1899/   *The Theory of the Leisure Class.* New York: Modern Library.
    1934

Veevers, J. E.
    1974   "Voluntary Childless Wives," in Arlene Skolnick and Jerome H. Skolick, eds., *Intimacy, Family, and Society.* Boston: Little, Brown.
    1977   "The Moral Careers of Voluntary Childless Wives," in P. Stein, J. Richman, and N. Hannon, eds., *The Family.* Reading, Mass.: Addison-Wesley.

Vincent, Clark E.
1961   *Unmarried Mothers.* New York: Free Press of Glencoe.
Vorenberg, Elizabeth and James Vorenberg
1977   "The Biggest Pimp of All," *The Atlantic,* Jan., pp. 27–38.
Waldorf, Dan
1973   *Careers in Dope.* Englewood Cliffs, N.J.: Prentice-Hall.
Walker, Lenore E.
1980   *The Battered Woman.* New York: Harper Colophon Books.
Walker, Marcia J. and Stanley L. Brodsky, eds.
1976   *Sexual Assault.* Lexington, Mass.: D. C. Heath.
Walkowitz, Judith R.
1980a   *Prostitution and Victorian Society.* Cambridge: Cambridge University Press.
1980b   "The Politics of Prostitution," *Signs,* 6 (Autumn), 123–135.
Waller, Willard
1936   "Social Problems and the Mores," *American Sociological Review,* 1 (Dec.), 922–934.
1937   "The Rating and Dating Complex," *American Sociological Review,* 2 (Oct.), 727–734.
Walshok, Mary Lindenstein
1971   "The Emergence of Middle-Class Deviant Subcultures: The Case of Swingers," *Social Problems,* 18 (Spring), 488–495.
Warren, Carol A. B.
1974   *Identity and Community in the Gay World.* New York: Wiley.
Weissman, Myrna M.
1980   "The Treatment of Depressed Women," in Carol Landau Heckerman, ed., *The Evolving Female.* New York: Human Sciences Press.
Weisstein, Naomi
1972   "Psychology Constructs the Female," in Vivian Gornick and Barbara K. Moran, eds., *Woman in Sexist Society.* New York: Signet Books.
Wertz, Richard W. and Dorothy C. Wertz
1979   *Lying-In: A History of Childbirth in America.* New York: Schocken Books.
West, Candace and Don H. Zimmerman
1977   "Women's Place in Everyday Talk," *Social Problems,* 24 (June), 520–529.
Wikler, Norma J.
1980   "On the Judicial Agenda for the 80s: Equal Treatment for Men and Women in the Courts," *Judicature,* 64, p. 207.
Willis, Ellen
1981   "Nature's Revenge," *The New York Times Book Review,* July 12, pp. 9, 18–19.

Winick, Charles and Paul M. Kinsie
    1972   *The Lively Commerce.* New York: Signet Books.
Wiseman, Jacqueline P.
    1970   *Stations of the Lost.* Englewood Cliffs, N.J.: Prentice-Hall.
Wolf, Deborah Goleman
    1980   *The Lesbian Community.* Berkeley: University of California
            Press.
Wrong, Dennis H.
    1980   *Power: Its Forms, Bases, and Uses.* New York: Harper Colophon
            Books.
Yarrow, Marian Radke, Charlotte Green Schwartz, Harriet S. Murphy,
    and Leila Calhoun Deasy
    1955   "The Psychological Meaning of Mental Illness in The Family,"
            Journal of Social Issues, 11, 12–24.
Young, Gail
    1981   "A Woman in Medicine: Reflections from the Inside," in Helen
            Roberts, ed., *Women, Health and Reproduction.* London: Rout-
            ledge and Kegan Paul.
Zimmerman, Mary K.
    1977   *Passage Through Abortion.* New York: Praeger.
Zita, Jacquelyn N.
    1981   "Historical Amnesia and the Lesbian Continuum," *Signs,* 7
            (Autumn), 172–187.

Index

Fashion industry, 67, 68, 80
Fasteau, Marc, 12
Fear of men, 123
Fear of women, 118–120
Feinbloom, Deborah Heller, 58
Femaleness:
  intrinsic devaluation of, 7, 15
  psychotherapy and, 212–213
Feminist theory, 11, 19
Ferguson, Ann, 131
Ferrero, William, 16
Fetal abnormalities, 99, 102, 109
Fetal monitoring, 95
Feyerherm, William, 216
Firestone, Shulamith, 35, 88, 117, 209
Fishel, Diane, 116–117
Fishman, Pamela M., 59
Flanagan, Timothy J., 155, 194, 196
Flynn, Edith E., 224
Fodaski, Linda, 150
Forceps deliveries, 95
Forgery, 215, 217, 218
Forisha, Barbara, 141
Foucault, Michel, 31, 116
Foster care, 224
Fowlkes, Martha R., 111
Frank, Jerome, 224
Fransella, Fay, 27, 40
Fraud, 215, 217
Freeman, Jo, 11, 55
Freidson, Eliot, 23, 93, 198, 208
Fremont-Smith, Eliot, 178
Freud, Sigmund, 209, 211
Freudianism, 209–211
  modification, 212
Friedan, Betty, 25, 209
Frigidity, 115
Frost, Kay, 27, 40

Gagnon, John, 111, 174, 181
Garfinkel, Harold, 17, 22, 24, 29
Garrison, Howard H., 41
Gay liberation movement, 131
Geis, Gilbert, 146, 155, 183
Geis, Robley, 146, 155, 183
Gelles, Richard, 158
Gender, sex distinguished from, 10

Gender norms, 51–110, 187, 235
  appearance (*see* Appearance norms)
  deviances, tables of, 53
  psychotherapy and, 208–211
German measles, 99
Gerson, Kathleen, 83
Gill, Derek, 85, 87
Gilman, Charlotte Perkins (Stetson), 211
Giordano, Peggy C., 218
Glueck, Eleanor, 16
Glueck, Sheldon, 16
Goffman, Erving, 5, 17, 18, 22, 24, 29, 31, 35, 36, 38, 39, 52, 54, 55, 57, 72, 79, 121, 148, 197
Goldberg, Philip, 26, 27, 40
Goldman, Emma, 165
Goode, Erich, 193, 194, 196
Goode, William, 87, 88
Goodman, 70
Gordon, George, N., 182
Gordon, Linda, 96, 98, 108, 118
Gordon, Michael, 116
Gornick, Vivian, 23, 35, 40
Gottfredson, Michael R., 155, 194, 196
Gough Adjective Check List, 121
Gould, Meredith, 10
Gouldner, Alvin W., 14
Gove, Walter, 6, 201, 202, 203
Graham, Hilary, 94, 96
Granberg, Donald, 109
Grand Larceny, 227–228
Gray, Susan H., 177
Greer, Germaine, 68–69
Grier, William H., 39
Griffin, Susan, 174, 178–179, 181
Grosfeld, Sharon, 152
Group for the Advancement of Psychiatry, 102–103
Group homes, 224
Group sex, 117
Gusfield, Joseph R., 6, 9, 44

Hacker, Helen Mayer, 38, 39, 41
Hackett, Bruce M., 91
Halleck, Seymour, 209, 210
Handicapped persons, 17, 22–24, 37

ABOUT THE AUTHOR

Edwin M. Schur is professor of sociology at New York University, where he formerly was chairperson of the sociology department. He has also taught at Tufts University and Wellesley College and has been a visiting scholar at the University of California at Berkeley and the Harvard Law School. A graduate of Williams College, he received his doctorate from the London School of Economics and also holds a law degree from Yale University. His many books on deviance and social control include *Crimes Without Victims, Labeling Deviant Behavior,* and *The Politics of Deviance.* An early critic of restrictive abortion laws, Professor Schur also served as a member of the NIMH Task Force on Homosexuality and edited *The Family and the Sexual Revolution: Selected Readings.*